INDUSTRIALIZATION IN WEST AFRICA

CROOM HELM INDUSTRIAL GEOGRAPHY SERIES
Edited by Ian Thompson, University of Glasgow

The Industrial Geography of Canada
Anthony Blackbourn and Robert G. Putnam

INDUSTRIALIZATION IN WEST AFRICA

J.O.C. ONYEMELUKWE

CROOM HELM
London & Sydney

ST. MARTIN'S PRESS
New York

© 1984 J.O.C. Onyemelukwe
Croom Helm Ltd, Provident House, Burrell Row,
Beckenham, Kent BR3 1AT
Croom Helm Australia Pty Ltd, First Floor,
139 King Street, Sydney, NSW 20001, Australia

British Library Cataloguing in Publication Data

Onyemelukwe, J.O.C
   Industrialization in West Africa
   1. West Africa—Industries
   I. Title
   338.0966   HC1000
   ISBN 0-7099-1936-0

Library of Congress Cataloging in Publication Data

Onyemelukwe, J. O. C.
   Industrialization in West Africa.
   Includes bibliographical references and index.
   1. Africa, West—Industries. 2. Africa, West—
   Economic policy. 3. Industrialization. I. Title.
   HC1000.058 1984   338.0966   83-40175
   ISBN 0-312-41574-5

Printed and bound in Great Britain
by Billing & Sons Limited, Worcester.

CONTENTS

TABLES AND FIGURES

Tables

Figures

The economic development efforts of West African
countries have been featuring increasing interest
in industrialization, generally regarded as the
panacea for underdevelopment. The pervading faith
in industrialization seems to derive from a growing
realization that the marginal productivity of labour
in industry is higher than in primary (agricultural
or mining) activities and that a shift from the
primary to the industrial sector tends to assure
greater employment opportunities and raise the average product per worker for the entire economy,
thereby enhancing real income per head and the general quality of life in the country.
     This book reports the economic development ef-
forts of the sixteen West African countries (comprising the West African region) through industrialization - their industrial resource management and
use, their methods and many problems of industrial
development - as an integral part of their overall
space economy. It is developed in eight chapters.
Chapter 1 presents the political and economic background against which the slow and unsteady pace of
industrialization in each country can be appreciated.
Chapter 2 examines the resource potentials, the
prospects and the problems of material and human resource management for effective industrialization.
Chapter 3 presents an historical perspective of industrial development - the gradual development from
a predominantly processing subsector preoccupied
with material export promotion to an import substituting industrial sector. Chapter 4 highlights
the structural characteristics of the West African
industrial economy - relatively small scale, import-
dependent production of consumer goods mainly by
assembly-type methods from a fund of low level technical knowledge. Chapter 5 discusses the various

factors and forms of change in the geographical incidence of industrial activity. Chapter 6 focuses
on the major problems that bedevil industrial development and frustrate efforts towards national
economic independence. Chapter 7 reports a case
study of Nigeria, and Chapter 8 concludes by considering remedial policy options open to West
African countries both individually and in a common market framework.

No attempt has been made to present the con-
ceptual and theoretical underpinnings of industrial
location and general economic development. Rather
than bewilder the reader with abstract notions and
technicalities, reference is from time to time made
to some of the well-known theoretical works which
can guide the interested reader. Only a few frequently used concepts considered unfamiliar to most
of the prospective readers are briefly explained in
the glossary, if not as footnotes.

This book is intended to meet the needs of
social science-oriented students whose courses cover
the economic development problems of the West African region. In particular, the target readership
comprises students of educational institutions in
Africa, Europe and North America - university under-
graduates studying geography, economics, political
science, urban and regional planning; polytechnic
and college of education students of geography,
economics and town planning; as well as postgraduate
students taking diploma courses in development planning and public administration. There is a dearth
of illustrative texts based on the economic (especially industrial) development experience of West
African countries. Although a number of studies
have examined some aspects of industrial activity of
either the entire West African region (Harrison
Church, 1980; Gleave and White, 1971; Udo 1978;
O'Connor, 1978) or parts thereof (Kilby, 1969;
Onyemelukwe, 1974; Schatzl, 1973), a full-scale
study focused on the region's industrialization as
an important part of an evolving space economy has
not previously been attempted. This book is intended to fill part of this gap.

My sincere appreciation and thanks must go to
my former university teachers - Professors K.M.
Barbour, A.L. Mabogunje and B.W. Hodder. Barbour
and Mabogunje provided the inspiration and encouragement that blossomed into my specialization
in industrial geography. Hodder painstakingly read
through this manuscript, literally pruned it down to

PREFACE

the present size and enhanced its quality greatly
through his most useful suggestions. Dr Nlogha E.
Okeke, my brother-in-law, kindly financed part of
my fieldwork. But my life-long debt of gratitude
must remain to my parents whose pioneering work in
Christianity and formal education in my home area
did so much to fashion my early life and intellec-
tual aspirations. To them I gratefully dedicate
this book.

   I am very pleased with the good typing work in
the Geography Department of the School of Oriental
and African Studies, University of London, and with
the exquisite cartographic work on most of the maps
and diagrams by Mrs Aderogba, Mr Faoye and Mrs
Babarinde of the Department of Geography, University
of Ibadan. I am equally grateful to all the dist-
inguished authors, world organizations, and pub-
lishers whose tables and textual information have
been used and duly acknowledged in this text.

University of Ibadan,   Joe Okezie C. Onyemelukwe
Nigeria 1982

Chapter One

THE WEST AFRICAN REGION: PRE-INDUSTRIAL ECONOMY
AND SOCIETY

West Africa is conventionally recognized as comprising fifteen mainland states and the Cape Verde Island group all of which together form the southern
part of the western bulge of the African continent.

Table 1.1: West African states: dates of political
independence

Country	Political Independence Date	Country	Political Independence Date
Liberia	July 26, 1847	Senegal*	Aug. 20, 1960
Ghana	March 6, 1957	Mali	Sept. 22, 1960
Guinea	Oct. 2, 1958	Nigeria	Oct. 1, 1960
Togo	April 27, 1960	Mauritania	Nov. 23, 1960
Benin		Sierra	
(Dahomey)	Aug. 1, 1960	Leone	April 27, 1961
Niger	Aug. 3, 1960	Gambia	Feb. 18, 1965
Upper Volta	Aug. 5, 1960	Guinea	
Ivory Coast	Aug. 7, 1960	Bissau	Sept. 24, 1973
		Cape Verde	July 5, 1975

*Senegal and the Gambia recently unified as Senegambia are
presented separately in this book. At the time of reporting
this study, no appreciable statistics on their post-unific-
ation economic development existed.

Although three of the sixteen states shown in Table
1.1, namely, Niger, Mali and Mauritania, extend well
into the heart of the Sahara Desert, West Africa
can still be roughly described as sub-Saharan in

location. Thus the Cameroun-Adamawa highlands to
the east and the Sahara Desert to the north serve
as the physical boundaries separating the West African region from the rest of the mainland states
of this giant but compact continent. To the south
and west lies the Atlantic ocean. Figure 1.1 presents the locational specifics of West Africa in
terms of both longitude and latitude and of the
region's relative areal size in the African continent. It also shows, as illustrated in Tables 1.2
and 1.3, that great diversity in the sizes - both

Table 1.2: Estimated population of West African
States

Country	Population (millions) in 1981	Annual Growth Rate
Nigeria	85.3	2.8
Ghana	11.7	2.3
Ivory Coast	8.8	4.3
Mali	6.8	2.5
Upper Volta	6.0	2.3
Senegal	5.8	2.7
Niger	5.4	2.8
Guinea	5.5	1.5
Sierra Leone	3.4	2.6
Benin	3.4	3.3
Togo	2.6	2.4
Liberia	1.9	2.0
Mauritania	1.6	2.4
Guinea Bissau	0.9	2.0
Gambia	0.6	2.4
Cape Verde	0.6	2.1

Source: World Bank World Development Report 1982 and Atlas 1979
as presented by Rake, A. (1981/82) New African Year
Book, p.11.

areally and by population - of the component states
is a major feature of this region. And it may well
be that in this element of diversity lies one of the
main driving forces behind the current effort at
regional unity and cooperation.

The diversity in population size shows Nigeria
at one extreme with over 56 per cent of the entire
West African population - put at slightly over 150

THE WEST AFRICAN REGION

Figure 1.1:   Location of West Africa

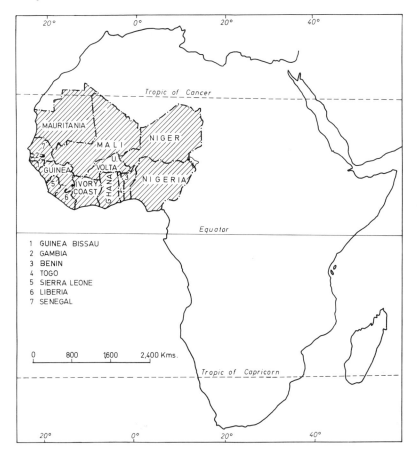

Figure 1.1:   Location of West Africa

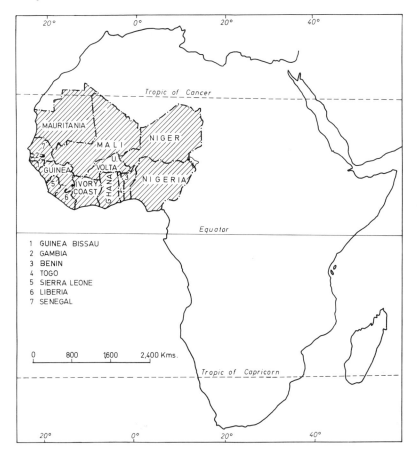

1 GUINEA BISSAU
2 GAMBIA
3 BENIN
4 TOGO
5 SIERRA LEONE
6 LIBERIA
7 SENEGAL

0   800   1600   2,400 Kms.

million in 1981; and at the other extreme are Cape
Verde, Gambia and Guinea Bissau, each of which has
less than 1 million people (Table 1.2). The diversity in areal size shows at one extreme the two vast
republics of Niger and Mali which together take up
over 40 per cent of the entire area of West Africa;
and at the other extreme are Cape Verde, Gambia and
Guinea Bissau, each of which occupies less than 1
per cent of West Africa (Table 1.3). The United
Nations' density figures in Table 1.3 show that
Mauritania, Niger and Mali had roughly 1, 4 and 5
persons respectively per square kilometre. These
figures compare very poorly with the 77 per square
kilometre in Cape Verde, 75 in Nigeria, or even
with the average of 21 persons per square kilometre
for West Africa as a whole.

West African states have annual population
growth rates ranging from 4.3 per cent in Ivory
Coast to 1.5 per cent in Guinea. All but one of
the sixteen states have at least 2 per cent annual
growth rates. At an average rate of 2.5 per cent,
according to World Bank 1981 estimates, the region's
population growth rate is rather high, though below
the average for the African continent (over 2.7 per
cent). Although the region's population growth rate
is impressive by world standards (especially when
compared with developed regions like Western Europe),
the fact of relatively very low density helps to explain why West Africa, like most of the African continent, cannot on the score of annual growth rate
alone be rightly described as in danger of over-
population. In other words, mere reference to annual population growth rates can be misleading in
the assessment of the population problems of West
Africa, or indeed of any other African region. The
factor of density must also be taken into account,
and density values are generally low in the region.

However, this does not in any way suggest that
the West African region does not have serious population problems to which high annual growth rates
may be related. Indeed, considerable population
problems do exist; but they arise more from the
patterns of population distribution than from the
total size of population of each West African state.
Just as there are considerable variations among West
African countries, so are there variations within
each state - all in response to a number of physical,
economic, social and, sometimes, political factors.

Whereas some factors, such as favourable physical environment, encourage agricultural productivity and population concentration, problems of

Table 1.3: Area and population density of West
African states

Country	Area (Sq. km.)	Percentage of entire region	Population Density (Per Sq. km.)
Niger	1,267,000	20.65	4
Mali	1,240,000	20.21	5
Mauritania	1,030,700	16.79	1
Nigeria	913,073	14.88	75
Ivory Coast	322,463	5.25	22
Upper Volta	274,200	4.47	23
Guinea	245,847	4.01	18
Ghana	238,540	3.89	44
Senegal	201,400	3.28	26
Benin	112,600	1.83	29
Liberia	111,400	1.81	16
Sierra Leone	71,740	1.17	41
Togo	56,000	0.91	43
Guinea Bissau	38,125	0.62	14
Gambia	11,036	0.18	50
Cape Verde	1,033	0.07	77
	6,136,357	100.00	21

Source: Various

high man/land ratios often arise and the annual population growth rate of over 2 per cent can become a
serious factor inhibiting economic progress.   But
this has been the case in only very few areas of
rural West Africa - notably in parts of Igboland and
Ibibioland in south-eastern Nigeria, in the area
around the city of Kano, and in the Mossi concentrations around Ouagadougou in Upper Volta.   In a
few other areas, like the cocoa belts of Ghana,
Nigeria and Ivory Coast, population problems take a
different form and mainly derive from labour immig-
ration rather than from natural population increase.
In general, the West African population problem relates more to its distribution than to the total
population size and rate of natural increase.   Many
parts are not inhabited as a result of their hostile
environment.   In Mauritania, for example, only 7 per
cent (the physically most hospitable southern section) of the 1 million square kilometres of the
country accounts for over 80 per cent of the coun-

try's population. The remaining 93 per cent of the
territory presents an inhospitable hot desert environment. Almost the same picture repeats itself
in Niger and, to a lesser extent, in Mali. Thus
even though Mauritania has an annual growth rate of
2.4 per cent and Niger 2.6 per cent, their density
figures of 1 person and 4 persons respectively per
square kilometre partly explain why the fear of
over-population cannot really be justified. Attention should rather be directed to resource availability on a per capita basis and the level of technology in each country for a better appreciation of
population problems in terms of the carrying capacity of the land.[1] Much of this issue of resource
availability and use is taken up in Chapter 2, especially to the extent that it relates to the industrial development problems and prospects of West
African countries.

MAJOR POLITICAL AND ECONOMIC FEATURES OF PRE-
COLONIAL WEST AFRICA

Pre-colonial West Africa witnessed the rise and fall
of a number of indigenous state systems. Notable
amongst them was the powerful Ghana Empire which
dominated the heartland of the grassland belt of
West Africa (Figure 1.2) from the 7th to the 13th
century A.D. This was superseded by the Mali
Empire from the 13th to the 15th century. More or
less contemporaneous with both Ghana and the Mali
administrations was the Hausa state which came to
the peak of its power from the 11th to the 14th
century. But the Songhai Empire, probably admini-
stratively the most efficient, emerged from the 15th
to the 16th century to overlap and supersede the
waning empires that pre-dated it.
    When each political administration was at the
zenith of its power, it strove to ensure political
order and loyalty as well as economic progress in as
many communities as it could control. However, its
strength and controlling influence invariably declined from the geographical centre of its power to
the distant communities at the periphery.   While
those state systems waxed and waned as more or less
loose federations of some indigenous communities,
many more small communities not under their political influence did exist independently and run their
own affairs. Also, like the more powerful empires
or states, they organized their own economies dominated everywhere by agriculture and craft industry

6

Figure 1.2: Notable kingdoms and empires of pre-colonial West Africa

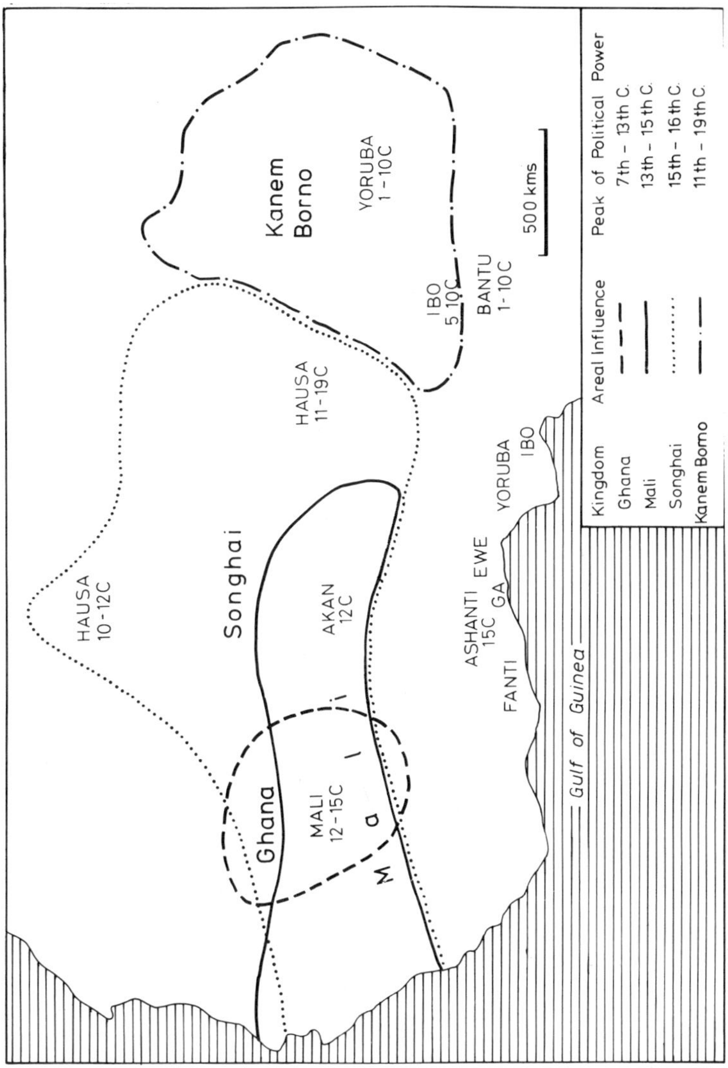

Kanem
Borno

YORUBA
1-10C

IBO
5-10C

BANTU
1-10C

500 kms

HAUSA
11-19C

Songhai

HAUSA
10-12C

AKAN
12C

YORUBA

IBO

ASHANTI
15C

EWE

GA

FANTI

Gulf of Guinea

Ghana

MALI
12-15C

M a l i

Kingdom	Areal Influence	Peak of Political Power
Ghana	————	7th – 13th C.
Mali	————	13th – 15th C.
Songhai	··········	15th – 16th C.
Kanem Borno	—·—·—	11th – 19th C.

which together provided the basis for lively trade
inter-actions with neighbouring and distant communities.

Agricultural activities were essentially of
two major categories - arable farming and animal
husbandry. Mainly in keeping with the dictates of
physical (especially climatic) factors, four broad
agricultural land-use belts developed across West
Africa. In the well watered (rain-fed) forest areas
and woodlands of the south, arable farming predomin-
ated, as is still the case. There the root crop and
tree crop economy (involving especially the oil palm
and kolanut) was prevalent in the wettest, non-
saline coastal belt. A root and grain crop economy,
involving in particular the production of yams,
cassava, onions, sorghum, maize, legumes and cotton,
featured, as now, in the moderately wet areas of
150 cm. to 25 cm. of annual rainfall further to the
north. Stock rearing dominates the desert fringes
where seasonal streams sustain animal husbandry and
the cultivation of date palms, wheat and millet.
Camels, goats and sheep constituted, as now, the
bulk of livestock reared in this belt. But the belt
immediately to the south and enjoying up to three
months of heavy rainfall annually featured both
stock raising involving cattle, sheep and donkeys
and the cultivation of such short-season drought-
resistant crops as groundnuts, millets, onions and
wheat.

Arable agriculture in pre-colonial West Africa
was largely of the subsistence type and based on
very rudimentary technology. Particularly in the
forest zone, it hardly involved any more than the
hoe and cutlass method; but in the politically and
economically better organized grassland communities,
ploughing with motive power provided by cattle and
donkeys and some rudimentary forms of irrigation
were practised. Livestock raising, involving considerable nomadic life in the search for water and
pasture, served as the basis for food (especially
fresh milk) and for trade in live animals. The
Fulani who then, as now, dominated the livestock
economy, depended heavily for food on milk rather
than on meat from their herds. So did the Wolofs,
who also put their premium for animal husbandry on
trade in livestock.

By and large, what have survived till now and
developed from those age-long economic pre-occup-
ations constitute the main elements of the region's
industrial resource base treated in some detail in
Chapter 2.

8

It is important to emphasize that it was the products of all these spatially varied agricultural activities that constituted the main items of the inter-regional and trans-Saharan trade of pre-colonial West Africa. Among the various trade relations that were then organized, the most important for their geographical scope and international economic implications were the trans-Saharan trade interactions with North African states and Europe. Trade flows across the Sahara Desert were invariably borne by camels which moved in caravans. Such flows involved at various periods some West African exports - considerable quantities of gold, ivory, hides, ostrich skins and leather goods (including well-made shoes); dyed cloths, kolanuts and slaves. Imports into West Africa from the Arab states of North Africa included salt mined in the North African region of Hoggar and Teghaza in the Sahara Desert; glass beads, silver and copper goods made in Europe; and cowrie shells imported from the Indian Ocean through Cairo. Towards the early 19th century, the range of imports into West Africa widened considerably to include more of European made goods like sword blades (then in high demand for frequent attacks and counter attacks during wars and on trade routes), needles, mirrors, gunpowder and sugar as well as Arab woollen dresses, red coral beads, and pepper.

Centres like Kumbi, Tirekka, Timbukto, Gao, Tekedda, Agades, Bornu, Bilma, Kano and Katsina (Mabogunje, 1968) flourished and declined with the social and economic vicissitudes of the political administrations within which they functioned as entrepots for inter-regional and trans-Saharan trade. They were very important centres for currency exchange and enforcement of trade regulations. Trade by barter (e.g. exchange of slaves with horses or with gold bars) later gave way to well-organized currency systems in which cowries, mithkal of gold (approximately one-eighth of an ounce) and iron pieces were used.

Another important feature of the West African economy and society throughout that period was the development and growth of craft industries. Most notable were leather works, spinning, weaving, dyeing and embroidery; gold and iron smelting/smithing; pottery, wood and calabash carving; and brass and bronze industries. These among others provided the main artefacts of the interregional and trans-Saharan trade. The pre-colonial period of the early 19th century may well be regarded as the zenith in the prosperity of craft activity in most

parts of West Africa. For as contact with European
powers developed over the years thereafter, the
elimination of products of local craft industries
by superior products of the industrial countries
gradually weakened the craft industry subsector of
the region's traditional economy.

However, at the height of the prosperity of
craft industry in pre-colonial West Africa, a number
of places were famed for the specialized development
of certain crafts. In each case the factor of favourable physical environment, especially in terms of
resource endowment, was a very important deter-
minant. Kano area was, for instance, noted for textile and leather goods - both cotton fibre and
leather being abundantly produced in the vicinity.
Textile products, according to Barth, included a
wide variety such as <u>tobe</u> or <u>riga</u> for men and <u>tur-
kedi</u> for women the export of all of which was organized from Kano to different parts of West and
North Africa. Mabogunje quoting Barth (1865,
p. 510) showed that cloth export from Kano to Timbukto alone amounted to at least 300 camel-loads
annually. The account of Robinson (1896, p. 113)
gives a vivid picture of Kano as a centre of craft
(textile) industry and trade:

> Any European who will take the trouble to ask
> for it, will find no difficulty in purchasing
> Kano-made cloth at towns on the coast as widely
> separated from one another as Alexandria,
> Tripoli, Tunis or Lagos.

The leather goods are mainly what Barth described as
"sandals and shoes made with great neatness, and,
like the cloth, are exported to an immense distance
... and to North Africa" (Barth, 1865, pp. 513-4).

In the Katsina area leather works, preparation
of hides, skins and dried beef for export were extensively carried on (Denham <u>et.al.</u>, 1828, vol. 2,
p. 392). The same activities flourished around
Timbukto and Gao. Also in Bornu weaving of linen
by what Denham described as "crude machinery" was
adroitly and extensively undertaken for local use as
well as for export. Rock salt (natron) mining and
processing were also major economic activities for
export trade especially to the coastal areas.

At the height of the Songhai Empire, Agades (in
Niger) was a major trade centre renowned for leather
works based on the local abundance of hides and
skins. In fact, the artistic excellence of Agades
leather artificers had a great influence on the

development of leather works in Katsina, especially
after the collapse of the Songhai Empire and the
consequent migration of many craftsmen from Agades
to Katsina (Mabogunje, 1968).

Gobir, also in the present Niger Republic,
north of Katsina, was famed for linen production and
leather works. According to Leo Africanus, "here,
(in Gobir) are great stores of artificers and linen
weavers, and here are such shoes made as the ancient
Romans were wont to wear".[2]

In the wetter forest and woodland belts, wood
carving and bronze making in the Old Bini kingdom
and pottery and metal working in the Igbo-Ukwu-Awka
area of the Igbo heartland (Onwuejeogwu, 1975,
p. 41) were highly commercialized age-long industries; spinning, weaving and dyeing of cotton cloths
were well established in the Oyo-Iseyin area of
Yorubaland. And over a widely scattered area, particularly between the present site of Ghana and the
Middle Niger, ivory and gold processing attracted
almost world-wide attention. Indeed it was largely
the international attractions of slaves, gold and
ivory that initially encouraged the direct participation of Europeans in West African trade - to the
extent of bringing into effect a reorganization of
West African trade. There was change from its
former Saharan orientation to what has since become
Atlantic coast-oriented sea-borne commerce.

In concluding our brief account of the political and economic scene of pre-colonial West Africa,
attention must be drawn to a very important point
often missed, namely, that in the rise and fall of
one imperial or state administration after another
among the indigenous communities of the region,
numerous towns and cities emerged. Such centres
played their role, as in other parts of the world,
in the articulation of civil administration and
trade and in the diffusion of innovations throughout their respective tributary areas. Also, as part
of the innovation process a wide-ranging currency
and exchange system was effectively used to promote
local and inter-regional commerce. It would therefore be reasonable to argue that pre-colonial West
Africa had effective political and economic institutions consistent with and necessary for a considerable measure of socio-economic advancement. Thus
the concept of Africa as the "Dark Continent" has
been particularly significant especially to the extent that it reflected the colossal ignorance outside
Africa about the characteristics of African peoples
and their traditional economies.

POLITICAL AND ECONOMIC CHANGES IN COLONIAL WEST
AFRICA

From the foregoing account, it is clear that there
were some forms of organized political administration and civil order before the advent of foreign
(European) political administrative systems in West
Africa. There was evidence of fairly well organized
economic (trade) relations within the region as well
as between it and other parts of the world, particularly northern Africa and southern Europe. There
was also evidence of European presence and activity
in West Africa, not as administrators but as busin-
essmen, long before the issue of colonies and political power relations arose. Indeed, the Portuguese
had been in close touch with their West African
partners in business - particularly the business of
slave trade - as early as the 15th century, thanks
to the patronage and foresight of Prince Henry the
Navigator. But when the European powers turned
their attention to the African continent to divide,
rule and exploit it, the political and economic
picture of the West African region began to experience drastic changes that hae had very far-
reaching consequences. It is to those changes and
some of their consequences that attention is now
directed, albeit rather briefly.

As early as the 18th century, many European
nations - Portuguese, British, Dutch, Danes, French,
Brandenburgers and Swedes - which had established
trading posts on the West African coast had also
been keen on gaining political footholds in certain
parts of Africa, including West Africa. In the
process of this political quest - which implied
territorial control - clashes of interest inevitably
arose. The historic Berlin Conference of 1884-5 was
indeed a forum for resolving such clashes of interest and for prescribing a standard procedure for the
European "scramble" for Africa. This is not the
right place for the historical account of the par-
tition of Africa, of which West Africa is part. It
serves our purpose to state briefly that it was in
line with the Berlin Conference decisions that West
Africa, like the rest of the African continent, had
to be parcelled out among the rival European powers.
The states that today make up West Africa were the
creations of foreign political interests in total
disregard of the interest of the indigenous communities of West Africa.

In such circumstances, where what are today
national boundaries were drawn up without regard to

12

the political and socio-cultural interests and pre-
ferences of the African communities, it is perhaps
not surprising that single sedentary communities
have been forced to belong to two different countries; and there has been the merging of very disparate cultural groups as one country. For example,
the Nigeria-Benin (Dahomey) boundary put one part of
the Yorubas in Nigeria and the other part in Benin.
The Ewes of Togo have many of their kinsfolk on the
other side of the border in Ghana; also the Hausas
find themselves in Nigeria, Niger and Benin. On the
other hand, Nigeria embraces over five large ethnic
groups - the Hausa-Fulani, the Igbo, the Yoruba, the
Efik-Ibibio and the Kanuris - each of which could
have constituted a separate and viable political
unit but now forms a component of a giant territory
in which over 250 different languages are spoken.
Such a collection of very disparate ethnic and cultural groups under one political administration has
had far-reaching political consequences even after
the political independence of the West African countries affected. In a number of cases, particularly
in Nigeria, Benin (Dahomey), Togo, Ghana and Sierra
Leone, political stability has not been easy to
forge amidst inter-ethnic cleavages. This has in no
small measure served as a drag on the economic progress of these countries.

THE SPATIAL PATTERN OF COLONIAL RELATIONS WITH
EUROPE

Another strong politico-economic impact of colonial
rule in West Africa was the division of the region
into two major language and currency groups - the
Francophone (franc) group and the Anglophone (sterling) group. German influence was rather short-
lived, ending with the sharing of the former German
territory of Togoland between French Togoland (now
Togo) and the British Gold Coast (now Ghana).
Portuguese influence was limited to Guinea Bissau
and the Cape Verde Island group.
    With the imposition of French as the lingua
franca in French colonies, and the English language in
British colonies, the stage was set for a very far-
reaching cultural and economic reorientation and re-
conditioning of West African people - to the extent
that even after over twenty years of political independence in most of those West African countries,
the cultural and economic attachments to their former colonial masters have continued to be very

strong indeed.

Until 1958, all the Francophone countries (altogether nine) in West Africa maintained strong political and economic links with France. The French government's decrees of 1895 and 1904 had the effect of stepping up French efforts towards tight economic and political control. The first four countries to be so harnessed were Senegal, France's earliest foothold, Guinea, Sudan (now Mali), and Ivory Coast. By 1904 all the four territories had been placed under the jurisdiction of a single governor-general residing in Dakar, Senegal. In 1906 Niger was brought in; Mauritania followed in 1910, and Upper Volta (carved out from Niger, Ivory Coast and Sudan) in 1920. In 1922 the eastern part of Togoland became a mandated territory of France according to the League of Nations' ruling.

The assimilationist policy of France which, as will be shown shortly, was very different from the British policy in West Africa, regarded all French territories in West Africa as part of Greater France (France Outre Mer) and their inhabitants as black French people. The latter were by a peculiar political arrangement represented in the French legislature by elected fellow Africans as deputies in Paris. French direct rule also involved the use of French administrative officers in many parts of French West Africa seen, not only in theory but also in practice, as the overseas provinces of France. Another element of direct French rule was the factor of direct control of all land in West Africa by the Paris-based state government. By this means it was easy to grant large concessions to foreign (non-West African) firms for cash crop plantations.

One major factor that facilitated the direct, strong political and economic link-up of French West African countries was their geographical contiguity (Fig. 1.3). This contiguity factor helped to minimize physical distances, encourage transport and communication link-ups of the various territories and facilitated commodity flows.

France's main interest in West Africa, like Britain's, was the exploitation of natural resources whose exports and the imports of French manufactures were left largely in the hands of a few French corporate monopolies. The most notable among such bodies were (and are) S.C.O.A. (Societe Commercial de l'Ouest Africain) and C.F.A.O. (Compagnie Francaise de l'Afrique Occidentale). To stimulate economic activity, the French introduced a number of measures. One was taxation by which the indigenous

Figure 1.3: Official language groups of West Africa – evidence of persisting impact of external influence

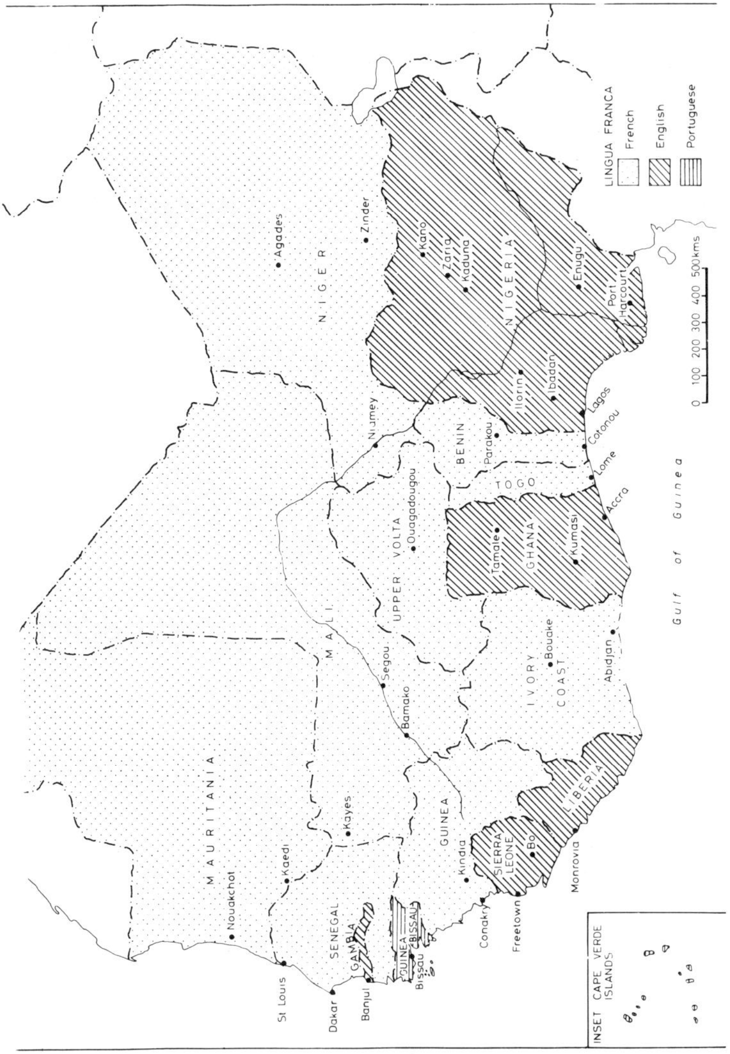

LINGUA FRANCA
French
English
Portuguese

0 100 200 300 400 500kms

Agades
Zinder
NIGER
Kano
Kano
Kaduna
Enugu
NIGERIA
Port Harcourt
Niamey
Ilorin
Ibadan
Lagos
Cotonou
BENIN
Parakou
Lome
TOGO
Accra
Ouagadougou
UPPER VOLTA
GHANA
Tamale
Kumasi
Segou
MALI
Bamako
IVORY COAST
Bouake
Abidjan
Gulf of Guinea
MAURITANIA
Kayes
GUINEA
Kinda
Nouakchot
Kaedi
LIBERIA
SIERRA LEONE
Bo
Conakry
Freetown
Monrovia
St Louis
Dakar
SENEGAL
Banjul
GAMBIA
GUINEA BISSAU
Bissau

INSET CAPE VERDE ISLANDS

people were obliged to produce for cash sales or
seek paid work. The second was the encouragement
and, sometimes, enforcement of the cultivation of
cash crops. Prominent in the cash crop economy were
coffee, cocoa, oil palm and bananas in the wetter
areas of the forest zone, and cotton as well as
groundnuts in the drier interiors.

     As if taxation were not an effective instrument
for promoting resource exploitation and the development of railways and roads in the colonies, forced
labour was also introduced. Africans were, until
1946, compelled to work on public projects like
railways and roads and also on European plantations.
The plantation economy was generally on such a large
scale as to leave the indigenous people providing
the bulk of the labour but hardly capable of exer-
cising appreciable entrepreneurial control. The
economic landscape thus presented a picture of an
enclave economy - with scores of large European-
owned plantations amidst thousands of tiny farmlands
for the African subsistence economy. Between the
millions of African small-scale producers and the
scores of European monopolies featured the Lebanese
middlemen who thus provided the remaining link in
the chain of economic exploitation of African
peoples.

     So strong have been the politico-economic ties
of the Francophone states with France that even
after the political independence of these countries,
a number of formal relations expected to be mutually
beneficial have continued to be organized and nur-
tured. Among such supranational and unifying organizations, the most important is, perhaps, the
Communaute Financiere Africaine (C.F.A.), otherwise
known as the Franc Zone. It embraces all countries
the currencies of which are linked with the French
franc at a fixed rate of exchange and which agree to
hold their reserves mainly in the form of French
francs. Many other benefits, besides currency exchange facilities, also accrue to member states
which include all Francophone states of West Africa
except Guinea and Mauritania. For example, French
assistance is received in the form of foreign aid
like technical assistance and budget support as well
as subsidies on commodity exports. In Chapter 8 the
various post-independence economic groupings of
Francophone and other states of West Africa are
examined. Meanwhile it is necessary to note how
strong and far-reaching the influence of France has
been on the politico-economic affairs of the Francophone states of West Africa from the colonial to

post-colonial times. The political dimension of
France's influence is probably not fully appreciated
until it is realized that up till now - after over
twenty years of political independence - most of the
Francophone states of West Africa still consult with
the French government before taking a stand on certain international issues which promise far-reaching
economic and political consequences. This may well
be seen as a sign of confidence in the assimilationist policy of France by her former colonies. But
the fact remains that the latter have hardly any alternative, given their heavy economic dependence on
France, their deep-rooted cultural and ideological
transformation by France, and, of course, their
weakness in modern technology and the gross inadequacy of their managerial skills and entrepreneurial
capabilities - themselves part of the legacies of
the French colonial period.

The Anglophone part of West Africa, as shown in
Figure 1.3, comprises five countries, namely Nigeria,
Ghana (formerly Gold Coast), Liberia, Sierra Leone
and Gambia. All but Liberia are former British
colonies. Liberia was largely a creation from
settlements sponsored from the United States in the
process of rehabilitating the emancipated slaves and
descendants of slaves taken from different parts of
Africa to the United States.³ It became an independent state in 1847. Therefore it is only to the
extent that the Liberians speak English as their
common language that Liberia is here regarded as
Anglophone.

With the exception of Sierra Leone the British
territories were, as in the French case, the result
of Britain's exploits during the "scramble for
Africa". Sierra Leone, which got its name (meaning
Lion Mountain) from the Portuguese, who made their
first known contact with the area in 1461, was, like
Liberia, a settlement for freed slaves as early as
1787. Although the Creoles - descendants of the
freed slaves - developed an identifiable culture and
their own language (Krio), the British take-over and
control of the territory as a protectorate from 1896
helped to impose the English language as the territory's lingua franca.

Through a series of open rivalries with other
European powers - the French in particular - and by
a number of treaties with the local chiefs and
village heads (sometimes after some show of force),
Britain secured the political control of the Gambia,
Ghana and Nigeria between 1873 and 1900. Contrary
to the assimilationist policy followed by France,

Britain was from the beginning of her colonial rule
in West Africa bent on giving each colony some form
of guidance towards separate existence and self-
rule. The issue of African representation in the
British House of Commons did not arise. Britain's
administration was in many cases by indirect rule -
through the traditional rulers of the people, or, in
their absence (and less successfully), through warrant chiefs (Afigbo, 1972). The active participation of the local people in the day-to-day affairs
of government, as well as the involvement of local
people in the various aspects of civil administration and economic exploitation, demanded certain
levels of literacy and education of a non-technical
nature. With the help of voluntary (especially re-
ligious) organizations, a good number of primary
schools and a few grammar schools were set up to
provide the education needed for achieving the objectives of Britain's colonial rule in West Africa.
Thus, not only did Britain's policy of indirect rule
help to preserve the traditional system of political
administration through the traditional rulers; it
also went a long way in the modernization of local
administrations through formal education and adaptation to the Westminster system of parliamentary
democracy.
     Unlike the French-controlled parts of West
Africa, land alienation to foreign developers was
discouraged. The intention was to prevent the dep-
rivation of the local people of their land and the
creation of a landless class of peasantry who might,
as in the French-ruled neighbouring territories, be
obliged to sell their labour in large foreign-owned
plantations. In other words, the local people were
encouraged to produce all the cash crops in which
Britain was interested. And through a few highly
capitalized ologopolies - invariably foreign - local
export products were assembled from millions of tiny
farms and village markets and bulked for export to
Europe. It was in 1948 that local produce marketing
boards in each territory were set up to coordinate
produce buying and export along the lines initiated
on a regional scale just prior to World War II. A
great deal of work has been done on the history and
economic performance of such produce marketing
boards, and the reader is referred to a few of such
works, especially by Bauer (1954), Helleiner (1966)
and Kriessel (1968b). It is enough to state here
briefly that, by allowing the mass of small farmers
to produce the cash crops the collection and sale of
most of which were coordinated by powerful marketing

institutions also manned by local people, the British, much more than the French, organized a wide system of income distribution among the indigenous people and gave them a measure of apprenticeship in decision-making which was to become vital for more effective administrative take-over at the start of political independence.

However, largely on account of considerable physical separation of the British colonies from one another, much less of the collaborative or block economic organization known in colonial and post-colonial Francophone West Africa has developed in Anglophone West Africa. For example, unlike the French efforts towards an all-connecting rail network, the British territories of West Africa, except Gambia, each have their separate railway system. In fact, the few attempts at formal regional cooperation were short-lived. Typical examples were the West African Produce Marketing arrangement which began in 1937 but was superseded in 1948 by Marketing Boards set up on an individual country basis, especially in Nigeria and Ghana. Another was the British West African Airways which later gave way to country-by-country air services. Also, in place of the West African Institute for Oil Palm Research there are now such research institutes on a local (national) basis. The West African Court of Appeal and the West African Currency Board have each been superseded by national bodies. It must be added that besides the attenuating effects of physical separation arising from the spatial disposition of the British West African colonies, the non-assimil-ationist Westminster policy did contribute in large measure to the practical difficulties of working out and sustaining supra-national organizations in British West Africa.

PRE-WORLD WAR II STATE OF NATIONAL ECONOMIES

From the foregoing, the picture of West African eco-nomy and society would seem to be clear. The in-habitants of the West African region live in two major ecological zones - the forest people in the more coastal south, and the grassland people between the forest zone and the Sahara Desert. We have also seen how, as a result of the wide variety of natural resources from those two major ecological zones, there was enough produce upon which both regional and inter-national trade could be based. The trans-Saharan trade that developed long before the Euro-

peans of various nationalities set up their trading
posts on the West African coast had to experience a
slow but steady decline with the re-orientation of
international trade towards the West African coastline. This reorientation meant not only greater
direct participation of Europeans in West African
trade but also a complete takeover of political and
economic control of West African administration by
European powers. Such a control was at its peak at
the start of World War II; and it was such that the
West African region was essentially a raw material
source and an expanding market for the manufactures
of Europe in particular. Although large concessions
had developed for cash crop production in Francophone territories, unlike in the British territories,
the bulk of agricultural produce being exported
from West Africa came from the smallholdings of poor
farmers operating with very primitive implements and
on a scale that hardly could pass as commercial.

As a result of policies designed, so it could
be argued, to keep West Africa perpetually economically dependent on European industries and technology, there was in all West Africa very little
that could pass as modern industrial development.
The non-provision of technical training for the
local people went a long way to frustrate the diffusion of modern industrial innovation. Besides the
small amount of manufacturing that existed before
World War II - notably printing works and bakeries
(Onyemelukwe,1978a) mainly organized by expatriates
for their own immediate needs - the main efforts in
the industrial sector had to do with raw material
processing for more effective promotion of foreign-
controlled exports of the natural resources of West
Africa. This widespread practice of material processing is discussed in some detail in Chapter 3.
However, the point to emphasize here is the fact
that although pre-World War II West Africa witnessed
some forms of industrial activity, yet virtually the
entire region depended almost entirely on goods manufactured in the industrial countries. And the more
such goods penetrated the region, the less was indigenous craft industry able to stand the stifling
competition of obviously more superior foreign manufacturing. In other words, craft industry had already been on the decline before World War II; the
craftsmen had in many parts - like the cocoa area of
Nigeria and Ghana as well as the cotton and groundnuts zones of the savanna - been faced with the alternative of a lucrative participation in the production and processing of those cash crops for ex-

port. With the middlemen increasingly demanding
much higher levels of capitalization and entrepreneurship which the average West African could not
afford, the majority of West African peoples were
apparently obliged to content themselves with their
small-scale farming and processing and the production of local foodstuffs on a subsistence basis.

Operations on such a small scale meant low financial returns which in turn implied very low per
capita incomes under conditions of high birth rates
and large family sizes. The implications of low per
capita income are indeed many; but the ones that
came into the open in pre-World War II West Africa
were widespread malnutrition, a high incidence of
death from preventable diseases and the inability of
most parents to educate their children in the fee-
paying primary schools established mainly by various
voluntary agencies.

Under such conditions of mass poverty, the in-
stitution of taxation became a major factor compel-
ling many a young man into the mines - tin in the
Jos Plateau, coal in Enugu, gold, diamond and manganese in the former Gold Coast, and diamond and
iron ore in Sierra Leone. Also migrations to the
plantations and the major cash crop areas were encouraged. From the grassland areas of northern
Nigeria and of the Mossi area of Upper Volta many
migrants drifted southwards to the forest zone: to
the cocoa and mining areas of southern Ghana as well
as to southern and central Ivory Coast; from northern and eastern parts of Nigeria, streams of migrants drifted into the cocoa and rubber belts of
south-western Nigeria; and from the central Sudan
(now Mali) the farming migrants (the *navetanes*)
drifted seasonally into the groundnut zones of
Senegambia.

In concluding this chapter, it can be argued
that although colonialism had the effect of trans-
forming the economic landscape of most parts of West
Africa, particularly through the introduction of the
cash crop economy, large-scale mining, rail and road
transportation and by more fully monetizing the West
African economy, yet mass poverty and a general inability to exploit the region's potential for modern,
albeit modest, industrialization remained outstanding problems in pre-World War II West Africa.
Furthermore the failure to involve the educated
elites in the political administration and in economic decision-making where the largely uneducated
traditional rulers were used (particularly in
British colonies) created considerable disenchant-

ment among them. On account of that as well as of their enlightenment and better understanding of the workings and objectives of colonial policies in Africa, the educated elites acted in the vanguard in the agitation for self-determination. It was under such conditions that greater public awareness and politicization gathered momentum as part of "the wind of change" that brought in its wake political independence in West African countries, beginning in 1957. Such indigenous political authority was necessary in the introduction of policies for industrialization as a vital element in the process of national development in all West African countries.

NOTES

1. This is in line with the concept of Critical Density of Population (CDP) defined as the human carrying capacity of an area in relation to a given land use system. In terms of persons per square kilometre, it is, therefore, the maximum population density which a system is capable of permanently supporting (Allan, 1965). With advances in agricultural and industrial technology, the carrying capacity of land in most rural West Africa is likely to be increased considerably.

2. See Mabogunje, A.L. (1968) Urbanization in Nigeria, London University Press.

3. Between 1822 and 1890, over 16,000 freed black slaves settled in that part of the Grain Coast (under the auspices of the American Colonization Society) as "Amerigo-Liberians" (Schulze, 1981). From the onset the latter relegated the native Africans found in the territory and dominated the political and economic scene.

Chapter Two

THE RESOURCE BASE FOR INDUSTRIALIZATION IN WEST
AFRICA: PROSPECTS AND PROBLEMS

INTRODUCTION

For successful industrial development, consideration
must first be given to the resource base. Without
adequate quantity and quality of requisite resources,
efforts at industrialization on an appreciable scale
are bound to be hampered if not seriously frustrated.
This is particularly the case where, as in West Africa, modern manufacturing is as yet rudimentary and
progress is at a relatively very low rate. Because
of very low levels of technological competence,
there is still heavy dependence on foreign expertise.
West African countries striving to industrialize
have need to be as self-supporting as possible in
most material resources in order to reduce to man-
ageable proportions their degree of dependence on
external sources - particularly sources outside the
West African region. In this chapter, the industrial resource base of West Africa is examined with
particular attention to its spatial variation. Attention is also drawn to the prospects and the problems of resource management for industrial development in a region that has seen considerable exploitation and control by external powers. The resource
base is divided into three major areas - land,
labour and capital resources - and these are examined
in that order.

LAND RESOURCES

In its economic sense, land comprises not only the
territory or the land as usually understood, but
also what is within it (minerals) and what is above
it, including the elements of weather. Thus for our
present purpose, the discussion of land covers agri-

cultural resources including forestry and fishery
resources; minerals including fossil water sources;
and such elements of weather as temperature, radiation, wind and rainfall - all of which can profitably be harnessed for industrial and other economic
development purposes. It is necessary to point out
at this juncture that these resources are capital-
yielding - either by being sold for cash incomes, or
by being directly used to manufacture things. Thus
the distinction between land resources and capital
is generally not clear-cut as will be appreciated
later, especially in Chapter 7.
     West Africa is particularly rich in a wide
variety of land resources. Virtually every country
in West Africa has extensive tracts of land suitable,
under normal conditions, for some form of agricultural activity. For a region covering the entire
tropical climate - from the equatorial forest climate type to the hot desert type - almost all varieties of tropical products have a chance of large
scale production, given the right technology and
market conditions. However, wide variations do exist from country to country in relation both to lat-
itudinal location and to each country's size and economic policy regarding resource management and use.
Maps 2.1 and 2.2 provide a generalised picture of
vegetation types and major vegetable products respectively of West Africa. The whole region is generally hot. But, whereas only slight differences in
maximum shade temperatures exist between stations of
widely varying latitudes, great differences in annual temperature range occur between stations on
such latitudes.
     West Africa has considerable solar energy re-
source potential for economic development purposes,
though the prospects for use of solar energy in commercial quantities are greater in the sub-Saharan
states with less cloudy skies and therefore greater
solar intensity than in the southern, coastal countries experiencing greater cloud cover and the dam-
pening effect of luxuriant vegetation. The solar
power plant at Dire, an isolated town on the banks
of the River Niger in Mali, is an example of an
attempt to tap the vast energy potential that exists
in the drier parts of West Africa. The plant equipped with 3,200 square metres of heat collectors was
the world's biggest set of its kind in 1978. It was
then expected to pump drinking water to an estimated
population of 10,000 people and to irrigate over 20
hectares of otherwise dry land. It was also planned to supply electricity to a tourist centre, to an

Figure 2.1: The main vegetation belts of West Africa

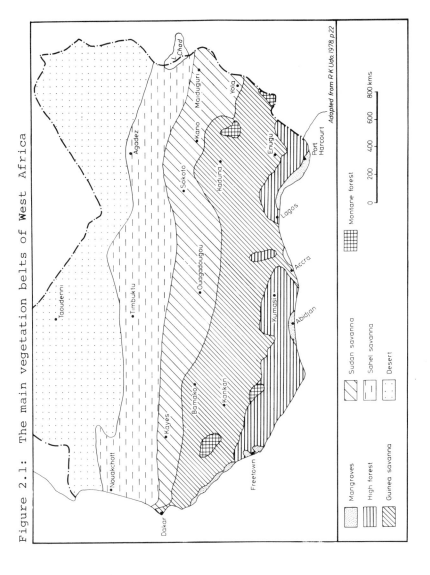

Adapted from R K Udo, 1978, p 22

0   200   400   600   800 kms

Mangroves

High forest

Gunea savanna

Sudan savanna

Sahel savanna

Desert

Montane forest

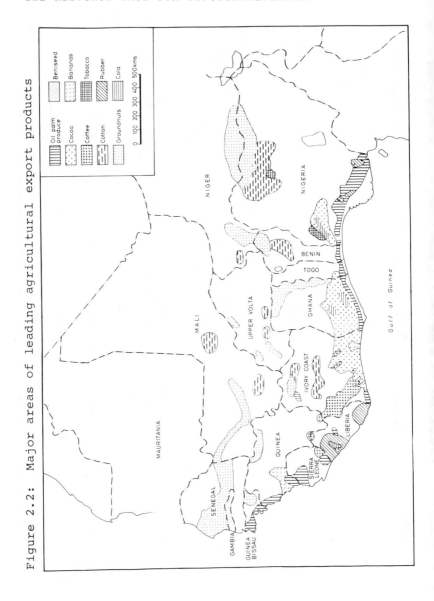

Figure 2.2: Major areas of leading agricultural export products

agricultural cooperative refrigeration unit, and to local manufacturing plants. Before the start of the Dire project, experiments on that method of tapping and using solar energy had been successfully carried out in Niger, Upper Volta, Mauritania and other parts of Mali. Increases in the price of oil, no doubt, make experiments in solar energy very worthwhile economic ventures, especially among the non-oil producing countries of West Africa.

AGRICULTURAL PRODUCTS

The agricultural economy of West African countries is still largely primitive, especially in the sense that it is still lacking in modern methods of production and largely being operated at near-subsistence level. That such agricultural methods are still prevalent even in the face of rising population and growing demands from domestic and foreign markets is, to some extent, accounted for by favourable climatic factors. The warm and moist climate of the greater part of West Africa is congenial to plant growth and makes much less demands on human ingenuity than are required even for subsistence agriculture in the cold latitudes. However, this is not to say that under the prevailing agricultural system West African countries have been finding it easy to meet their needs from their agricultural sector. Each country's efforts, particularly through a series of development plans, draw attention to the prospects and the problems that exist. From the outset, emphasis has mainly been on effective competition in, and foreign exchange earning from, the world market. The desire to develop the local industrial sector from the same agricultural resource base has been growing since the political independence of the majority of the countries in the late 1950's and the early 1960's. Thus, from the agricultural angle, the development of land as a resource base is along the same lines for both the long-existing primary export trade and the relatively new industrial economy.

The major agricultural (including forest) products being developed with an eye both to the export market and to the resources needed for local manufacturing, are in particular, cocoa, coffee, palm oil and kernels, groundnuts, rubber, cotton, timber and livestock, especially cattle for hides, meat and milk as well as sheep and goats for meat and skins. Maps 2.3 and 2.4 show in general terms their dist-

Figure 2.3: Production of major agricultural export products

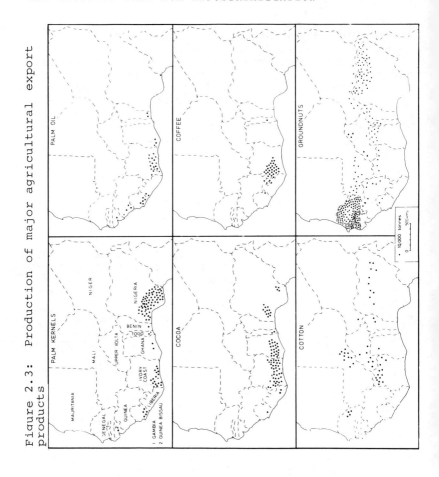

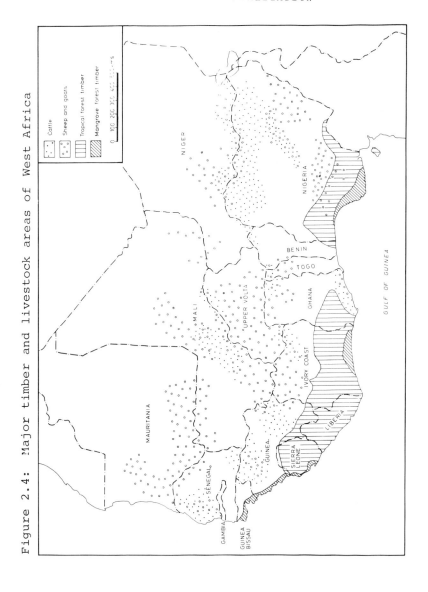

Figure 2.4: Major timber and livestock areas of West Africa

ribution over the region - largely in response to
climatic and edaphic factors.

Some progress has been made, particularly quantitatively, in the production of these items, thanks
to the demands of the First and Second World Wars
and their after-effects in the form of post-War re-
construction needs (Aboyade, 1968). But the relatively little progress made must be seen against the
background of the global economic recessions of the
1930's, the drought problems and, particularly in
Nigeria, the recent distractions by a highly competitive oil economy. However, to better appreciate
the nature of the agricultural resource base for
present day and future industrialization in West
African countries, it would be sufficient to focus
on what the situation is at present or has been in
the recent past.

Cocoa
The three main producers of cocoa in West Africa are
Ghana, Ivory Coast, and Nigeria. Ghana which, until
recently, was the foremost producer, turned out over
309,000 tonnes in 1975 (Table 2.1). However, she
has now been relegated to second place in the region
and in the face of her raging political and economic
crises, even the most progressive of her productive
sectors have been experiencing difficult times.
Agricultural export products are among the most seriously affected.

Ivory Coast, which was producing only an average of 140,000 tonnes of cocoa per year between 1965
and 1969, has since 1974 displaced Nigeria to become
the world's second largest producer. 430,000 tonnes
of cocoa were produced in 1981. Giant strides have
continued to be taken, especially in the form of
large scale plantation schemes. By 1976 over 80,000
hectares were under cocoa. Plantation acreages are
still rising besides the increasing efforts of small
private farmers.

Nigeria lost her second place in world ranking
in 1974 - at the height of her oil "boom" - mainly
as a result of too much preoccupation with the oil
industry, to the neglect of agriculture. Her cocoa
output declined from over 300,000 tonnes in 1970 to
a low of 155,000 tonnes in 1980. However, with her
current economic recession (sequel to the rather
suddent decline in oil revenue), Nigeria is gradually moving back into agriculture, with due emphasis on cocoa.

Table 2.1: Cocoa Production in West African Countries

Country	Production ('000 tonnes) in:							
	1970	1975	1976	1977	1978	1979	1980	1981
Ghana	309.5	339.0	320.0	310.0	265.0	296.0	250.0	230.0
Nigeria	302.4	220.2	200.2	210.0	160.0	160.0	155.0	160.0
Ivory Coast	168.0	241.0	257.0	240.0	312.0	379.0	400.0	430.0
Togo	23.2	14.6	17.8	17.0	13.0	14.0	16.0	15.0
Sierra Leone	6.6	7.5	8.0	6.0	7.0	9.0	7.0	9.0

Sources: (i) For 1970-1976 Economic Commission for Africa (1979)
Survey of Economic and Social Conditions in Africa;

(ii) For 1977-1978 Rake, A. (1981-2) New African Yearbook 1981-2

(iii) For 1979-1981 F.A.O. (1981) Production Yearbook Vol. 35, p. 185

Coffee

Coffee production is, as in the case of cocoa, confined to the forest zone of the Atlantic coast countries of West Africa, as shown in Map 2.3. The
countries of note are Ivory Coast, Sierra Leone,
Guinea, Togo and Liberia. Ivory Coast is Africa's
largest producer of coffee and the third in the
world - after Brazil and Colombia. Production, as
of cocoa, has been on the increase. Between 1965
and 1969 output averaged 240,000 tonnes: in 1970
Ivory Coast produced 274,000 tonnes. Production
rose to 324,000 tonnes in 1976. The highest ever
was 350,000 in 1981. Price rises on the world market have led to increases in acreage and output.
Sierra Leone produced 22,000 tonnes of coffee in
1970. As shown in Table 2.2, there has been an appreciable decline in output ever since.
    Guinea is the third largest producer of coffee
in West Africa. By 1969, production was at the level of 13,000 tonnes; by 1974, it was around 16,000
tonnes. A sharp decline from 1977 seems to have
been over since 1979.
    Togo produced over 13,000 tonnes of coffee in
1970, but the enthusiasm to expand production has
not been as much as pervades in Ivory Coast. However, the potential for increased coffee production
awaits exploitation. Liberia has picked up in recent years and is showing promises of superseding
Guinea and Sierra Leone before long.

Oil Palm

The forest lands of West Africa are ideal environments for the oil palm. Although largely growing in
scattered small farms and forests rather than in
huge plantations as in South-east Asia or in Zaire,
the oil palm is a major crop of West Africa. Its
main products - palm oil and kernels - are among
the leading exports of West Africa and one of the
basic raw materials for local industries. According
to estimates by Harrison Church (1980), 190,000
tonnes of palm oil would be sufficient to make about
275,000 tonnes of high quality soap. The same ton-
nage of palm kernels could provide enough oil for
over 200 tonnes of margarine. Explosives are also
made using glycerine extracts from palm kernel.
West Africa was, by 1957, supplying 80% of the
world's palm kernels and 33% of palm oil. As an important food item in many parts of the region and a
raw material for local industries, palm oil is mainly consumed locally.
    Nigeria was, by 1900, producing the bulk of the

Table 2.2: Coffee Production in West Africa

Country	Production ('000 tonnes) in:							
	1970	1975	1976	1977	1978	1979	1980	1981
Ivory Coast	274.0	254.0	324.0	291.0	196.0	277.0	250.0	350.0
Sierra Leone	22.0	21.0	22.0	10.0	10.0	14.0	10.0	6.0
Guinea	13.0	16.0	n/a	5.0	5.0	14.0	15.0	15.0
Togo	13.0	7.7	8.5	12.0	12.0	6.0	10.0	9.0
Liberia	4.9	4.5	4.6	12.0	12.0	8.0	13.0	13.0

Sources: (i)   For 1970–1976: E.C.A. (1979) Survey of Economic and Social Conditions in Africa

(ii) For 1977–1978: Rake, A. (1981–82) New African Yearbook 1981–82, p. 17

(iii) For 1979–1981: F.A.O. (1981) Production Yearbook, Vol. 35, p. 183

33

world's supply of palm oil. The acid sands of the
lower Niger basin and of most of the forested parts
of former Eastern Region, as well as the Basement
Complex rock region to the west of Benin, favour the
oil palm. In fact, the main constraint on the expansion of production has been competition from less
labour-demanding crops. As the oil palm grows tal-
ler, the harvesting process (involving risky and
tedious tree-climbing) becomes more difficult and
expensive. This has affected output to a considerable extent, as the requisite type of labour (the
young able-bodied man) increasingly prefers underemployment in the town to remunerative but tedious
oil palm trimming and harvesting in the countryside.
Just before the Nigerian civil war in 1967, the
country exported 520,000 tonnes of palm oil and
440,000 tonnes of palm kernel. Production went down
during the civil war to 8,000 tonnes for palm oil
and 176,000 tonnes for palm kernels in 1969. Table
2.3 shows that production has lately come close to
pre-civil war levels. Export figures are, however,
very low as local industries absorb the bulk of the
output.
    Other West African countries with sizeable oil
palm economy are Ivory Coast, Sierra Leone, Benin,
Ghana, Liberia, Guinea, Guinea Bissau and Togo, in
that order of importance (Table 2.3). Considerable
expansion programmes have, as for cocoa, been undertaken in Ivory Coast since the 1970's. Progress in
palm produce output is evident in the fact that in
1981 as much as 190,000 tonnes of palm oil were produced, compared with only 48,000 tonnes in 1967.
    Oil palm expansion programmes in many West
African countries have been in response to local
(including industrial) needs rather than to any
stimulus from world prices as in the case of coffee
and cocoa. The production potentials that exist are
still immense.

Groundnuts
Groundnuts are the major crops of the less humid
savanna zone of West Africa where annual rainfall is
from 14 to 35 inches (355 - 890 mm). The rich sandy
soils on which the groundnut crop does very well are
common features of the drier savanna - the Sudan
savanna - of West Africa which is the world's major
source of groundnuts (otherwise known as peanuts).
Besides the use of groundnut oil as a highly val-
uable cooking oil, considerable industrial use is
made of the product in the form of oil, cake, and
meal for a variety of products ranging from margar-

Table 2.3: Palm kernel and palm oil production in West Africa

Country	Production of Palm Kernels ('000 tonnes) in:			Production of Palm Oil ('000 tonnes) in:		
	1979	1980	1981	1979	1980	1981
Nigeria	335.00	345.00	350.00	650.00	675.00	675.00
Ivory Coast	26.04	30.00	30.00	132.00	170.00	190.00
Sierra Leone	32.73	30.00	30.00	45.00	48.00	50.00
Benin	69.50	73.00	75.00	30.00	34.00	34.00
Ghana	30.00	30.00	30.00	21.00	21.00	21.00
Liberia	8.00	7.20	7.00	26.00	27.00	20.00
Guinea	35.00	35.00	35.00	40.00	42.00	42.00
Guinea Bissau	26.00	30.00	30.00	4.80	4.70	4.70
Togo	17.22	19.00	20.00			

Source: F.A.O. (1981) Production Yearbook, Vol. 35, p. 141

ine to animal feedstuffs.

Senegal is the chief producer of groundnuts in West Africa. Production for export has been the pre-occupation of Senegal since as early as the 1840's. The opening of the railways from Dakar to the interior of former French West Africa gave considerable stim-ulus to groundnut production. Output of groundnuts in a normal year was estimated at over one million tonnes. World market prices have been providing some stimulus just as the recent (1969-73) Sahelian drought had adversely affected output. The 900,000 tonnes of 1981 amounted to a substantial improvement on the figures for the late 1970's.

Gambia is a country whose economy is based al-most entirely on groundnut production. That her Gross Domestic Product has, since 1965, shown con-siderable improvement has been due mainly to the groundnut economy and favourable world market prices. Production in the last three years was slightly over 100,000 tonnes on average. A peak of 140,000 tonnes had been reached in 1975.

Nigeria used to be the world's chief exporter of groundnuts. Production for export existed since the first decade of the present century. The con-struction of the railways for effective evacuation of the produce became a major stimulus to groundnut production from 1912 when the rail line first reached Kano, the centre of groundnut production in the country. Production rose to a peak in 1966/67 when 1,026,000 tonnes of output were recorded. In spite of the 1967-70 civil war in the country, and of the relative neglect of agriculture at the height of the country's "oil boom", groundnut exports in the form of nuts, cake, meal and oil amounted to 785,000 tonnes in 1969 (Nigeria, 1970). However, production later dropped sharply, as shown in Table 2.4. The growing disillusionment with the oil economy is helping to turn official attention once again to increased agricultural outputs. This may raise groundnut output to pre-civil war levels.

Mali has been making remarkable progress in groundnut production, especially after the 1969-73 droughts. The 1979-81 production figures of over 160,000 tonnes per year on average were much above the pre-drought (1967/8) output of 119,000 tonnes. Ghana and Gambia respectively produced an average of over 100,000 tonnes of groundnuts during the 1979-81 period, as the table shows. The potential for higher output is hardly in doubt. The same is true for Niger, Guinea, Upper Volta, Benin, Ivory Coast, Togo, Guinea Bissau and Sierra Leone, also

involved in groundnut production, but on a less impressive scale.

Table 2.4: Groundnut* production in West Africa

Country	Production ('000 tonnes) in:		
	1979	1980	1981
Senegal	676	489	900
Nigeria	540	570	580
Mali	179	130	190
Gambia	100	80	130
Ghana	107	100	90
Niger	81	100	100
Guinea	82	83	83
Upper Volta	75	77	77
Benin	66	60	60
Ivory Coast	52	53	54
Togo	35	35	35
Guinea Bissau	35	30	30
Sierra Leone	20	20	20

* in shell

Source: F.A.O. (1981) Production Year Book vol. 35, p. 127

Cotton
Cotton has much wider tolerance than groundnuts,
cocoa and the oil palm; its production is therefore
geographically most widespread. It grows as well in
the wetter savanna, otherwise known as the Guinea
savanna, as in the drier Sudan savanna. In the
latter, where it competes with groundnuts and such
important food crops as millet, cotton dominates in
areas of relatively heavy loam soils less suitable
to groundnuts. As the principal source of fibre for
textile production, cotton is grown both for export
and for local factory and craft industries. Craft
activity is very widespread in West Africa and traditionally age-old in a number of places.
     Output by West African countries, especially
for export, is generally very low. Table 2.5 gives
some indication of recent production levels in many
countries of West Africa, showing Mali and Ivory

Coast in the lead. The scope for increased production is still very wide and likely to be greater as
demands of modern industrial development underscore
the use of local raw materials. Expansion for domestic industrial needs in particular has been going
on in Ivory Coast where farmers are being encouraged
by high cotton prices to increase their acreage
and quality of seed cotton.

Table 2.5: Seed cotton production by major sources

Country	Production ('000 tonnes) in:		
	1979	1980	1981
Mali	136	158	114
Ivory Coast	115	143	134
Nigeria	110	90	85
Upper Volta	60	78	71
Senegal	27	22	35
Benin	26	16	24
Togo	13	20	20
Niger	9	4	6
Ghana	7	6	7

Source: F.A.O. (1981) Production Yearbook, Vol. 35, p. 135

Rubber
Rubber (Heva brasiliensis) thrives in the tropical
rainforest of West Africa. Production is very pro-
nounced in Liberia and Nigeria, and less so in Ghana.
By 1975, over 130,000 hectares had been planted with
rubber in Liberia. Annual production was then about
90,000 tonnes. Efforts to increase acreage have
continued through both the big foreign firms and the
small Liberian planters. Production in 1980 stood
at about 100,000 tonnes. In Nigeria, rubber growing
has yet to regain its prominence lost as a result
mainly of both the impact of synthetic rubber and
the recent local preoccupation with the oil economy.
Production in 1966 was just over 70,000 tonnes, but
declined to 56,000 tonnes in 1969. In 1975, it
stood at 50,000 tonnes. Ghana, which   by 1974
had   a total of 27,000 acres under rubber, produced only 9,700 tonnes then. Efforts to double the
rubber acreage by 1980 did not meet with success.

THE RESOURCE BASE FOR INDUSTRIALIZATION

West African rubber now has another chance of increased attention, the rising cost of oil having
caused a sharp rise in the price of synthetic rubber and diverted much attention to natural rubber.
Also, the greatly increased attraction of radials
in tyre technology preferring natural rubber is
raising considerable promise for natural rubber output, particularly in Liberia and Ivory Coast where
the foreign concessions have taken the new trend
into account in their expansion programmes.

Timber
Belonging ecologically to the forested parts of West
Africa where rainfall is above 60 inches (over
1520 mm.), timber is abundant. A wide range of
species exists. Many have, in fact, not yet been
discovered as industrially important and still remain unexploited for either the export market or
local industrial uses. Even the already identified
commercial trees awaiting exploitation are still
very substantial in many parts of West Africa. The
countries with great timber potential are Nigeria,
Ghana, Ivory Coast, Guinea and Liberia.
     Of Nigeria's estimated 120 usable tree species,
only about 30 are at present exploited. About 50
million cubic feet of industrial wood is taken annually from Nigerian forests; and about 50 per cent
of this gets into the export market in one form or
another.
     In Ghana, timber exploitation is on a large
scale, especially in the well-watered south-west.
Timber is second only to cocoa in Ghana's export
trade. By 1971, log shipment was above 500,000
tonnes and sawn timber exports amounted to about
130,000 tonnes.
     Timber resources in Ivory Coast are immense.
The country's third largest source of foreign exchange is timber. Carefully programmed reafforest-
ation schemes are not only to ensure a smooth export trade, but also to prepare the ground for
local industries needing special species. For example, eucalyptus is being planted as a long-term
measure to support the country's giant pulp mills.
The latter are designed to start with ordinary trees
and brushwood left after the commercial trees have
been removed for export.
     Guinea, like Ghana and Ivory Coast, is striving
to put her timber industry on a firm footing. In
1969, a large-scale programme for timber exploitation from the vast reserves was begun with Bul-

39

garian assistance. The objective was to provide for
domestic industrial use as well as for the export
market.

Fisheries
West African fisheries, from the Gulf of Guinea to
the territorial waters of Mauritania, are yet to be
exploited on a large scale. All the coastal countries consider fishing important, but their fishing
methods are as yet not fully modernized. Traditional fishing methods are still common, accounting
for more than 50 per cent of output. Fishing with
commercial boats and trawlers is gradually developing. Until there is full modernization of fishing,
the fisheries resources will likely remain considerably underexploited. However, the main point
is that, barring substantial increases in water pollution along the shores of West Africa as well as
trespasses from other parts of the world, the region's fisheries resources are still immense and
can be looked upon as a base for successful fish-
based industrial activities. Table 2.6 shows levels
of fishery resource exploitation associated with all
the countries of West Africa, some of which, like
Nigeria and Ghana as well as some landlocked states,
also have large inland (lake and river) fisheries.
For example, out of an average of 440,000 tonnes
produced annually by Nigeria between 1969 and 1975,
70,000 tonnes (16 per cent) came from Lake Chad, the
major inland source. The Kainji Lake, which then
accounted for only 8,000 tonnes, is yet to develop
into a major fishery for the country. So is the
Volta Lake fishery in Ghana.
      On the whole, the fish needs of West African
countries are as yet far from met from local cat-
ches. The need to minimize fish import which has
been a long-standing practice and source of foreign
exchange drain underscores the importance of modernizing the fishing industry by West African countries.
The implications of such modernization for industrial development are clearly positive and far-
reaching, as will be shown in later chapters.

Livestock
A larger part of West Africa has climate and vegetation characteristics conducive to livestock raising. However, on account of such environmental
problems as tsetse infestation and the 1969-73
Sahelian drought, areas for commercial stock rearing
have been very variable from year to year. Most of
the countries, like Niger, Mali and Upper Volta,

40

Table 2.6:   Fish production in West Africa, 1974-78

Country	Total catch ('000 tonnes) in:				
	1974	1975	1976	1977	1978
Benin	27.80	25.90	25.50	24.90	25.50
Cape Verde	3.43	3.90	2.02	8.33	8.33
Gambia	10.80	10.80	n.a	n.a	n.a
Ghana	n.a	n.a	237.70	268.10	264.00
Guinea	12.10	13.40	9.90	9.10	10.00
Guinea Bissau	n.a	0.87	1.62	1.91	n.a
Ivory Coast	n.a	n.a	77.00	83.40	79.00
Liberia	n.a	16.00	16.60	16.50	18.80
Mali	n.a	100.00	180.00	100.00	100.00
Mauritania	34.20	29.00	31.00	37.00	34.20
Niger	n.a	9.10	4.70	7.40	8.80
Nigeria	473.20	466.20	496.90	504.00	518.60
Senegal	n.a	362.90	362.00	288.80	345.80
Sierra Leone	67.70	68.60	53.80	52.70	50.10
Togo	11.15	14.42	11.38	8.44	n.a
Upper Volta	n.a	n.a	6.00	6.00	7.00

n.a.:   not available

Sources: F.A.O. Fishery Statistics (as published by Europa
Africa South of the Sahara, London, 1981)

largely covered by the Sahel and the Sudan vegetation, depend on their livestock, notably cattle,
sheep, goats and pigs, for a great deal of their
Gross Domestic Product accounted for by agriculture.   In Upper Volta, for instance, livestock are
the greatest source of the country's foreign exchange, accounting for 36 per cent of total export
earnings in 1975.   Livestock exports are in the form
of whole animals, and as hides and skins. The livestock products serve as part of the agricultural
resource for agro-based industrial activities ranging from meat-packing and bone-milling to leather
tanning and shoe industries.
       Table 2.7 shows the distribution of cattle,
sheep, goats and pigs in selected West African
countries - selection being largely on the basis of
size of output.   The distribution of production reflects the greater importance of predominantly
savanna and Sahel countries compared with countries

in the forested south. Poultry keeping, which has
been more modernized that any other aspect of stock
farming, if not of agriculture in general, has been
the most widespread aspect of animal husbandry.
Both the drier sub-Saharan and the coastal territories have been making considerable progress. The
effect of drought has however been felt on the pace
of progress as grains for feedstuff production become scarce on account of drought.

The phenomenon of food shortage, particularly
the issue of low protein content, is a general problem among West African countries. The endeavour to
cut down on food import bills is being given practical effect in programmes for food production. The
current Green Revolution programme in Nigeria and
the recent Operation Feed Yourself in Ghana have
been typical of such nationwide efforts. The most
outstanding stride in the direction of national
self-sufficiency concerns rice, sugar cane, fruit
and poultry. Although targets set have not been
consistently approached or met by many countries
owing to official lethargy in most cases, substantial successes have been recorded by some countries. For example, Ivory Coast, which was importing up to 100,000 tonnes of rice in the early 1970s
was by 1975 a net exporter of rice after recording
a production of 500,000 tonnes of paddy. Also the
country was able to export 70,000 tonnes of fresh
pineapples, then becoming the world's leading exporter (Rake, 1978). In the grip of political and
economic crises, Ghana has fitfully been demon-
strating similar enthusiasm but has yet to come up
with   target-reaching results comparable with
those of Ivory Coast or Senegal. At any rate, the
point to note is that all these efforts towards
domestic self-sufficiency in food supplies have
positive implications for the manufacturing industry sector, particularly the processing subsector which will be discussed in the next chapter.

Minerals
West Africa is richly endowed with a variety of
minerals. As a result, mining has been a major
economic activity in most West African countries.
It has played a very important part in the economic
development of most of those countries - not only
by contributing substantially to the GDP of the
country but also by influencing the provision and
spatial setting of such basic infrastructure as
railways, roads and ports. For example, Mauritania,
Nigeria, Liberia and Guinea are today deriving over

Table 2.7: Livestock production in selected West African countries 1979-81

Country	Cattle (million)			Sheep (million)			Goats (million)			Pigs (million)		
	1979	1980	1981	1979	1980	1981	1979	1980	1981	1979	1980	1981
Nigeria	12.00	12.30	12.50	11.35	11.70	12.00	24.20	24.50	25.00	1.05	1.10	1.15
Mali	6.00	6.25	6.35	6.00	6.25	6.35	6.50	6.75	7.00	0.04	0.04	0.05
Niger	3.11	3.21	3.30	2.77	2.80	2.85	6.87	7.00	7.20	0.03	0.031	0.032
Upper Volta	2.71	2.71	2.80	1.80	1.86	1.90	2.70	2.78	2.90	0.17	0.17	0.18
Senegal	2.53	2.34	2.26	1.07	2.07	2.08	0.95	1.10	1.15	0.17	0.20	0.20
Mauritania	1.14	1.20	1.07	4.90	5.20	5.20	2.55	2.60	2.60	n.a	n.a	n.a
Guinea	1.70	1.76	1.80	0.43	0.44	0.44	0.40	0.41	0.42	0.04	0.04	0.04
Ghana	0.73	0.75	0.75	1.65	1.70	1.70	2.00	2.10	2.10	0.40	0.42	0.42
Ivory Coast	0.65	0.70	0.72	1.15	1.20	1.25	1.20	1.25	1.30	0.32	0.34	0.36

Source: F.A.O. Production Yearbook, 1981, vol. 35, pp. 203 & 205

60% of their export earnings from mineral resources,
just as Libya and Zambia. The 675 kilometre F'
Derik-Nouadhibou railway line of Mauritania was constructed principally for handling the iron ore on
which the country so much depends. The Takoradi-
Tarkwa-Prestea railway of Ghana was initially designed to facilitate mineral evacuation from the
Tarkwa-Prestea Gold area to the export port of Tak-
oradi. So was the Port-Harcourt-Enugu rail line originally designed to handle coal from Enugu. The
process led to the opening of Port Harcourt as Nigeria's second port, and Aba, Umuahia and Enugu as
the major planned towns of the former Eastern Region
of Nigeria. However, in our consideration of the
importance of minerals (which are essentially non-
renewable assets) within the context of the industrial
resource base, attention should be on the winnable
reserves on which the foundations of future industrial development can be safely laid.

Table 2.8 shows what prospects there are for
iron ore. Although a great deal of exports of iron
ore has been going on from Mauritania, Liberia,
Guinea and Sierra Leone while commercial mining is
yet to begin on the Nigerian, Ghana, Benin, Mali and
Senegalese deposits, it is on these reserves that
the iron and steel mills of West Africa are later to
depend. Such mills will hopefully be providing the
long-awaited foundation for manufacturing on reasonably large and competitive scales. Supplementation
of raw material outside the import trade can only
come from domestic scrap iron trade - a very small
source indeed within the West African region.
Therefore for a region that is yet to set up its
iron and steel mills, export of the basic raw material - iron ore that is a wasting asset - calls for
cautious and long-term planning in the interest of
meaningful local industrialization.

Coal
West Africa has very limited coal reserves; the limitations are as much in quantity as in quality. So
far, the only reserves of note are those in Nigeria
as shown in Map 2.5. Nigeria's proven reserves a-
mount to a total of over 800 million tonnes, lig-
nites or brown coal excluded. Over 50 per cent of
Nigeria's coal is of the soft   semi-bituminous
type which does not coke well for iron smelting purposes, and for other thermal uses it has lower cal-
orific value than non-coking anthracite coal. By
and large, the region's coal resources are likely to
be in greater demand for other uses than iron ore

44

Figure 2.5: Distribution of important minerals and hydro electric power stations

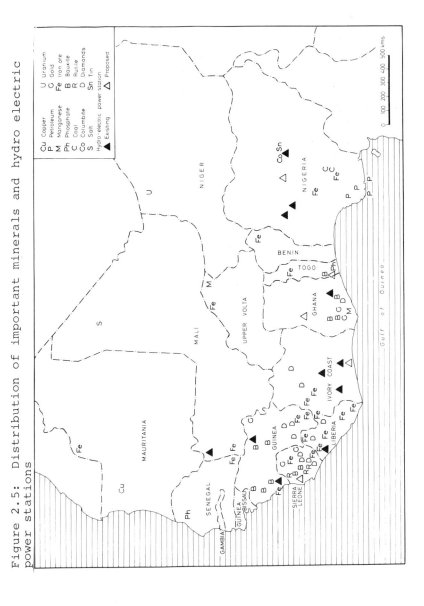

45

Table 2.8: Major iron ore reserves in West Africa

Country	Estimated Reserves (Mil. tonnes)	Estimate year
Liberia	12,000	1978
Mauritania	2,000	1977
Guinea	2,000	1977
Sierra Leone	1,200	1978
Senegal	1,200	1978
Ghana	700	1977
Ivory Coast	500	1978
Nigeria	300	1980

Source: Various, including E.C.A. Statistical Yearbook (several years); Udo, R.K. (1978), A Comprehensive Geography of West Africa; Rake, A. (1978) New African Yearbook

smelting. There are several such uses. They include: use as general fuel for firing manufacturing
plants like cement kilns and factory boilers; use as
raw material for the production of tar, dyes and
paints, as well as several chemicals for industrial
uses. Also such coal varieties can be converted into oil as the need arises, as is now the case in
India, sequel to the recent steep rises in the price
of petroleum. The process of oil liquefaction provides hydrocarbon oils that supplement chemicals and
fuel obtainable from petroleum.

Petroleum
West Africa's petroleum potential is immense and yet
to be fully estimated. Besides Nigeria, which is
among the top ten producers of crude oil in the
world, Ghana, Ivory Coast, Senegal and Benin have
reserves the sizes of which are yet to be determined.
However, put together, the oil reserves of West
Africa are over 35 per cent of Africa's, and should
form a strong base for large scale production of
fuel oils, lubricants, petro-chemicals and a host of
other possible derivatives. Nigeria's proven reserves at the end of 1975 were estimated at 2,700
million metric tonnes. Output in 1976 averaged
2.024 million barrels per day. It was 2.3 million
barrels per day in 1974. It dropped below 1 million
barrels per day towards the of the 1970's but is

46

gradually picking up once more as world market conditions improve.

Gas

Gas has been found in vast reserves in West Africa,
particularly in Nigeria - mainly in the same area as
petroleum. There is on average 750 cubic feet of
gas per barrel of crude oil in Nigeria (World Bank,
1974). Exploitation on any appreciable scale is yet
to begin. Unfortunately, there has been considerable loss of natural gas in Nigeria through inten-
tional flaring. With improved technology the bulk
of the product now being wasted will constitute a
major source of electricity and liquefied gas products for industrial and household uses.

Bauxite

West Africa is rich in bauxite, the ore of aluminium. There is therefore a good material base for an
aluminium industry. This is of special significance
at a period when aluminium is becoming more and more
important vis-a-vis the traditionally well-known
metals like steel and copper. The geographical distribution favours Guinea, Ghana, Ivory Coast and
Sierra Leone. By 1977, Guinea had an estimated reserve of 2,400 million tonnes, i.e., more than 33
per cent of total world high grade reserves (Rake,
1978, p. 143).

Manganese

Manganese reserves in West Africa have so far been
in Ghana, Ivory Coast and Upper Volta. In each
country, the size of the deposit is yet to be determined even though exploitation has existed in Ghana
for over fifty years now. In that country, the main
carbonate ores in Nsuta district are estimated to be
about 28 million tonnes. There are also deposits of
the less valued ores for manganese oxide nodules,
which have been estimated to be about 100 million
tonnes. But the size of the medium and the low
grade deposits, though very substantial, is yet to
be determined. At any rate, the reserves in various
countries of West Africa are by any standards great,
and can be considered as a stable source of alloys
for a West African steel industry. Manganese is one
of the most important alloys existing in West Africa; others are chrome and nickel. The quantity of
chrome ore available in Sierra Leone, Mauritania,
Togo and Ivory Coast is yet to be more precisely determined. So is the reserve of nickel in the Tombao
district of Upper Volta.

Tin, lead, zinc, columbite, rutile, phosphate, copper and other industrially important minerals shown in Map 2.5 have not yet been found in vast quantities. Their exploitation (excepting in the case of diamonds and gold), however, has generally been fitfully embarked upon, mainly in response to world prices.

Power Resources
West African streams are very important power sources which can complement other sources already identified - solar energy, coal, wood, petroleum and gas - to present a composite picture of the vast power potentials in the region. Map 2.5 shows both the developed and the proposed hydro-electric power stations on the many streams of West Africa. Particularly noteworthy are the Volta power dam, the Niger dam complexes comprising the Kainji, the Shiroro and the Lokoja dams in Nigeria, the Selingue barrage in Mali, the Bandama river power dams complex comprising the Kossu dam, the Taabo dam, and the Soubre dam; and the proposed Senegal river power dam at Manantali in Mali for joint use by Senegal, Mali and Mauritania.

Table 2.9 provides a representative pattern of energy development and use in West Africa. The appalling inadequacy of energy use per capita can be appreciated from the fact that industrial economies had, on average, over 7,000 kg per capita during the same period.[1] The region's energy resources are still grossly underdeveloped. A typical example of underdevelopment of generating capacity is provided by the Kainji Dam power scheme in Nigeria. By 1970, only four of the twelve generating sets provided for in the dam had been installed and in use. Although there was a problem of the low level of the Kainji Lake water, there was a good possibility of increasing the generating sets to six. This was not done until 1978! At any rate, West Africa's power resource endowment is great and very adequate in most of the countries for coping with future demands of large-scale industrialization,given the right resource management. The geographical distribution of power resources is uneven and some countries seeking for cheap power sources must go beyond their borders. To that end, bilateral and tripartite arrangements in electric power distribution have been in existence and augur well for the future. Even before the inauguration of the Economic Community of West African States (ECOWAS), there had been electricity distribution from the Volta power dam in Ghana to

Table 2.9:   Energy consumption per capita, 1979

Country	Per capita Consumption (coal equivalent)	Country	Per capita Consumption (coal equivalent)
Liberia	425 kg	Guinea	84 kg
Ghana	258 kg	Nigeria	80 kg
Senegal	253 kg	Benin	65 kg
Ivory Coast	230 kg	Niger	46 kg
Mauritania	196 kg	Mali	28 kg
Togo	112 kg	Upper Volta	26 kg
Sierra Leone	84 kg		

Source: World Bank, <u>World Development Report 1982</u>, p. 122

Togo and Upper Volta, and from Nigeria's Kainji Dam
to Niger. The plan to supply Mali, Senegal and
Mauritania with power from the Manantali Dam also
predated ECOWAS. The inauguration of the latter and
the progress it has so far made hold out much promise for closer and more lasting cooperation on energy and other economic development programmes.

LABOUR RESOURCES
West African economies in general have been experiencing many problems related to manpower development. Skilled labour needed for such specialized
functions as industrial operations and business management is in very short supply. As a result, many
positions requiring certain grades of labour are
either not filled at all or occupied by less qualified hands. Certain aspects of some countries' indigenization policy are often very difficult, if not
impossible, to implement without losing expatriate
services critical for economic progress. Yet it is
the same countries that also experience fast rising
rates of unemployment. These two situations of
acute shortage of labour and rising levels of unemployment in the same region may seem paradoxical.
However, a close study of the structure of available
manpower and the nature of posts required to be
filled will help to show that both situations are
two sides of the same coin - inadequate manpower development and distribution. This needs to be appreciated in any effort to understand the problems
and prospects of industrialization in West Africa.
And to that end, a few statistical details on West
Africa's labour resources can be helpful.

Table 2.10 shows the percentages of economically active population in 1980 compared with percentage rates of adult literacy per country. Economically active population is a term used to embrace,
according to the International Labour Office, all
employed and unemployed persons, including those
seeking work for the first time. This definition
covers employees, persons working on their own account, salaried employees, wage earners, unpaid family workers, members of producer cooperatives and
those serving in the armed forces (ILO, 1973, p.20).
It is perhaps needless to say that all the above
categories of persons should be aged 15 years and
over. Adult literacy rates, on the other hand, refer to the percentage of the total population aged 15
years and over able to read and write. Since the
two values in Table 2.10 refer more or less to the
same population and age group, it can be appreciated

Table 2.10: Economically active population and
adult literacy rates as percentages of total adult
population in West Africa

Country	Crude active rate* (%) in 1980	Adult literacy rate[@] (%) in 1977
Benin	51	25
Cape Verde	n.a	n.a
Gambia	n.a	n.a
Ghana	51	n.a
Guinea	53	20
Guinea Bissau	n.a	n.a
Ivory Coast	53	41
Liberia	50	25
Mali	52	9
Mauritania	52	17
Niger	51	5
Nigeria	50	30
Senegal	52	10
Sierra Leone	53	n.a
Togo	51	18
Upper Volta	53	5

Source: World Bank (1982) World Development Report, 1982

* p. 146, @ p. 154

how high the level of illiteracy is among the economically active population of the countries shown.[2]
Even among the literate group of each country's active labour force the level of the type of skill
needed for effective manufacturing and industrial
management functions is generally low. The structure of formal education in West Africa in general
has not changed significantly since political independence of most of the countries in the late 1950's
and early 1960's. The low technical content of the
type of education inherited from the former colonial
powers is still one of the common features of education in West African countries. Thus, given the
inadequacy of facilities for technical manpower development, and the continued emphasis on   non-
technical education, the development of manpower appropriate for industrial growth is generally very
slow.

Furthermore, although, as shown in Table 2.10,
the percentage of the economically active population in West Africa was generally over 50 per cent
in 1980, the non-agricultural component was indeed
very small. Table 2.11 shows that, with the exception of Benin, Ghana and Nigeria, the West African countries in 1980 had each over 65 per cent of
their economically active labour force engaged in
agriculture. It was even as high as 91 per cent in
Niger.

In addition to the young primary school leavers, it is mainly the youth among the agricultural
labour force that constitute the core of rural-urban
migration which has for some time now assumed alar-
ming proportions. It is to those unskilled and hardly educated, if literate, groups that the bulk of
the unemployed in the urban centres of West Africa
belongs. Thus, although West African countries have
fast-growing populations and large cohorts of economically active labour force, their skilled manpower
needs have continued to grow. Official efforts to
grapple with the problem of inadequate industrial
manpower are beginning to reflect the type of urgency and priority that should have been demonstrated
soon after political independence. The past few
years, particularly since 1976, in Nigeria have witnessed crash training programmes involving over four
thousand young people in technical training in Europe and North America. Also, Ghana's 1975-80 Development Plan gave some prominence to the training of
skilled manpower. Efforts to train technical manpower both locally and overseas have been made and
will be continued when practicable. Meanwhile the

unrelenting economic problems of the country constitute a serious constraint.

Table 2.11:   Sectoral distribution of active labour
force, 1960, 1980

Percentage of labour force in:

Country	Agriculture		Industry*		Service	
	1960	1980	1960	1980	1960	1980
Benin	54%	46%	9%	16%	37%	38%
Ghana	64%	53%	14%	20%	22%	27%
Guinea	88%	82%	6%	11%	6%	7%
Ivory Coast	89%	79%	2%	4%	9%	17%
Liberia	80%	70%	10%	14%	10%	16%
Mali	94%	73%	3%	12%	3%	15%
Mauritania	91%	85%	3%	5%	6%	10%
Niger	95%	91%	1%	3%	4%	6%
Nigeria	71%	54%	10%	19%	19%	27%
Senegal	84%	76%	5%	10%	11%	14%
Sierra Leone	78%	65%	12%	19%	10%	16%
Togo	80%	67%	8%	15%	12%	18%
Upper Volta	92%	82%	5%	13%	3%	5%

*including non-manufacturing establishments in the indust-
rial sector.

Source: World Bank, World Development Report 1982, p. 146

CAPITAL RESOURCES
One major problem of West Africa is that of capital
accumulation and use for economic development. The
region is as a result one of the poorest in Africa
which itself is the poorest of the world continental
blocks. By 1975, Africa's gross national product
per capita was less than half the world per capita
average. As shown in Table 2.12, the average per
capita GNP in West Africa in 1980 was US $410. The
range was from $160 in Guinea Bissau to $1,150 in
Ivory Coast. By world standards, West Africa is a
region of very poor countries. As many as 17 out of
the 35 countries of the world earning less than $200
per capita by 1975 belonged to Africa. Also, out of
the ten African countries which had less than $150

per capita in 1975, five belonged to West Africa.
All these help to put the degree of poverty of West
Africa into graphic form. Since modern manufacturing activity involves considerable capital investment - much more than is locally available - West
African countries have had to depend on the sale of
their natural resources in the agricultural (including forestry) and mining sectors to be able to fin-
ance, albeit partially, their major industrial projects. But quite often there is a heavy leaning on
external sources of capital to supplement the foreign exchange earned from primary export promotion
under unfavourable conditions of declining terms of
trade.

It should be a matter for concern to West African countries that such dependence on primary export promotion and external sources of aid has obvious dangers. The first is the danger of depleting
the vital, non-renewable resources (minerals) before
the exporting countries are financially and technically well placed to use such resources for the development of their own industrial economy. Sierra
Leone in 1975 was in danger of seriously depleting
her main iron ore reserve and obliged to stop iron
ore mining. However, the newly discovered ore deposits have given the country another chance of using
the local ore base for developing modern metallurgy
and for diversifying an economy that is essentially
primary or extractive. Niger is currently increasing her rate of export of uranium - a rare mineral
resource that a richer country would strive to conserve for more beneficial domestic use in future.

The second danger has to do with the terms
under which capital is borrowed from some of the
outside sources. West African countries, like most
Third World countries, have often been obliged to
exchange their natural resources or make other major
concessions for externally secured loans and aid on
terms clearly prejudicial to the long-term economic
interest of the receiving African countries.

Although some of these dangers are known to the
African countries, sometimes quite vaguely, the latter seem to be left with very few alternatives.
Such deals are often concluded in the hope that
sticky problems will somehow find ways of resolving
themselves before the worst comes to the worst! And
sometimes they do, as in the case of poor countries
like Libya and Gabon suddenly striking vast reserves
of oil, and Mauritania and Guinea discovering large
iron ore deposits. The new finds should serve as
the resource base on which modern economic growth

Table 2.12: Per capita gross national product in West Africa, 1980

Country	G.N.P. at market price per capita (U.S. $)
Benin	300
Cape Verde	300
Gambia	250
Ghana	420
Guinea	290
Guinea Bissau	160
Ivory Coast	1,150
Liberia	520
Mali	190
Mauritania	320
Niger	330
Nigeria	1,010
Senegal	450
Sierra Leone	270
Togo	410
Upper Volta	190
AVERAGE	410

Source: World Bank (1982) <u>World Bank Atlas: Gross National Product and Growth Rates, 1981</u>, p. 12.

and development can firmly begin. By virtue of the oil industry in Libya, the country had in 1980 a per capita GNP of $8,640 (US), one of the highest in the world!

Apart from such problematic sources of funds and aid, there are international organizations whose contributions have been one major source of assistance to developing countries including West African countries. For instance, out of a total assistance of $1,517.6 million (US dollars) from the Organization of Petroleum Exporting Countries (OPEC) to black African countries in 1975, West African countries received $76.1 million distributed as shown in Table 2.13. However, the total net receipt of each West African country from a variety of sources between 1976 and 1979 was as indicated in Table 2.14. The Sahelian countries were the main recipients, having been the main problem areas both because of their recent drought disasters and as a result of

Table 2.13: OPEC concessional assistance to West African countries in 1975

Recipient	Assistance (U.S. $ million)
Mauritania	47.6
Niger	15.3
Guinea	4.0
Mali	4.0
Senegal	3.0
Guinea Bissau	1.2
Upper Volta	1.0

Table 2.14: Net receipts of official development aid by West African countries, 1976-79

Receiving Country	Amount received ($ million) in: 1976	1977	1978	1979
Benin	54.4	49.3	61.1	81.2
Cape Verde	24.9	27.2	33.2	34.3
Gambia	11.9	21.6	35.2	35.7
Ghana	64.0	91.2	113.9	171.2
Guinea	11.7	22.1	60.2	57.3
Guinea Bissau	22.2	37.6	50.1	53.1
Ivory Coast	108.2	106.3	131.4	162.3
Liberia	26.9	33.7	48.0	82.2
Mali	89.0	112.8	161.5	189.7
Mauritania	180.3	164.7	216.7	165.5
Niger	129.4	96.8	156.5	172.0
Nigeria	53.3	42.4	37.4	25.7
Senegal	126.8	123.0	225.9	309.0
Sierra Leone	15.1	26.2	40.2	52.1
Togo	43.0	64.2	102.5	111.6
Upper Volta	84.1	110.3	159.4	199.3

Source: O.E.C.D., Annual Review (as reported by Rake, A. (1981/2) New African Yearbook, p. 12)

their permanent economic problems of relative isolation.

Besides the aid, bilateral relations with external bodies are also designed to supplement the
capital resources of the African countries involved.
For example, the sugar cane plantation scheme in
Ivory Coast, the bauxite industry in Guinea, the
rubber plantations and the iron mining operations of
Liberia as well as the technical skills training
programmes of Nigeria and Ghana are typical of projects receiving some form of external assistance toward the improvement of the resource base of West
African countries. Such supports by the more advanced countries or by bodies from such countries
are, however, less helpful in the long run if resource development in the African countries is not
carefully worked into a programme of sustained economic development and increasing economic self-
reliance.

Altogether, our survey of the resource base of
West African countries has highlighted some of the
prospects and problems of modern industrialization
in the region. Land resources in general seem to
have good prospects in terms of their potential for
sustaining industrial development. But much depends
on whether resource exploitation is carefully planned and executed with medium- and long-term development objectives in view. To that end, there is need
to relax the current hurry in the exploitation of
non-renewable assets like minerals for export as
primary products. Export-orientated primary production should rather concentrate on the agricultural (including forestry and fishing) sector. The
modernization of the agricultural sector of West
Africa should be pursued as an essential preliminary
to successful industrialization and continued export
promotion. This is for purposes both of earning the
badly needed foreign exchange and of providing the
basic industrial inputs and food for domestic needs.
The prevailing traditional systems of agriculture
characterized by small scale and rudimentary technology cannot adequately prepare the agricultural
sector for large scale industrialization.

The problems associated with both labour and
capital resources are indeed serious and deserving
of much more attention than they are at present receiving in most West African countries. On the issue of labour, the general dearth of technical and
managerial manpower calls for more than the crash
training programme currently being organized by a
number of countries. More importantly, it requires

the restructuring of the education system inherited
from the erstwhile colonial powers. A new structure
of education in West Africa and in other parts of
Africa should give more attention to the technical
content of modernizing education in order to make
the average educated inhabitants more receptive and
adaptable to technological innovations. Indeed,
without such technically biased education, the current campaigns for technological transfer can hardly
be translated in practical terms.

   Although the problems of poverty have been recognized all over West Africa as a major obstacle to
industrial development on any appreciable scale, it
is not certain that the danger of seeking solutions
through foreign loans and aid is fully, if widely,
appreciated. For one thing, aid in the form of
machinery and equipment often compromises some of the
economic objectives of the beneficiary. For example
if the donor countries are more interested in promoting their economic interest than in meeting the
needs of the recipient countries, sophisticated
labour-saving equipment may be introduced where employment generation is badly needed. The maintenance of such special equipment and the supply of its
spare parts remain the preserve of the donor country
thus well placed to manipulate the economic fortunes
of the recipient countries. Also the cost of loans,
even at low interest rates, serves to increase
rather than decrease the financial burden of recipient countries, particularly in the medium- and
long-term. This is more so when debt redemption is
based on primary exports by the recipients under
conditions of unfavourable terms of trade for the
primary product exporter. Under such trade conditions, West African countries, like other primary
product-exporting countries of the Third World, receive less for their increasing quantum of primary
products. At any rate, while continuing with the
prevailing unfavourable terms of trade, West African
countries would be well advised to conserve their
non-renewable resources for more effective future
use in the development of their own industrial sector.

NOTES

   1. Compare these low values for West African
countries with 1,018 kg. for Brazil, 771 kg. for
Turkey, and 645 kg. for Algeria.

2. It is also noteworthy that a good part of the so-called literate population in those countries are not literate in the <u>lingua franca</u> - English, French, or Portuguese - and can hardly fit into even the low grade jobs in the formal sector of each country's economy.

Chapter Three

HISTORICAL PERSPECTIVE OF INDUSTRIAL DEVELOPMENT IN WEST AFRICA

FACTORS IN THE POST-WORLD WAR II TRANSFORMATION TOWARD INDUSTRIALISATION

The colonial period in West Africa was one of large-scale primary production and export to industrial Europe and North America in particular. Up to the end of World War II, exports of agricultural and mineral products of West Africa were still on the increase. Indeed, post-War reconstructions and industrial rehabilitation efforts in war-ravaged Europe and Asia stimulated further increases in West African exports. The Korean war of the 1950s brought the demands for West African primary products to a peak. Most of the primary products involved are shown in Table 3.1.

Effective primary export promotion involves some form of commodity valorization - the process of enhancing product quality per unit of weight through processing. If by their low value per unit of weight or volume agricultural and mineral raw materials cannot profitably bear the cost of long distance transportation, processing of agricultural products and beneficiation of minerals become very necessary in the exporting country. Processing or beneficiation reduces the amount of waste in the raw material, and, thereby, the cargo space required for the commodity. Even for local needs, material valorization is the very first step in normal industrial activity.

The nature of first stage processing activity widely undertaken in West Africa is shown in Table 3.2. Traditional methods of manually extracting oil from the oil palm fruit began during the inter-war years to give way to the more efficient hand press by which the oil extracted increased and also the free fatty acid content of the oil decreased consider-

Table 3.1:   Major exports of West Africa by source
up to 1970

Product	Major Sources in West Africa
Coffee	Ivory Coast, Guinea, Togo, Liberia
Cocoa	Ghana, Nigeria, Ivory Coast
Groundnuts	Nigeria, Senegal, Mali, Gambia, Niger
Cotton	Nigeria, Mali, Ivory Coast, Niger
Palm Oil	Nigeria, Sierra Leone, Benin, Ivory Coast
Palm Kernel	Nigeria, Sierra Leone, Benin, Ivory Coast
Rubber	Liberia, Nigeria
Timber	Ghana, Ivory Coast, Liberia, Nigeria
Hides & Skins	Nigeria, Niger, Senegal, Mali
Bananas	Ivory Coast, Guinea
Gold	Ghana
Diamond	Ghana, Sierra Leone
Tin	Nigeria
Columbite	Nigeria
Petroleum	Nigeria
Uranium	Niger
Iron Ore	Liberia, Mauritania, Guinea
Phosphates	Togo, Senegal

ably, making the product more acceptable in overseas
markets. Furthermore, post-War increases in demand
for West African palm oil encouraged the introduction of factory-type "pioneer oil mills" which further increased the quality of palm oil.   In like
fashion, cotton ginneries (which first appeared in
Nigeria in the first decade of this century but
earlier in Senegal) and power-driven saw mills increased in numbers in the source areas for cotton
and timber. This had the effect of reducing the
share of more traditional or rudimentary processing
methods and of increasing rates and quality of output. Noteworthy is the subregional concentration of
processing activities as supply-based enterprises.
While palm fruit, cocoa, coffee, timber and rubber
processing units concentrate in the forest zones in
the more coastal south, cotton ginning and the processing of groundnuts, hides and skins feature prom-
inently in the savanna and the Sahel zones. In both
zones it is in the rural environs of the main col-
lecting centres, rather than in the centres themselves, that this first stage processing is mainly
undertaken. A notable exception is groundnut oil
milling in big cities like Kano, Dakar and Bamako.

Table 3.2: First-stage processing activity in West Africa

Material	Activity	Product
Oil Palm fruit	Oil-extraction	Oil
Oil Palm nut	nut-cracking	Kernels
Seed Cotton	Ginning	Cotton lint
Rubber latex	Crepe making	Crepe
Cocoa pods	Extraction and drying	Cocoa beans
Coconut	Kernel extraction and drying	Copra
Groundnuts	Shelling and crushing	Nuts and oil
Coffee	Extraction and drying	Coffee
Cassava	Peeling, grating and roasting	Gari
Paddy	Hulling and threshing	Rice
Logs	Saw milling	Sawn lumber
Hides & Skins	Tanning	Leather
Casiterite	Separation and dressing	Cassiterite

However, although the main aspect of West Africa's industrial economy was processing activity, it was by no means the only form of industrial activity known before the exit of the colonial powers. A study of Nigeria's pre-1945 industrial scene (Onyemelukwe,1978a) shows that there were additionally manufacturing enterprises engaged in finishing functions. Table 3.3 shows industrial establishments that could be identified by offical surveys as operating before 1945 and employing ten or more workers.[1] Of the 47, only 21 (about 45 per cent) were actually engaged in the production of processed commodities. The remaining 55 per cent which produced goods in their finished forms were in bakery and printing industries which catered for a relatively small clientele, particularly the few foreign (mainly European) administrators, missionaries, and merchants. Thus in spite of its numerical strength, the finishing aspect of the industrial economy was far more circumscribed in its influence compared with the processing activity geared to the rapidly expanding export trade. The Nigerian example largely mirrors the pre-1945 West African scene.

When world prices were good (as in the mid 1950s) primary export trade had the effect of putting big cash crop producers at the top of local income groups. A rise in income normally increases

Table 3.3:   Pre-1945 industrial establishments in Nigeria by type

Industrial Type**	Frequency	Product Type	
		Processed	Finished
Meat Processing	1	1	–
Saw milling	1	1	–
Fruit processing	1	–	1
Vegetable & Animal processing	3	2	1
Bakery	6	–	6
Food processing	1	1	–
Line and Block	1	–	1
Cotton ginning	10	10	–
Wearing Apparel	1	–	1
Tannery	3	3	–
Drugs and Medicine	1	–	1
Furniture and Fixtures	2	–	2
Printing and Publishing	9	–	9
Soap	1	–	1
Coal Products	1	–	1
Rubber Processing	3	3	–
Wood carvings	1	–	1
Total	47	21	26

Source: Industrial Directory, Federal Ministry of Industry, Lagos, 1971.

* Excluding many processing establishments whose start-up years and/or sizes (employment) were not known.

** Excluding Mining and Service establishments listed in the Directory.

the possibility of greater savings and investments. Although it does not always follow that greater income leads to greater saving and investment (it could lead to greater consumption), there is generally a greater propensity to save. Also, even when some savings are made, and the propensity to invest is strong, very much depends on the choice of what to invest in. In the case of many West African primary producers who had hitherto been exchanging their primary products with imported manufactured consumer goods, the desire to invest in simple processing

plants, assembly plants and in rudimentary forms of
modern manufacturing soon became as strong as the
propensity to spend on imported consumer goods.
Thus as more and more of the imported consumer goods
got popularized and their market widened in each
country of West Africa, the urge to produce some of
such imported items locally increased.

The groups of West Africans best placed financially to try out the entrepreneurial innovation of
simple manufacturing and higher-stage processing
were the relatively well-to-do export-promoting primary producers. So also were the powerful middlemen
operating between Produce Marketing Boards and the
small farmers as licenced buying agents. After all,
one of the major constraints on manufacturing enterprise is capital; and it was the cash crop farmer or
such big time intermediaries as the licenced buying
agents who at that time were best placed to own or
loan the capital required. However, it soon became
clear that it required much more than capital to set
up an industrial enterprise that could effectively
compete with overseas manufacturers. The badly
needed technical and managerial skills were virtually lacking; also with political control still in the
hands of European powers, it was not easy to create
the political climate conducive to industrial development. Attainment of political self-determination
was thus expected to provide a major solution to
problems of industrial development in West Africa.
And it did to a great extent from the late 1950s.
The gradual exodus of the colonial powers from the
West African scene had led to a substantial increase
in the political decision-making power of West Africans (Aboyade, 1968). By 1957 Ghana had attained
full political sovereignty. Guinea followed suit in
1958, and Senegal, Mali, Togo, Ivory Coast, Benin
and Nigeria in 1960. By the end of 1965 all but
Guinea Bissau and Cape Verde had attained political
independence. As should be expected, one of the
evidences of political self-determination was the
evolving of industrial development policies by the
emergent independent countries' governments. Definite budgetary allocations to the industrial sector
under a ministry of industry became a feature of the
first post-independence government of each West African country.

THE IMPORT SUBSTITUTION STRATEGY

The practice of import substitution has been embraced as the most convenient way of developing the industrial sector towards decreasing dependence on external sources for consumer goods. It is convenient in the sense that it does not call for as much technical expertise as would be necessary for undertaking most capital goods manufacturing. Capital goods like machinery, tools and spare parts are imported in preference to consumer goods which can be locally produced, mainly in assembly-type operations. As pointed out in Chapter 2, West African countries were (and are still) generally weak in technology; also they are short in the capital resource required to set up heavy industries even if the requisite technical know how were locally available. Therefore on attainment of political independence, the need to cut down on foreign exchange expended on consumer goods and also to diversify their economies that were essentially agricultural was given official expression by the various West African governments through strategies of import substitution. Necessary promotional fiscal measures were taken, particularly in the form of tax exemptions granted to infant industries, and import restrictions designed to protect local industries from the crippling effects of foreign competition. The setting up of industrial development banks, as in Nigeria, and the special use of existing and newly established commercial banks for the task of promoting manufacturing enterprises became a common feature of official strategy in industrial development.

Another important step taken by many West African governments was the encouragement of small industrial promoters through the development of industrial estates. It was realised that most aspiring industrial entrepreneurs had inadequate capital and could best be helped by the provision of industrial estates and zones in major urban centres. The rationale for such official decisions is manifold. First, most prospective industrial promoters hardly have enough capital to rent adequate urban space and set up the structures and the manufacturing plants as well as cope with the running costs involved, especially at the teething stage of industrial projects. Providing them with space and buildings to rent at reasonable prices is therefore a considerable assistance. Secondly, even where the promoters have the financial resources for providing such physical needs as land and factory structures, there is often great difficulty of obtaining a lease of suitable land in the big cities. This can be obviated by the provision of industrial estates. Thirdly, where industrial estates are properly planned and equipped with the necessary infrastructure - power, water supply, cheap accessibility, particularly by means of roads and railway sidings, among others - industrial promoters enjoy external economies that would have been non-existent were they to take up isolated locations. Industrial estates attract several manufacturing firms to the same place. Fourthly, in addition to providing some of the facilities that are cost-reducing, industrial estates raise the prospects of such economies as inter-factory linkage benefits, the pooling of labour and of certain common services, and the isolation of urban activities not conducive to industrial development. All these benefits arising directly and indirectly from the establishment of industrial estates collectively accrue to firms as urbanization economies. They can, however, arise outside industrial estates, but generally take a longer time to evolve. Industrial estates, therefore, have the effect of hastening the realization of such economies.

A point to note well is that industrial estates in West African countries are not necessarily designed for import substitution activities only; any form of industrial activity has as much chance of being promoted as any other. The fact remains that when the idea of industrial estates was bought by most West African countries during the early 1960s, official industrial preoccupation was with the import substitution strategy.

Capital goods imports are sometimes for purposes of establishing higher-stage processing of local raw materials hitherto exported after first-stage processing. Although at a more sophisticated level of material processing there is need for much more technical know how than would normally be required in first-stage processing described earlier (Table 3.2), considerably less factor (especially material) combination is normally involved than in most finishing operations, even for simple consumer goods. Therefore, making less demands on modern technology that is in very short supply in West Africa, high level or multi-stage processing has generally had an earlier start as a more feasible economic proposition than the finishing functions. Consequently during the post-independence period when import substitution became a major policy objective of most West African governments, high level

processing of such industrial materials as are shown
in Table 3.4 was a prominent feature of the slowly
changing economic landscape in many parts of West
Africa. Indeed, this higher-stage processing activity became an outstanding feature from the immediate post-War years to the first half of the post-
independence decade (i.e. the mid 1960s) of the industrially most active countries - Ivory Coast,
Senegal, Nigeria and Ghana (Fig. 3.1). During the

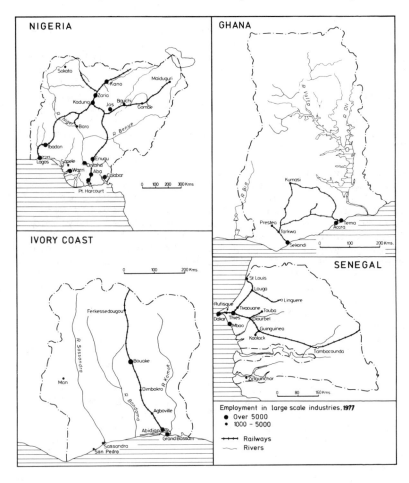

Figure 3.1: Major industrial concentrations in
leading industrial countries of West Africa

1950s, for instance, Treichville on the Petit Bassam
Island, immediately south of Abidjan in Ivory Coast,
had become a busy centre for advanced level processing of coffee, cocoa, timber and fruits. A coffee
mill capable of annually converting 15,000 tons of
hulled coffee into soluble coffee was established
soon after 1950, sequel to the successful rail-sea
link-up through the Vridi Canal.[2] A cocoa butter
processing plant, a plywood factory and a number of
fruit canneries also went into production in Ivory
Coast. In Abidjan itself were post-World War II
mills crushing palm kernels, cocoa and shea butter
both for export and for local use in soap production. Pineapple canning factories were established
in Abidjan and Gagnoa. In Senegal, peanut oil ex-
traction had begun in Dakar with one small mill in
1924. By 1950, mills with much larger capacity had
been established at Kaolack, Diourbel, Louga,
Rufisque, Zinguinchor and Tambacounda, thanks to the
impetus of World War II. Dakar and Zinguinchor have
fish processing and tinning factories. All these
plants have been material rooted, or supply based
for economic reasons that will be considered in
Chapter 4.

In Nigeria, groundnut oil and cake processing
was first undertaken as factory activity in Kano in
1949. By 1965 no less than seven such mills had
been set up - five in Kano and one each in Maidguri
and Zaria. The two palm kernel crushing mills in
operation by 1965 were in Lagos. Between 1956 and
1964 there were six meat processing and freezing
plants - three in Lagos and one each in Kano,
Port Harcourt and Ukpor which is about 4½km. east
of Onitsha. As shown in Table 3.5, all the five
fish processing and canning factories during the
period 1945 to 1965 were located in Lagos. Port
Harcourt and Lagos had then one flour mill each. Of
the five tobacco processing factories during the
same period, two were located in Ibadan; Port
Harcourt, Zaria and Ilorin each had one factory.
The only sugar cane processing factory then went into production in 1964 in Bacita. There were altogether clearly more than the forty-two plants shown
in this table engaged in advanced stage processing in
Nigeria between World War II and 1965. But many of
the establishments which did not co-operate during
the survey by the Federal Ministry of Industry could
not be included. However, the survey did show a
clearly rising trend in high-level processing activity existing side by side with the more common first
stage processing.

Table 3.4: Higher-stage processing activities in post-1950 West Africa

Material	Product
Hulled palm kernels	Oil, glycerine
Hulled groundnuts	Groundnut oil, cake
Cocoa beans	Cocoa butter, cocoa powder, cocoa cake
Sawn lumber	Veneer, plywood boards, match sticks
Pulp wood	Wood pulp
Bones	Bone meal
Iron	Iron pellets
Manganese Carbonate	Manganese oxide nodules
Alumina	Aluminium
Fruit	Canned fruit, jam
Cured tobacco leaf	Cigarettes, cigars
Hulled wheat	Flour
Fresh fish	Frozen fish
Limestone & clay	Clinker
Cotton seed	Oil, cake
Peeled and dried yam	Yam flour
Maize	Maize flour
Milk	Butter, condensed milk, powdered milk
Marble	Marble chips
Fresh meat and fish	Canned meat and fish
Hulled coffee	Coffee extracts
Sugar cane	Granulated sugar, alcohol
Cassiterite	Tin

Ghana was at that period operating fewer but relatively large-scale high-level processing plants while having a very large sub-sector of first-stage processing industry based on the vast mineral and agricultural products of the country. The major processing centres are Tema, Accra, Kumasi and Sekondi-Takoradi. The most notable high level processing establishment in Tema is the giant VALCO (Volta Aluminium Company) factory smelting alumina from imported bauxite. Tema also has a number of fish processing, cigarette and cocoa butter processing plants. In Accra, Kumasi and Secondi-Takoradi the production of veneers from local timber has been very important; the earliest veneer plant was started in 1950. According to Harrison Church (1980), Ghana had no export of veneers before World War II.

Table 3.5: Advanced stage industrial processing in Nigeria – location and type, 1945-65

Location	Meat Processing	Veg. oils*	Dairy	Fruit	Grain milling	Fish	Sugar Cane	Food	Tobacco	Cordage & Ropes	Plywood & Veneer	Tin	Petroleum	Total
Lagos	3	2	–	–	1	5	–	2	–	2	–	–	–	15
Kano	1	5	–	–	–	–	–	–	–	–	–	–	–	6
Port Harcourt	1	–	–	–	1	–	–	–	1	–	–	–	1	4
Aba	–	–	–	1	–	–	–	–	–	–	–	–	–	1
Ukpor	1	–	–	–	–	–	–	–	–	–	–	–	–	1
Obudu	–	–	1	–	–	–	–	–	–	–	–	–	–	1
Ibadan	–	–	–	2	–	–	–	–	2	–	–	–	–	4
Agege	–	–	1	–	–	–	–	–	–	–	–	–	–	1
Bacita	–	–	–	–	–	–	1	–	–	–	–	–	–	1
Awka	–	–	–	–	–	–	–	1	–	–	–	–	–	1
Zaria	–	1	–	–	–	–	–	–	1	–	–	–	–	2
Ilorin	–	–	–	–	–	–	–	–	1	–	–	–	–	1
Sapele	–	–	–	–	–	–	–	–	–	–	1	–	–	1
Calabar	–	–	–	–	–	–	–	–	–	–	1	–	–	1
Jos	–	–	–	–	–	–	–	–	–	–	–	1	–	1
Maiduguri	–	1	–	–	–	–	–	–	–	–	–	–	–	1
Total+	6	9	2	3	2	5	1	3	5	2	2	1	1	42

* Milling of processed (shelled) nuts to produce oil and cake.
+ Only plants whose start-up years were known to the Federal Ministry of Industry are included here.

Source: Industrial Directory, 1971.

But in 1957 the country exported 140,000 cubic feet of veneers worth £287,000 sterling. Also since the War those centres have developed large-scale cocoa butter production among others.

During World War II, high level processing of groundnuts into oil and cake developed at Koulikoro in Mali, at Bobo Dioulasso in Upper Volta and at Maradi in Niger, and has since the War extended to Bamako and Banjul (Bathurst). Tobacco processing into cigarettes was developed in Mali in 1968; palm kernel crushing also began in 1968 at Wellington, near Freetown in Sierra Leone. In 1970, a plant processing bauxite into alumina was set up in Guinea to become the first of such highly demanding units in West Africa based on local bauxite. With increasing local capital and technology over the coming years, West Africa will witness considerable increases in high-level processing involving the region's vast agricultural and mineral resources. Already there are plants for pelletizing iron ore in Buchanan, Liberia, and for processing the enormous reserves of Nigeria's natural gas which has been continuously flared since 1958. The more the countries of West Africa are able to engage in high-level material processing, the better are their future economic prospects with regard to material export promotion and local industrial development. For one thing, such a level of processing allows a country much greater flexibility in dealing with the uncertainties of world market demands for industrial raw materials. This is especially to the extent that high-level processing makes a commodity more easily handled, stored or put into alternative uses. Part of the alternative use is in the local industrial sector which has hitherto depended rather heavily on many imported material inputs that have a resource base in West Africa. Typical examples are wood pulps and crude oil derivatives. Nigeria, for instance, is still dependent on imported woodpulp for the bulk of paper produced in the country. Like countries that have as yet not discovered crude oil in commercial quantity, Nigeria largely depends on imports for petro-chemical products (intermediate goods) and refined gas derivable from her crude petroleum and associated sources.

The problems associated with dependence on imported material inputs include high import bills as well as disruptive supply bottlenecks, all of which collectively weaken the import substitution strategy of each country. High production costs make local manufactures less competitive than imported goods.

In spite of these problems and several others which will be discussed in some detail in later chapters, industrial programmes of all the West African countries have continued to retain import substitution as a major policy objective. Examples taken from a number of countries will serve to show how strong the import substitution drive has continued to be.

According to Ghana's Five-year Development Plan 1975-80 (1977), the import substitution strategy adopted by the country soon after her independence concentrated on the production of consumer goods. The leading industries, at least since 1972, have been food processing, textiles and basic metal industries which in 1972 together accounted for 46.2 per cent of the gross output by manufacturing. In 1964 wood, tobacco, beverages and chemical products had been the leading industries respectively contributing 20 per cent, 15.4 per cent, 13.3 per cent, and 12.6 per cent of the gross output by the manufacturing sector.

Most of those industrial activities are import substituting and have as a matter of policy been striving to meet domestic demands. According to the Government of Ghana,

> To the largest degree possible, domestic substitutes should be produced for those manufactured staples of consumer demand for whose supply Ghana is now entirely dependent upon foreign sources and expends large sums of foreign exchange each year...The attainment of the targets for the production of stable consumer goods will be given priority over all other aspects of the industrialization programme. (Ghana Planning Commission, 1964, p. 93).

Although this policy statement was meant to cover the first post-Independence decade, it in fact represented the industrial state of affairs up to the launching of the country's 1975-80 development plan.

In Nigeria, the same pattern of industrial development as is found in Ghana obtains as shown in Table 3.8. The preponderance of import substituting industries is attested to by the evident prominence of such industries in the eleven leading industries of Nigeria in 1972. The industries shown in this table were the only groups accounting for over ₦30 million gross output each. The eleven of them together accounted for 62.86 per cent of total gross output by manufacturing in 1972. The situation was

Table 3.6: Leading manufacturing industries of
Nigeria, 1972

Industry	Gross Output (₦ '000)	% of total Gross Output by manufacturing
1. Textiles (Spinning, Weaving, Finishing)	136,959	13.09
2. Beer Brewing & Spirits Distilling	89,377	8.55
3. Petroleum & Coal Products	69,475	6.64
4. Fabricated Metal Products	65,475	6.26
5. Soap, Perfumes, Cosmetics	59,541	5.69
6. Tobacco	57,535	5.48
7. Vegetable oils	44,663	4.27
8. Sugar and Sugar Confectionery	38,882	3.72
9. Grain Milling	33,405	3.19
10. Structural Metal Products	31,269	2.99
11. Printing	31,136	2.98
Total	657,535	62.86

₦: Symbol for Naira, Nigerian currency (₦1 = 100 Kobo =
US $1.7)
Source: Annual Abstract of Statistics, Federal
Office of Statistics, Lagos, 1973, p. 45.

not structurally significantly different from what
it had been in the 1960s; compare Table 3.7 with
Table 3.6. The ten industrial groups shown are
predominantly import substituting, with textile
manufacturing (including spinning, weaving and finishing functions) being the most important both in
1968 and 1972. The main difference is in the increased value of gross output contributed by each
industrial group - after taking care of the effect

Table 3.7:   Leading manufacturing industries of
Nigeria, 1968

Industry	Gross Output (₦ '000)	% of total gross output by manufacturing
1. Textile	36,159	14.38
2. Vegetable Oils Milling	23,603	9.38
3. Beer Brewing	18,187	7.23
4. Food and Tobacco	12,399	4.93
5. Soap, Perfume, osmetics	12,361	4.91
6. Fabricated Metal Products	12,198	4.85
7. Basic Metal, Cutlery and Tools	11,486	4.77
8. Motor Vehicle Assembly	10,959	4.36
9. Sugar and Sugar Confectionery	6,978	2.77
10. Cement	5,629	2.24
Total	150,459	59.82

Source: Annual Abstract of Statistics, 1970, p. 45.

of inflation.   However, in spite of evident increases in the output of such goods meant to replace
imports, the need to further expand import substituting industries has continued to be quite strong in
the face of substantial import bills.   For instance,
Table 3.8 shows that as much as N264 million was
spent in 1974 on a few of the many consumer goods
that continue to bulk large in Nigeria's annual imports.   While there can be no question about the
need for continued imports of manufactured goods, the
whole objective of the import substitution strategy
is the minimization of foreign exchange commitment
to goods that Nigeria can produce within her borders.

Table 3.8: Nigeria's imports of selected items by value in 1974

Imports	Value (₦ '000)
Cotton piece goods	7,293
Rayon piece goods	10,451
Footwear	10,454
Petroleum oils	45,969
Commercial vehicles	58,363
Private cars	97,003
Cement	34,802
Total	264,338

Source: Digest of Statistics, Federal Office of Statistics, Lagos, 1975, p. 48.

But the achievement of this objective by Nigeria or by other West African countries except Ivory Coast is not as yet in sight.

Ivory Coast is the one West African country that has demonstrated a sustained ambitious effort to meet her import substitution objectives since her political independence in 1960. Manufacturing industry which grew by 23 per cent between 1970 and 1974 (Rake, 1978) has since the early 1960s been taking giant strides in the pursuit of import substitution objectives. The impressive gap between achievements in 1960 and those in 1967 attests to this point.[3] The leading industrial productions are food and tobacco, chemicals and fats, textiles, wood products and metal products industries. Those alone accounted for over 94 per cent of the total output by the country's industrial sector in 1960, and for 86.87 per cent in 1967.

Since the 1970s Ivory Coast has been making long-term plans for the promotion of textile, garments and paper pulp industries among others within the manufacturing sector. Cotton textile manufacturing which was first started by Gonfreville at Bouake in 1921 did not quite find its feet until 1963 when a modern factory was set up by the same firm to start using the high grade Allen cotton grown in the northern parts of the country. With the successful achievement of such inter-sectoral linkage (between the local agricultural sector and

Table 3.9:   Leading manufacturing industries of
Ivory Coast, 1960, 1967

Industry	Gross Output and % Share in 1960		Gross Output and % Share in 1967	
	(Mil. CFA Francs)	%	(Mil. CFA Francs)	%
Food & Tobacco	3,313	31.49	16,019	31.95
Chemicals & Fats	2,221	21.12	7,603	15.17
Textiles	1,648	15.67	6,931	13.83
Lumber products	1,605	15.26	8,167	16.29
Metal products	1,103	10.49	4,829	9.63
Total	9,890	94.03	43,549	86.87

* 214 CFA francs = $1 (USA)   See Appendix C.

Source: Le Moniteur Africain, 18 Juillet, 1968, pp. 9-11
Chambre d'Industrie Bulletin

the textile manufacturing sector), both cotton growing and textiles manufacturing are being promoted
with considerable foreign capital and expertise.
UTEXI, COTIVO and UNIWAX enterprises are foreign companies now in partnership with the Ivorian government for the production of what is likely to be West
Africa's biggest output of very high quality cotton
textile fabrics and prints for home needs and exports. The Blue-Bell complex near Abidjan is a producer of ready-to-wear clothing. By 1975 it was
making 1.8 million items per year and then was aim-
ing at 5.6 million by 1978 - to become one of the
largest of such complexes in the world.
     Paper pulp production is being developed, star-
ting with the use of ordinary local trees and brushwood but later on switching over to the exploitation
of eucalyptus and other exotic plants currently
being massively grown. This probably makes Ivory
Coast the first country in West Africa to develop
giant pulp mills based on tropical woods. Besides,
the country is still looking ahead into the future
for her import substitution programme through heavy
investments in silk, polyester, chemical and vehicle
tyre industries among others. The objective of im-

port substitution having been achieved in certain
areas of industrialization, the role of manufactured
export promotion is increasingly catching the fancy
of Ivory Coast while countries like Gambia, Mauritania and Guinea Bissau are yet to find their feet in
their own domestic markets. This kind of very small
beginning in Cape Verde can be appreciated from
Table 3.10.

Table 3.10: Manufacturing outputs of Cape Verde

Product	Quantity ('000 tonnes) in:			
	1974	1975	1976	1977
Salt	35.00	21.00	14.00	31.00
Canned Fish	0.10	0.20	0.2	0.2
Tobacco (manufac.)	0.10	n.a	0.8	0.8
Bread	1.00	1.00	1.00	1.00
Pozzolana*	15.40	15.40	15.40	15.40
Alcoholic beverages+	-	1.00	-	1.00

* Estimates only
+ In hectolitres

Source: Europa <u>Africa South of the Sahara</u>, London, 1981,
p. 256

MANUFACTURED EXPORT PROMOTION

The objective of any country striving to develop its
industrial sector is not only to be able to meet
most of the needs of the inhabitants but also to engage fruitfully in export promotion involving finished and intermediate goods. Much more than the
import substitution aspect of industrialization,
export promotion is very demanding and therefore
very challenging. For one thing, export involves
direct competition with outsiders in the foreign
market. Such export, therefore, calls for competitive quality and prices for each manufactured item of
export. But in the face of their low technology and
short supply of managerial manpower, developing
countries generally contend with high production
costs incurred mainly through high import bills,
heavy leaning on costly foreign expertise, small
scale production and infrastructural bottle-

necks among many other cost-raising problems. A
successful entry into the export subsector by developing countries is a major indicator of significant
progress in industrialization.
  Just as the problems involved are many and difficult, so are the benefits or economies that export
promotion promises enormous and attractive. To be
sure, the ability to put manufactured goods on external
markets secures to the manufacturer a much wider
market and more sales potential than may be found
within his base country. This is of particular importance for manufactures based on poor countries.
Mainly on account of their very low income per
capita, West African countries individually constitute narrow markets that are too small for large
scale manufacturing. But Nigeria and Ivory Coast
are a great deal bigger and better than many others.
The development of the export subsector opens the
way to a larger market and to the economies of scale
(especially in the form of low production costs)
which can accrue from large scale production for an
enlarged market. It is against this background that
efforts so far made and the levels of achievements
by countries in West Africa are now examined.
  Generally speaking, very little export promotion outside the processing subsector has as yet
been achieved by West African countries. As shown
earlier, the most industrially progressive amongst
them are still mainly preoccupied with the perfec-
tion and expansion of their import substitution programme, while many others have yet to make a modest
beginning at the import substitution stage. It is
in the industrially more advanced countries that what
little export industry there is has developed in West
Africa. The export list of Nigeria in 1973 amounted
to ₦52.96 million. However, there was a preponderance
of products at the higher stage of processing. Bulking
very large and, in fact, dominating the export list,
were processed materials like groundnut cake worth
₦17.96 million, cocoa butter worth ₦14.97 million,
cocoa cake worth ₦5.4 million, animal feed and food
waste worth ₦4.04 million, and wood materials -
veneers and plywood boards etc - worth ₦2.87 million.
Indeed, but for petroleum products worth ₦5.69 million, no fully manufactured or finished product exported in 1973 by Nigeria was worth up to ₦0.4 million. The noteworthy capital goods on Nigeria's
long list were organic chemicals worth only ₦340,919,
explosives and pyrotechnic products worth ₦5,998 and
inorganic chemicals ₦3,205. Most of the remainder
were very simple consumer goods. There were no such

capital goods as machinery and heavy equipment,
which is a reflection of the technological constraint still very present in Nigeria. Senegal,
Ivory Coast and Ghana have each been promoting manufactured exports of similar composition to
Nigeria's. Much less in total volume and value,
each country's export list has a remarkable preponderance of processed and simple consumer goods.
However, when the expansion of the textile and the
garment industries comes into full swing in Ivory
Coast, the latter will probably have a much more impressive volume of consumer goods exports. The Blue
Bell Company products of jeans and overalls as well
as the cotton prints by the UNIWAX and UTEXI groups of
companies have been leading the way in Ivory Coast's
successful exports of finished consumer goods to
Europe.

It is important to emphasize, by and large,
that the few but noteworthy achievements observed in
the export subsector of the West African region are
rather confined both in space and time. Spatially,
it is particularly in Nigeria, Ivory Coast, Senegal
and Ghana that exports involving finished manufactured products have been significant. And historically, it is since the 1970s that exports of manufactured (not merely processed) goods have become important in the foreign trade of those few countries.
The current development plans particularly in Nigeria, Ivory Coast and Senegal have been strongly
geared to export-promoting heavy industries. For
example, in Nigeria, the iron and steel mills at
Ajaokuta are already under construction; a ₦390
million gas-based direct reduction steel plant is in
production at Aladja near Warri, and it is proposed
to complete the setting up of nitrogen fertilizer,
petrochemical, gas liquefaction, machine tools and
parts factories before 1985. In Ivory Coast there
are the textile and the paper pulp mills, whilst in
Senegal development programmes involve textiles and
chemical industries. If all goes well with those
national development programmes, West Africa as a
region will have in the 1980s a much firmer hold on
the industrial export markets than the 1970s have
witnessed.

On the whole, industrial development in West
Africa has generally been marked by slow progress,
largely as a result of gross inadequacy of capital
resources and managerial and technical know how. However, because of the wide spatial variation of those
vital factors of industrial development as well as
of natural resources, much of which has been dis-

cussed in Chapter 2, progress in industrial development has also been spatially varied in West Africa.
Countries like Nigeria and Ivory Coast have made
relatively substantial progress in the volume, variety and value of their industrial outputs since
their political independence, thanks to their better
resource endowment. But many, like Gambia, Upper
Volta, Mauritania, Togo and Guinea Bissau, have,
mainly for the reasons of resource constraints, yet
to develop the consumer goods, let alone the capital
goods, subsectors. Future progress will in general
largely depend on efforts made to improve the conditions related to technology, capital and manpower
resources in each country.

NOTES

    1. By that time, many more small scale indust-
rial units had been in existence. The industrial
survey by Aluko, (1973) shows that there
were 125 industrial establishments before 1945 out
of a sample total of 8,537 plants of the small scale
category in Lagos, Mid-West, and Kwara States of
Nigeria. However, the sample included non-manufacturing service undertakings like bicycle and clock
repairs. The actual number of manufacturing plants
in the sample cannot be determined to ascertain the
real size of small scale manufacturing units before
1945.
    2. The Vridi Canal providing the major access
from the Atlantic shores to the Abidjan-Petit Bassam
core area was opened in 1950.
    3. More outstanding progress was recorded in
the 1970s. For instance, value added by manufacturing was 3.8 times higher in 1977 than in 1970
(ECA, 1979, p. 125).

Chapter Four

STRUCTURAL CHARACTERISTICS OF MANUFACTURING INDUSTRY
IN WEST AFRICA

The need to take account of the structural characteristics of industrial production units in any in-
depth consideration of plant location and profit-
ability is well known. Hardly any objective appraisal of industrial performance and location patterns can be undertaken without a clear understanding of the structural characteristics of the industries concerned. The present chapter is intended to
identify and analyse the structural characteristics
of modern manufacturing in West Africa. The structural variables identified will help to provide part
of the necessary background to a fuller appraisal of
the spatial organisation and economic development
problems of the industrial sector in the West African
region.
    As much as data allow - in terms both of avail-
ability and of comparability among West African
countries - illustrative cases are taken in as many
countries of the region as possible. In a number of
cases it is sufficient to base illustrations in the
region on data from a couple of West African countries. And unless otherwise stated, such illustrations are intended to represent the general picture of the relevant phenomena.

SOME ELEMENTS OF INDUSTRIAL STRUCTURE

Theoretically, the three most important aspects of
industrial structure to which attention is here
being directed embrace the physical (non-spatial),
the organizational and the spatial elements. The
physical elements include labour force or employment
characteristics; material inputs; industrial outputs; industrial capital; and industrial floor space.

The organizational aspect covers such elements as
ownership types; nature of market organization; and
nature of linkages or integration of production processes. The spatial variables of industrial structure refer particularly to the geographical distribution and interaction of industrial units over a
given landscape.

PHYSICAL ELEMENTS

Labour as a physical element of industrial structure
may be viewed in a number of forms. These can be in
terms of size of employment. It can be in terms of
categories of skills - i.e. whether a given industrial unit is dominated by a highly skilled or unskilled
labour force. Labour may also be characterised in
terms of sources - i.e. whether local or foreign.
In newly independent countries where indigenization
of the industrial labour force is a major policy objective, the need to emphasize this aspect of the
work force in a close study of an industry's physical structure seems quite justified. Consider the
increasing importance of various governments' policy
on indigenization and expatriate quota. Nigeria's,
Ghana's and Guinea's indigenization programmes are
typical.
     The main material inputs for industrial produc-
tion are other elements for determining the structural (physical) characteristics of industrial units.
Wide-ranging structural variants are revealed through
the relative importance of weight/bulk-losing,
weight/bulk-adding and perishable or non-perishable
materials forming an industry's inputs. Also the
state of such inputs at the point of entry into the
industrial production process helps to give the industry a structural character. A wide variety of
industries use materials in their raw, semi-proc-
essed or fully processed state, or as intermediate
goods. Whether the materials are home-based or
foreign is crucial. In view of the cost and technological implications of the use of various material
inputs, the industrial promoter's decision-making
must be guided by such implications so as to minimize production costs and ensure a reasonable margin.
For example, an industrial plant, like a cement or a
brick factory, using weight/bulk-losing material (in
which case the material index is well above 1) is,
under normal conditions, locationally constrained to
the material source. Nearly all West African integrated cement plants are resource rooted. But the

plant owner mainly dependent on intermediate goods
as inputs is likely to take a different decision,
being more footloose as a result of the plant's input requirements. This is the case with pharmaceutical, chemical, radio assembly and paint plants
in all West African countries. The plant owner
mainly dependent on weight and bulk-gaining material
which bulks large in the overall production cost
structure would prefer market location. This is
generally the case with soft drinks, furniture and
brewing establishments for instance.

Industrial structure may be identified by the
nature of the <u>industrial products</u>. Such products
may be highly perishable, like ice-cream or daily
newspapers requiring prompt distribution to nearby
consumers. The products may be high or low in value
which largely determines their range (Christaller,
1933), they may be either consumer goods meant to
serve as import substitutes, or capital goods which
could serve both domestic and export markets.
Whichever is the case puts the industry in a somewhat particular group and more or less influences
the decision-making of the industrial entrepreneur
especially in choosing plant location. Illustrations from West African countries will later be
used to demonstrate more of the spatial implications
of industrial structure.

<u>Capital</u> as an element of industrial structure is
to be seen in its wide economic sense as comprising
capital stock, like equipment and machinery, which
can be regarded as produced means of production, and
capital funds which generally refer to working capital
for taking care of all sorts of expenditure in the
production process. The amount and type of capital
involved in getting an industrial unit off the ground
and functioning well vary quite considerably from one
industry to another and therefore help to give an industry a structural identity. For instance, certain
industries like basic steel, chemical and petrochemical industries are highly demanding of capital
stock which is essentially fixed and expensive, but
relatively less demanding of working capital. The
reverse is the case for a number of industries such
as textile and clothing industries. Mainly because
of the heavy structural demands of iron and steel,
petrochemical and basic chemical industries, West
African countries are still lacking such major and
basic projects while proliferating the much less
capital intensive assembly plants of various kinds.

One more example of the physical elements of
industrial structure is <u>floor space</u>. Certain in-

dustries, such as aircraft and motor industries, are highly space-demanding; others, like precision instruments, printing, battery assembly and electrical product industries, have much less need for floor space. Such physical characteristics are clearly reflected in the choice of plant location which itself largely affects the geography of the economic welfare of the societies concerned.

ORGANIZATIONAL ELEMENTS

The nature of industrial ownership is a very important organizational element which helps to give the industrial unit its structural character. Most Third World countries, like those of West Africa, are very short in investment capital as well as in technical and managerial know how, and there is a strong reflection of these constraints in the ownership structure of their manufacturing industry. The wide range of existing ownership structures extends from a mixture of foreign and indigenous ownership to fully foreign and fully indigenous ownership. Other less important sub-sets of ownership types in this particular respect include joint state and private ownership, fully state ownership and fully private ownership.

From another viewpoint, ownership structure can be sole or corporate, the latter including partnerships, private companies and public companies. Each of these directly or indirectly reflects the need and attempt to get around one or several of the problems identified above. For instance, the need for joint foreign and indigenous ownership often arises in West Africa from inadequacy of technical and managerial know how and sometimes capital. The same is largely true of most other corporate ownerships of industrial ventures in the region. Since certain ownership structures have considerable implications for the control of business and the distribution of profits, particularly internationally, ownership structures are of particular interest in the West African region and frequently feature in policy statements and programmes of most West African governments. This will be illustrated with the Nigerian case studies in Chapter 7.

Industrial units are also structurally identifiable in terms of their marketing organization. In this sense, marketing structures with which industrial enterprises may be associated include monopolies, oligopolies and varied forms of imperfect

market. Perfect market structure (which hardly exists) is one which gives an industrial unit the
image of one out of a large number of competitors
none of which is individually capable of influencing
prices, output, and wage rates in the industry.
West African countries are generally characterised
by imperfect competition in which prices and qual-
ities of commodities are widely varied, and market
information is so defective that commodity quality
and prices cannot be properly estimated.

Organizational elements also include types of
industrial integration or linkage that industrial
firms arrange. Linkages refer to mere business relationships involving the dependence of one firm on
other firm or firms, each of which controls its own fir
ances and decision-making process. Integration is a
much stronger form of linkage relations. The distinction lies in the fact that integration involves
a firm's full control of the finances and the decision-making of all the associated production units.
A typical example may serve to make this point clear.
If a steel producing firm depends for its iron ore
and scrap iron on other independent firms, the situation is one of linkage relations between the steel
firm on the one hand and the ore and scrap iron
firms on the other. But if the linkage relations
are such that the steel firm also controls the finances and decision-making in the ore and scrap production units, the complex (including the steel mill
and the ore and scrap metal units) is an integrated
enterprise. If the linkage or the integration involves successive stages of a production process,
the integration or the linkage is vertical - backward from steel making to ore mining and processing,
forward from steel making to the production and distribution of steel-based products.

Thus, if the steel enterprise supplies other
industrial units with its outputs like steel wire or
sheets needed as intermediate goods for the production of final goods (like nails, pins and cutlery) a
situation of forward relationship (linkage or integration as the case may be) with those units then
exists. Similar structural patterns exist in
other industries.[1]

As can be appreciated from all these, considerable economies accrue (though not automatically)
from linkage relations. The countries of West
Africa are beginning to put much premium on the development of inter-industry linkages intranationally
rather than internationally. On account of technological inadequacies, West African countries have

for a long time been obliged to develop strong backward linkages that extend to their sources of industrial inputs, namely, the industrial countries of
the world. The direct consequences include leakages
(foreign exchange drain) to the industrial countries.

SPATIAL ELEMENTS

In spatial terms, the structural features of manufacturing industries refer to the various patterns of
industrial distribution over a given landscape.
These can be identified as variants of industrial
concentration and dispersal. Variants of industrial
concentration include industrial agglomerations
which embrace a variety of industrial types dominating the economic activity of a specific area.
Industrial localization occurs where an agglomer-
ation is dominated by a particular industry - such
that the share of the industry in the total labour
force or total value of fixed capital in the agglom-
eration is not only the highest but also constitutes
a significant proportion. Where industrial agglom-
eration of any of these two types is a result of
policy decision, an industrial zone or an industrial
estate develops. The latter is distinct from the
former especially in the sense that the necessary
infrastructural facilities including factory buildings as well as service units are officially provided for industrial entrepreneurs expected to rent
factory buildings and avail themselves of the facilities provided. But an industrial zone is hardly
more than an area set aside by legislation for industrial activity. The firms provide their own factory buildings and some of their other needs normally provided by the management of industrial estates. The purpose of establishing industrial estates is mainly to stimulate economic development.
In particular it is to promote small-scale industrial activities which would otherwise be handicapped
if not incapacitated by shortage of the start-up
capital. Developing countries have in general embraced the concept and practice of industrial estates first developed in Western Europe and the
United States (Pearson, 1969). West African countries' experience typifies this general enthusiasm.
    Another variant of industrial concentration is
an industrial complex which is usually spatially a
much larger concentration than an industrial agglom-
eration and in which the presence of various service
industries also contributes in no small measure to

85

the geographical extent and the welter of economic
activity mix of the complex. Only a couple of industrial complexes exist as yet in parts of West
Africa, notably in Nigeria (Lagos) and Senegal
(Mbao).

Industrial complexes of nearby cities may merge
into continuous stretches to become industrial conurbations. A clearly distinct elongation of such
conurbations is typified by the London-South Lanca-
shire axial belt in Britain. Such a spatial structure can be referred to as a development corridor or
development axis. None of these has as yet developed in any part of West Africa.

At the other lower end of the scale of the
spatial structure of industries, there are isolated
collections of industrial plants in small towns, as
well as a dispersal of numerous industrial units in
rural areas. Unlike the large industrial concentrations, there is a remarkable absence of external
economies as well as of a large and nearby market
for the products of such relatively isolated plants.
Much of this is a feature of West African countries.

The foregoing serves as a theoretical background. The structural characteristics of West
African countries are now closely examined in the
rest of this chapter on the basis of statistical information available.

THE WEST AFRICAN PICTURE OF INDUSTRIAL STRUCTURE

Owing to the paucity of relevant data and the fact
that the figures on individual countries do not
often relate to the same elements of industrial
structure, comparability of situations across the
region can hardly be graphically demonstrated. This
is made even more problematic by the fact that industrial survey statistics for particular structural
characteristics cover different years for different
countries. Also the methods adopted or the yard-
sticks used in data collection and grouping vary
quite widely among the various countries. The data
available cannot, therefore, have more than an illustrative value and do not lend themselves to the
many computational analyses that an in-depth study
of this nature demands. There is, as a matter of
fact, hardly any other source of data than the industrial surveys conducted by the individual countries of West Africa - surveys known to be very few
and far between in most, if not all, of the countries. In view of this serious problem of data

limitation, we are constrained to examine only a few
of the many elements of industrial structure the
theoretical exposition of which has just been made
in outline.

SIZE CHARACTER OF WEST AFRICAN INDUSTRIES

Measures of industrial size which could apply to
West African countries relate to such variables as
employment, total amount of fixed capital, and gross
value of industrial output. In terms of employment,
a common feature of West African industrial establishments is smallness. Industrial statistics for
most countries cover plants with as low a work force
as ten persons. This is not to say that plants with
less than ten workers are negligibly few. In fact,
the contrary is the case: there are many more plants
with below ten workers than there are plants with
more than ten workers in each country. The factors
underlying the preponderance of small-scale industry
are mainly capital, market and technological constraints. With little capital, often arising from
personal savings, and poor understanding of the
technical and organizational demands of industrial
production, most industrial promoters tend to play
safe by starting their project on a scale they can
more easily cope with on a trial-and-error basis.
Bank loans are possible, though at much lower frequency than in developed countries; but most entrepreneurs feel safer to plunge into the unknown and
experiment with their own savings. However, among
the well informed, the difficult problems of obtaining bank credit facilities contribute a great
deal to the common resort to personal and other
informal sources which are hardly enough to support
medium-scale industrial operations.
     According to the official industrial statistics
published by some West African countries, the vast
majority of plants employing ten or more workers
belong to the small and medium-scale group of 10-200
workers.[2] An illustration from seven West African
countries listed in Table 4.1 shows that there was
an average of 171 workers per industrial establishment in Nigeria during 1971, 144 in Ghana during
1970, and 104 in Togo during 1970. In Ivory Coast
it was 80 workers per plant in 1971, and 72 in
Liberia in 1972. The rather low averages of 66 and
47 in Senegal (1967) and Benin (1966) respectively
might have been accounted for by time factor - the
fact that they represent much earlier years of in-

Table 4.1:   Industrial establishments and work force
in selected West African countries

Country	Year	Number of Establish-ments	Total Industrial Work Force	Average Em-ployment per establishment
Liberia	1972	24	1,723	72
Nigeria	1971	870	148,568	171
Ivory Coast	1971	404	32,128	80
Ghana	1970	386	55,711	144
Togo	1970	24	2,486	104
Senegal	1967	204	13,400	66
Benin	1966	17	805	47
Average		275		98

Source: Statistical Year Book, Economic Commission for
Africa, Part II, 1972

dustrial development in those newly independent
countries. Much later figures, say, in the early
1970s, would probably have shown a considerable rise
in employment size per industrial unit.

At any rate, the main point to note is that
even on the basis of low labour demands of plants in
developed countries (where, on account of high labour costs, greater use is made of labour-saving devices), the average of 98 workers[3] per plant among
the seven selected West African countries is indeed
very low. This low figure is an indication of the
predominance of small-scale industrial plants in the
countries listed. Even within a wider African context, the West African average is relatively small.
Table 4.2 shows that the average industrial plant in
25 African countries was by 1972 employing about 111
workers. Also, whereas there were on average less
than 300 industrial establishments per West African
country in the early 1970s there were on average
over 700 per country in the U.N. sample of 25 African countries during the same period.

The size character of manufacturing plants
shows considerable variation among industrial types,
grouped according to the International Standard
Industrial Classification (ISIC) system. For example, the heavy industries, like chemicals and chemical products as well as basic metal industries, in

Table 4.2: Some structural features of manufacturing in 25 selected African countries

| | | Average number of: | |
ISIC No.	Industry Type	Establishments	Worker per plant
31	Food, Beverage & Tobacco	192.96	74
32	Textile, Clothing	216.00	90
33	Wood & Furniture	84.84	48
34	Paper, Printing & Publishing	32.84	79
35	Chemicals & Petrochemicals	45.92	135
36	Non-metallic products	46.68	70
37	Fabricated metal products	102.92	70
38	Basic metal industry	2.96	407
39	Other industries	23.76	28
	Total Industrial Types	716	111

Source: Computed from Economic Commission for Africa, Survey of Economic Conditions in Africa, Part I 1972, p. 127

taking advantage of scale economies, can afford to be high on both labour and capital. But those like textile and clothing industries using low wage labour can be long on labour and short on capital. What do we find in West Africa? This pattern of variation is not very evident from Table 4.3 owing partly to great differences in the industrial survey dates and partly to varied levels of industrial development among the countries. However, although these explanatory factors are somewhat reflected in the overall average in the last column of the table, it is still possible to pick out the textile, clothing and leather industry group as the most important industry according to plant size measured in labour terms. The basic metal industry is second in importance. By and large, by world standards, a work force of 228 persons per cotton textile plant or 187 persons per basic metal plant is indeed very small. Comparative figures in developed countries are in each of the two industries generally well above 500, in spite of much greater efforts towards labour-saving devices. The overall averages would have been lower for all West African countries,

89

since the countries covered by the table are the
most important industrially. Nigerian textile mills,

Table 4.3: Average employment per plant by industry
type in leading industrial countries of West Africa

Industry Type	Average in:				Overall Average
	Ivory Coast	Ghana	Nigeria	Senegal	
Food, beverages, tobacco	68.40	139.46	123.64	79.1	102.7
Textile, clothing, leather	207.93	186.10	343.26	172.7	227.5
Wood & Furniture	144.12	165.86	92.97	-	134.3
Chemicals & Chemical products	75.04	98.04	184.53	61.9	104.9
Basic metal industry	14.00	334.00	211.97	n.a	186.7
Non-metallic mineral products	74.64	110.47	141.00	n.a	108.7
Fabricated metal products	78.23	107.31	194.50	31.4	102.9

Source: E.C.A., Statistical Year Book, Part II, 1972

-: not applicable; n.a: not available

for instance, employed between 1,000 and 4,000 workers each during the period. Compare with Liberia
where in 1975 the 309 textile plants in operation
had a total work force of 964[4]. On account of
scarcity of investment capital as well as of technical skills, and also owing to a surplus of semi-
skilled and unskilled manpower in such countries,
resort to capital-intensive production should, in
the interest of meaningful development, be discouraged as much as practicable. Generation of employment is expected to be one major contribution of
industrialization in West Africa. To embark upon
labour-saving devices negates the objective of employment generation and of wider distribution of income
in a poor country.

The cotton textile industry is a typically
labour-intensive industry; almost every developing
economy begins its industrial development from that
subsector in which much technical skill is not a
necessary entry requirement and the skill needed is
normally acquired on the job. Also developing countries embrace cotton textile industry not only for
its capacity for generating unskilled employment,
but also to minimize the ugly foreign exchange implication of heavy dependence on imported capital
(including raw materials) and expertise. However,
the very low average of 228 workers per plant in
table 4.3 is an indication that textile and leather
goods plants in most West African countries probably
operate on a very small scale. And at such a scale
(determined in terms of labour employed), it would
be difficult to meet the technological threshold of
the industry without being unduly capital-intensive,
i.e. without substituting capital for labour.
Capital-intensive production in West African countries is necessary only in such heavy and capital
goods industries as steel, petrochemical, basic
chemical and basic metal industries which can afford
to take full advantage of scale economies and thereby penetrate external markets.

In the absence of the requisite data for ascertaining how much more capital-intensive such industries
are vis-a-vis the consumer goods industries of West
African countries, an alternative approach is to examine the value of their output per worker. It is
expected that capital-intensive industries more
capable of taking advantage of scale economies would
generally show much higher value of output per worker. The value is ascertained by matching the monetary value of total output (gross output) against
total labour force. Table 4.4 shows that in spite
of considerable variation among the countries covered, the Basic Metal industry had by 1971 the highest
value of output per worker, with an average of US
$111,827 per worker per year. This is quite in
keeping with theoretical expectations from the heavy
industry subsector. That the Chemicals and Chemical
Products industries with US $17,753 and Non-metallic
Mineral products industries with US $14,708 per wor-
ker were also high up (in the third and fourth positions respectively after the food industries with
$17,823) is in conformity with our theoretical ex-
pectation: such heavy industries should reflect their
greater proneness to capital-intensity and economies
of scale, compared with the generality of light industries in each country. However, the prominence

Table 4.4: Output per worker by industry type in selected countries

Industry Type	Value (in US $) of output per worker in:					Average for a year
	Ivory Coast (1971)	Ghana (1970)	Nigeria (1971)	Senegal (1967)	Benin (1966)	
Food, beverages, tobacco	18,903	7,921	21,600	27,420	13,270	17,823
Textile, clothing, leather	12,484	3,050	10,328	10,084	n.a	8,987
Wood and furniture	4,911	1,587	3,382	-	30,841	10,180
Chemicals, chemical products	27,460	6,220	22,580	24,083	8,424	17,753
Basic metal industry	58,411	2,624	274,430	n.a	n.a	111,827
Non-metal mineral products	30,337	4,572	9,214	n.a	n.a	14,708
Fabricated metal products, machinery equipment	22,341	4,256	12,096	16,939	8,213	12,769
Other industries	14,223	2,799	5,894	n.a	10,494	8,353

-: not applicable as data grouping is different. n.a: not available
Source: Computed from same source as Table 4.1

of Food industries is a common feature of West
African countries. Table 4.5 on Liberia alone,
though based on a different system of industrial activity grouping, seems to mirror the pattern shown
in Table 4.4 for our sample of five West African
countries. The Cement industry, Explosives, and Petroleum refining (all heavy industries) with US $31,935,
$29,412 and $26, 889 respectively per worker were in
the lead in 1969. These were followed by the Food
industries subsector featuring Fish processing
($17,000), Soft drinks ($16,324) and the Brewery
industry ($9,036).

However, compared with the average situation in
most of independent Black Africa represented by the
UN sample of twenty-five countries[5] (Table 4.6), the
picture in West Africa seemed slightly different
during the late 1960s and early 1970s. This was
with particular reference to the value of industrial
output per worker. While the wider African picture
showed gross output highest in Food industries with
the basic industries closely following, it was the
other way round in West Africa during the same period. However, the greater importance of the heavy
industries (in terms of value of output per worker)
compared with the light industries subsector can be
appreciated from sub-sector averages of US $7,050
for the heavy industry subsector and $6,471 for the
light industry sub-sector. This agrees with the
West African picture roughly represented by Table
4.4.

Again, comparing the West African (Table 4.4)
with the wider African structures revealed by Table 4.6,
one point that comes out quite clearly is the much
higher value of gross output per worker in West African countries. For example, output per worker in
the food industry was $11,161 in most of Africa but
$17,823 in the selected countries of West Africa.
Also in the heavy industry sub-sector, while the
average value of output per worker in the Chemicals
and Chemical products industry was only $8,481,
it was as high as $17,753 in our West African sample
during the period. There is, however, the probability that the values for West Africa would go down
quite visibly if all the West African countries were
to be covered. Our sample included the four industrially most developed West African countries -
Nigeria, Ivory Coast, Ghana and Senegal. Although a
drop would also be expected in an all-Africa average,
it is likely that the rather wide gap observed
in these tables would have been narrowed but not removed by total census counts. The margin that would

Table 4.5: Output per worker in Liberian industries, 1969

Industry	Value of Output ($'000 US)	Total Employment	Value of Output per Worker (US $)
Footwear, (plastic canons, leather	434	116	3,741
Umbrella & scarves	195	30	6,500
Bakeries	572	101	5,663
Distillery	210	41	5,122
Soft drinks	4,812	111	16,324
Brewery	1,500	166	9,036
Cement	1,980	62	31,935
Paints	98	26	3,769
Plastics	41	54	759
Explosives	3,000	102	29,412
Soap	300	56	5,357
Refinery (Petroleum)	7,986	297	26,889
Furniture	695	433	1,605
Building materials	2,488	400	6,220
Fish processing	3,500	200	17,500

Source: Annual Report of the Department of Commerce and Industry, 1970 (as reproduced by S. von Gnielinski, Liberia in Maps, University of London Press, 1972, p. 94)

still remain in favour of West Africa can be explained by the smaller number of employees per plant in West Africa, vis-a-vis all the regions of independent black Africa (compare plant size by work force in Tables 4.1 and 4.2).

If the factor of smallness of work force per industrial plant in West Africa is accepted as an explanatory variable for the relatively high value of gross output per worker, then the corollary of capital-intensity deserves further consideration. There is hardly any reliable and usable information for estimating average capital (fixed capital) in-

Table 4.6: Industrial structure by employment and output per worker in 25 selected independent developing African countries

ISIC No.	Industry Group	No. of Employees per Establishment	Gross Output per worker per year (US $)
31	Food, beverages and tobacco	74	11,161
32	Textiles and clothing	90	3,934
33	Wood and furniture	48	3,288
34	Paper, printing and publishing	79	4,504
	Light industries	73	6,471
35	Chemicals, petroleum and plastics	135	8,481
36	Non-metallic mineral products	70	4,940
37	Basic metal industries	407	9,025
38	Fabricated metal products machinery and equipment	70	6,722
39	Other industries	28	4,153
	Heavy industries	142	7,050
	Total manufacturing	111	6,654

Source: Computed from E.C.A. Survey of Economic Conditions in Africa, Part I, 1972, p. 128

vested per industrial plant (from which the extent of capital-intensity can be directly estimated). There is also no statistical evidence to show that the marginal productivity of labour is significantly higher in West Africa than in the rest of independent black Africa. Other things being equal,

it can be argued that the higher value of
gross output per industrial worker in West Africa
compared with the rest is a result of a higher level
of capital-intensity. An industrial survey by the
present author in parts of the former Western State
of Nigeria (Onyemelukwe, 1972) and a similar study
in East Africa (Pearson, 1969) provide a rough basis
for comparing levels of capital-intensity inter-
regionally. Pearson in his study of industrial development in East Africa, found that fixed capital
investment per industrial worker amounted to an average of US $188 in Kenya and US $148[6] in Uganda
during 1963. The work on the Western State of
Nigeria showed an average of $940 of fixed capital
per industrial worker during 1972. The ten years
gap between the two sets of values makes comparison
very problematic. But assuming that on account of
continued growth in industrialization there is
greater capital-intensity (as Pearson envisages),
and making allowance for inflation, it would be

Table 4.7: Output per worker by industry type in
Nigeria, Ivory Coast and Togo, 1976

Industry Type	Value (in US $) of output per worker in:		
	Nigeria	Ivory Coast	Togo
Food, beverages, tobacco	11,160	33,000	1,500
Textile, clothing, leather	10,150	17,210	1,520
Wood products, furniture and fixtures	6,330	8,560	691
Industrial chemicals, synthetics, other chem. products, drugs	14,500	35,100	1,110
Iron, steel & non-ferrous metal	283	39,207	n.a
Metal products & machinery	21,660	31,700	n.a

Source: Computed from UN, (1979) Yearbook of Industrial
Statistics

reasonable to say that by 1972 the values for Kenya
and Uganda would have increased three-fold. That
would have amounted to $564 in Kenya, and $444 in
Uganda. If this rough estimate is anything to go
by, then it provides a basis for comparison between
parts of East Africa and a part of West Africa. And
clearly, our earlier argument that West African industries are more capital-intensive than those of
some other parts of independent black Africa seems
justified. The values for 1976 for Nigeria and
Ivory Coast (Table 4.7) indicate a continuation of
this pattern into the 1970s in some West African
countries. Data are not available for a more general picture. By and large, these independent and
localised studies cannot provide any more than a
very rough indication of support for the apparently
high level of capital-intensity of manufacturing
plants in West Africa. A more acceptable conclusion
will have to await the collection and analysis of
data on fixed capital investment in plants of specific industrial groups in several regions of independent black Africa over the same period.

By value added is meant the monetary value of
product less the cost of material inputs from other
producers. In other words, it is the contribution
by a production unit to the monetary value of a
good or service. As a structural component of manufacturing, value added is an important means of
characterising industrial performance. A low value
added is an indication of poor industrial performance. Where manufacturing consists mainly in the
assembly of imported components and parts, as in the
vehicle assembly and soft drinks bottling sub-sec-
tors of West African economies, value added is usually small. The same is also the case where manufacturing being undertaken consists mainly in mere
processing of raw materials, as in a good number of
material export preparations in West Africa. With
these as the dominant industrial activities in West
Africa, as in many developing countries,there is
generally low value added by manufacturing in the
region.

The major factor underlying the low value added
content of West African manufactures is the low level of technology. Owing to lack of technical and
managerial expertise, there is a low level of efficiency in factor combinations towards industrial
productivity. In consequence, there is very heavy
dependence on imported intermediate goods which are
then locally assembled. Even in Nigeria, probably
the most industrially developed and most resource-

STRUCTURAL CHARACTERISTICS OF MANUFACTURING

Table 4.8: Value added by manufacturing per worker in selected countries of West Africa

ISIC No.	Industry Group	Value added (in US $) per worker in:		
		Ghana (1970)	Senegal (1967)	Togo (1970)
31	Food, beverages and tobacco	4,942	8,640	2,836
32	Textiles and clothing	1,199	4,427	2,239
33	Wood and furniture	887	-	n.a
34	Paper printing and publishing	1,535	-	n.a
35	Chemicals, petroleum and plastics	3,152	7,908	n.a
36	Non-metallic mineral products	1,623	n.a	n.a
37	Basic Metal industries	1,617	n.a	n.a
38	Fabricated Metal products	1,223	7,314	n.a
39	Other industries	1,778	n.a	809

-: not applicable owing to mixed industry grouping.
n.a: not available
Source: Same as Table 4.1

endowed West African country, the import content of the manufacturing sector is very high. "For every naira of value added (by manufacturing), the economy spends 67 kobo[7] on (material) imports" (Nigeria, 1975c, p.149). As shown in Table 4.8, value added per industrial worker is highest in the food industry group involving a great deal more of processing than of finishing functions. It would have been much higher in the chemical industry group as well as in such heavy industry groups as fabricated metal product industries but for the generally heavy dependence on imported intermediate goods used as inputs. The Nigerian example helps to bring out the point about relative industrial performance in terms of value added. There was in 1974 an average value added of US$5,859 per industrial worker. Far below this general average were the saw milling industry ($1,882 per industrial worker) which is character-ised by material processing or export valorising functions, and the wearing apparel industry ($1,365 per worker) which is essentially assembly-type. But value added was well above the average in the Brew-ery and distillery industries ($33,946 per worker) and in the cement industry ($15,186 per worker), both importing proportionately negligible amounts of in-termediate goods as inputs, although in the case of the breweries barley is imported as raw material.

One major distinction between industries in developed and developing countries is that whereas the heavy industry groups in developed countries ac-count for the highest value added, depending as they do on locally developed technology and industrial inputs, it is the light industries of the food pro-duction groups that dominate in the industrial eco-nomy of developing lands. The factor underlying this major difference is mainly that of the wide gap in technology. Until the technological content of industrial production in West African countries im-proves considerably, heavy dependence on imported intermediate inputs will continue to reduce the value added shares of the technologically highly de-manding industrial production in the region.

INPUT STRUCTURE OF MANUFACTURING

From the foregoing it can be appreciated that West African industries can also be characterised struc-turally on the basis of their major inputs like their materials, their labour and their technolog-ical demands. Such characterisation aids decision-making in terms of what industry to profitably em-bark upon and where. The labour and the technolog-ical factors are almost inseparable. The constraints imposed by low level technology in West Africa, as in most of the developing countries, cannot but be reflected in the industrial structures. The majority of industrial productions in West African countries are local resource-based. In the bid to develop the import substitution strategy and thereby minimize foreign exchange losses, manufacturing activities which depend on local resources are generally given greater attention than the heavily import-dependent industries. This is one main reason for the emphasis on the cotton textile, cement, rubber goods, food and footwear industries. West Africa is a major source of the relevant material inputs: cotton, natural

rubber, limestone and leather. However, because of
low level technology, the development of such industries as chemical and petrochemical, steel, aluminium and paper pulp industries is visibly low in the
resource-abundant countries like Nigeria, Ivory
Coast, Liberia, Sierra Leone, Ghana, Mauritania,
Guinea, and Guinea Bissau, and almost absent in less
resource-endowed countries like Upper Volta, Mali,
Niger, Gambia, Benin, Togo and the Cape Verde Islands. The structure of industrial activities of
these countries brings out this emphasis on industrial activities that are least constrained by inadequacy of relevant resource base and technology.
Nigeria, Ivory Coast and Ghana, for their better
placing in terms both of resource endowment and
technology, are clearly more industrially divers-
ified than Upper Volta, Mali, Togo and Gambia at the
other end of the scale.

OWNERSHIP STRUCTURES

As has been theoretically outlined earlier in this
Chapter, organizational structures of manufacturing
units can also be differentiated in terms of ownership types. For our present purpose, the most important ownership types associated with industrial
promotion in West African countries are state ownerships, private ownerships that are either indigenous
or foreign, joint ownerships involving state governments and foreign firms, or the latter and private
indigenes of each country. Each of these ownership
types has in varying degrees from one country to
another influenced the policy, pace and pattern of
industrial development in the region. Since each
ownership type is to a large extent a means of
getting around certain economic or politico-economic
problems, it is of geographical interest to see the
pattern of industrial ownership that has emerged
over the West African region.
     One common feature of West African industrial-
ization is state direct participation in industrial
ventures. The degree of state direct participation
is widely varied among the countries. It is strong-
est in Guinea, Gambia, Mali and Guinea Bissau, and
weakest in Liberia and Ivory Coast. The rest of the
countries fall somewhere between these extremes.
     With Guinea turning socialist from the time of
her independence in 1958, state control and ownership of industrial investment and planning became a
fait accompli. The main objective was to use the

industrial sector as a major front in the war against capitalism and neo-colonialism. However,
owing to the capital, the technological and the manpower limitations of the country, the need for state
partnership with foreign industrial groups has been
quite real and given expression in official policy
statements and programmes. A typical example of
joint (state-foreign group) industrial venture is
the aluminium smelter at Boke set up in collabor-
ation with some oil-exporting Arab States. There
are also foreign investors - United States, Soviet
Union, Chinese, Japanese, Yugoslav and Belgian
nationals - not only in the ore (bauxite and iron)
mining sector, but also in the ore beneficiation
industry. A few are also in the import substituting
and agricultural material processing industries.

Gambia has only a very small industrial sector.
This is dominated by the processing of agricultural
export products including fish. Fuller government
participation in the industrial sector has since
1973 been demonstrated through the take-over of the
two vegetable oil refineries in the country by the
Gambian Produce Marketing Board. The former private
owners of the refineries were bought out. A cotton
ginnery recently set up at Basse in the Upper River
Division is also state-sponsored; so also are the
rice mills. However, there is as yet too little
manufacturing activity to require or attract substantial foreign participation or assistance. The
existing dyeing industry, silver and gold-smithing
as well as leather works operate on very small
scales and are tied to the slowly growing tourist
industry also largely state-sponsored and owned.

Guinea Bissau has since independence in 1973
adopted a state-owned or socialist economy. Within
that framework the small amount of industrial development that has taken place is characterised by
state ownership. Prominent, though as yet on a
small scale, are agro-based industries tied to the
centrally controlled agricultural economy. Sugar,
vegetable oil and salt refining, fish processing,
spirits from sugar cane, groundnut and rice milling
are as yet the country's leading industrial projects.
Groundnut and rice milling as well as fish processing are largely export-oriented industries. The
others are being developed as import substituting
industries.

A great deal of direct government involvement
in the industrial sector is a characteristic feature
of Mali's economy. From the days of Modibo Keita,
the small industrial sector of Mali has, as in

Guinea, been used as a show-piece of the country's socialist policy towards economic independence. Industrial productions are largely by state corporations and state-sponsored co-operative societies assisted by China. However, as a result of bureaucratic bottlenecks and lapses, the state-owned industrial projects have since the early 1970s had considerable problems. To save the worsening economic situation, the Malian government has since 1976 fallen back into the redeeming hands of the French government - rejoining the Franc Zone and in return getting France to cover much of the country's mounting deficit. Thus, although largely state-owned, the industrial sector now relies on the active participation of China and France - an indication of the fact that the ownership structure of Mali's industrial economy is gradually changing.

At the other end of the scale is the open-door policy of Liberia initiated and promoted by President Tubman from 1944. According to Tubman, the open door policy is essentially designed to induce foreign capital and technical know-how in the exploration and utilization of the country's natural resources:

> We shall encourage the investment of foreign capital in the development of the resources of the country, preferably on a partnership basis, and we shall accord to all investors the necessary protection and fairness of treatment (Tubman, 1944).

This open-door policy amounts in effect to virtually unrestricted private ownership of industrial and other economic enterprises in Liberia. According to Cole and Cassell (1970):

> Manufacturing, as a matter of policy, is in private hands under the free enterprise system. State participation, however, is done indirectly. And where there is no private entrepreneurship to start industries for which feasibility studies have shown prospects of profitability, such government agencies as the Industrial Development Corporation exist to initiate such industries (p. 76).

Thus in contrast with the ownership structures of manufacturing concerns in Guinea, Gambia, Guinea Bissau and Mali, Liberia's is a long way away from state ownership or control. The partnership ventures involving the state seem more of an exception to the general rule of private ownership. Such state involvement within the manufacturing sector is typified by the Liberia Refining Company which, by 1970, was processing crude oil at the rate of 10,000 barrels a day. Established with an investment of $17 million in 1969, the company's major shareholder has been the Sun Oil Company of Philadelphia, USA, while the minority interests are held by Hydrocarbon Research, Inc. of New York, USA, and by Liberian citizens. In the West African Shoe and Rubber Industries Limited sponsored by the Liberian Development Corporation, the state has the majority share. An example of totally private and foreign-owned industrial enterprise is the West African Explosives and Chemicals Limited formed with American and Canadian capital. It is still the leading explosives manufacturing firm in West Africa and produces blasting agents for both domestic needs and export to other West African countries. By and large, although all forms of ownership structures exist within the open-door framework of Liberia, private ownership prominently featuring foreign ownership ventures seems to dominate.

Between these two extremes are variants of joint ventures in which state and foreign interests are represented. The examples of Nigeria and Ghana are noteworthy. In Nigeria since 1972, under the country's enterprises promotion decree, industrial investments have been placed under three major categories. One category includes enterprises involving no more than $352,000 and into which foreign investors are not allowed. The second category includes industrial activities considered too important and strategic to be thrown open to foreign participation. Typical industries in this category include weapons, explosives and security printing industries. The third category comprises the rest of large scale industries not covered in the other two categories. It is in this area that foreign participation is encouraged. Even so, such participation must be jointly with Nigerian people, state or private, or both. Since 1976, foreign equity shareholding in most of such ventures has been pegged at 40 per cent. In other words, the ownership structures within the Nigerian framework have changed considerably over the past decade, featuring increased restriction on foreign ownership and control of the country's industrial sector.

The case of Ghana is another interesting one.

There was a swing in 1966 from the full state-
ownership structure which came with Nkrumah's socialist economic policy to a more or less open-door
policy though not as loose as Liberia's or even as
Ivory Coast's. As in Nigeria, a certain category
of industrial activities is exclusive to Ghanaian
entrepreneurs. However, the areas open to foreign
interests are not, as in the Nigerian case, subject
to stringent limits as regards foreign equity shareholding. For example, whereas in the Nigerian
framework foreign shareholding in certain areas does
not exceed 40 per cent, in Ghana's case, foreign
shareholding ranges from 45 to 75 per cent. A more
graphic illustration of the Ghanaian ownership
structures is presented in Table 4.9.

By and large, ownership structures have noteworthy implications for industrial location, size
and prosperity, and sometimes influence the type of
inter- and intra-industry associations that exist in
West Africa as in any other regions. It is to the
issues of linkage structures that we now turn.

PATTERNS OF LINKAGES AND INTEGRATIONS

Applying to West Africa our earlier theoretical discussion of industrial functional relations in terms
of linkages and integrations, the picture presented
seems basically the same from one country to another.
Much of the distinction that can be made is one of
degree rather than of kind. Considerable linkage
relations exist inter-sectorally and such abound
between the manufacturing sector on the one hand and
both the mining and the agricultural sectors on the
other hand. One very important objective of official policy on industrial development is the exploitation and use of local resources in a bid to save
foreign exchange as well as to achieve wider distribution of the responsibility and benefit of economic development over a country. To that end, all
the West African countries, in their common experience of serious constraints imposed by acute shortage of capital and technical knowledge, put much
premium on industries that are **local resource-based**.

Because of the greater flexibility which linkage structures allow, and of the fact that mere
linkage relations are a great deal less capital-
demanding relative to integrated production functions, the inter-sectoral relationships (between the
industrial and the primary sectors) that have tended
to prevail are more of backward linkages rather than

Table 4.9: Ownership structures in the manufacturing industries of Ghana, 1975

Type of Ownership	Participants	Industrial types
i) State	Ghana Industrial Holding Corporations; National Investment Bank; ad hoc statutory corporations.	Industrial rehabilitation/expansion foundry, granite projects, silicate bricks, production of raw and building materials.
ii) Private (foreign and indigenous)	Wholly foreign; joint Ghanaian and foreign ownership (foreign equity participation to range from 50 to 60%).	Pharmaceuticals, cosmetics, plastics, metal containers, footwear, electrical equipment and assembly of vehicles.
iii) Private (indigenous)	Wholly Ghanaian individuals or partners.	Bakeries, printing of books and stationery, cement blocks, suitcases, briefcases, handbags, wallets, garments.
iv) State/Private	Government or statutory corporations; Foreign investors (45 to 75% equity share).	Basic necessities industries like sugar, soap, salt, fertilizers, matches, agricultural implements, cement, rubber products.
v) Co-operatives	Groups of Ghanaians	Cottage industries.

Source: Five-Year Development Plan, 1975-1980, Ministry of Economic Planning, Accra

backward integrations. For example, the cotton textile and ginning firms rely on independent farmers
or produce marketing boards for their seed cotton.
So do the groundnut milling firms depend on groundnut farmers, the rubber processing firms on
the rubber growing communities, and the fruit-
canning establishments on the thousands of independent fruit growers around. Similarly, the leather
and leather product factories depend on the stock-
farming communities for their raw materials, and the
furniture and construction firms on private producers of sawn timber not in any way concerned with the
production of industrial wood products.
     However, in specific industrial areas, it has
not been so easy, if economically feasible, to separate raw material production and the manufacturing
operations. This is particularly, but by no means
always, the case with industries that are mineral
resource-based. The oil refining industry, for instance, is undertaken by the same group engaged in
oil exploration, provided that the refining is carried on within the territory producing the crude.
This is the case with the Nigerian National Petroleum Corporation which undertakes both petroleum exploration, refining and marketing, and will soon be
refining gas and producing petrochemicals from the
same resource base. This kind of relationship is a
case of backward integration from the standpoint of
the secondary activity (refining). This is, however,
not the case in Ivory Coast, Ghana, Sierra Leone,
Liberia, Togo and in all other countries that depend
on imported crude oil for their refineries. Ordinary
linkage relations exist - linkage with external
sources of crude oil. The kind of backward integration in Nigeria is also typified by the aluminium
smelting industry at Boke in Guinea, but not by
Ghana's VALCO project which still depends on imported rather than local alumina. Again, a case of
integrated industrial structure is the backward integration of a pelletizing plant at Buchanan with
iron ore mining by the Liberian-American-Swedish
Minerals Company (LAMCO) in Liberia. The Nigerian
steel complex will by 1984 be producing steel from
its own iron ore mines. Meanwhile production depends on linkage relations with Guinea and Liberian
ore mines. In such areas as cement, brick and tiles
as well as glass and ceramic industries, integration
is more   the rule than the exception in West
Africa. The material source is in most cases owned
by the manufacturing firm, whether private or state.
The notable exceptions are the clinker-grinding

cement plants which are non-integrated and are in
linkage relation with other firms that supply clinker as an intermediate product. Such plants are few
in West Africa and are now in the process of being
replaced by resource-based integrated cement mills
in countries, like Nigeria, where clinker grinding
plants were once very important.

Integrated production is not by any means confined to mineral-based industries. A few examples
of agro-based integrated industrial processes are
noteworthy. Following on the development of agriculture on a large scale in plantation schemes,
forward integration of the manufacturing process has
been quite feasible and is gaining increasing popul-
arity in West Africa. Sugar cane growing concerns
in Nigeria, Ivory Coast, Liberia, Ghana, Guinea
Bissau, Mali and Upper Volta have extended their
activity to include cane sugar production. For
example, in Upper Volta, cane sugar refining which
was the largest industrial project in the country by
1976 is being based on a vast sugar plantation at
Zanfara. This is run by the Upper Volta Sugar Company which is a joint venture between the Upper
Volta government (with 71 per cent equity shares)
and a French company. Fruit canning has similarly
developed as an offshoot or a secondary activity of
large fruit plantation schemes, notably for pineapples in Ivory Coast. So has rubber processing
developed from huge plantation schemes in Liberia
and to a lesser extent in Nigeria. Paper pulp industry based on local pulp wood is in the process of
being developed in Nigeria and Ivory Coast in particular, where plantations of eucalyptus and gmelina
trees are being developed as the major sources of
integrated wood pulp and paper industry.

So far, we have been concerned with inter-
sectoral linkages and integrations in the various
countries of West Africa. But another form of this
organizational structure involves intra-sectoral
linkages and integrations. This structural feature
is much less in evidence in the industrial sector of
West Africa than the inter-sectoral relationships
just discussed. There are few cases within each
country where linkage relations have developed on an
appreciable scale between industrial units. Most of
the examples that exist are those of linkage relations between the processing plants and those engaged in finishing functions. For instance, the
cotton ginning establishments supply the cotton textile mills with cotton lint. The sawmilling plants
supply sawn lumber to the furniture and construction

firms. The hides and skins processing firms provide
the shoe and leather goods establishments with
leather and glue. And the vegetable oil mills supply oil to soap and margarine plants. In most cases
the inter-industry relations are of the mere linkage
type. The few cases of integrated production are
mainly to be found in countries where state ownership of production units is in vogue. In Mali,
Guinea and Guinea Bissau, integrated production processes exist particularly in the sense that industrial product types and their uses are state-deter-
mined and controlled.
     Inter-industry and intra-industry linkages in-
volving intermediate products are as yet on a low
scale within each country. The distinction between
inter-industry and intra-industry linkages is worth
making at this point. In line with our definition
of what an industry, an industrial firm and a plant
are respectively, inter-industry linkages refer to
functional relationships between different industries, say textile and chemical industries. But
intra-industry linkages refer to such functional
relationships between firms within the same industry,
for example, spinning linked with weaving in the
textile industry.
     A survey of cotton textile industry in Nigeria
(Onyemelukwe, 1972) showed that Kaduna Textile
Limited (KTL) was originally designed to produce
grey cloth needed as an intermediate good by other
cotton textile firms concentrating on the finishing
functions like wax printing. But in 1970 the mill
supplied only 3 per cent of its output for the year
to the textile mills in the country. The bulk of
its products is now directed to the final consumers,
especially in the northern part of the country where
the "riga" attire made with the product of the KTL
is traditional wear. The Calabar Cement Company
(CALCEMCO) established in 1967 at Calabar was originally designed to turn out 80 per cent of its products as clinker to be absorbed by the clinker-
grinding cement plants otherwise dependent on imported clinker. But before 1970 it had become clear
that the expected forward linkage with clinker-
grinding plants could not work. The CALCEMCO has
since switched from 20 per cent to 100 per cent
production of cement. The examples serve to buttress
the point that intra-industry linkages are still weak
in West Africa. The reasons for this derive partly
from the high production costs of local industries -
costs which are themselves largely the result of low
level technology and inadequate management skills as

well as of small scale production to which hardly
any economies accrue. These and many other problems
will be the main focus in Chapter 6. Suffice it to
say here that these problems are real and serious; in
the face of high costs and the sometimes poor quality
of local products, industrial firms are forced to
depend largely, if not entirely, on imports for such
intermediate products.

However, there are a few noteworthy examples of
linkage relations involving locally made intermediate
goods. In Nigeria, the glass industry near Sapele
produces glass sheets and bottles which are inputs
in a variety of manufacturing industries, particularly the breweries and the soft drinks bottling establishments. Also the sugar company at Bacita produces
the bulk of the alcohol being used as an intermediate
good by the spirit distilleries in the country, as
well as sugar used by the beer breweries, the ice-
cream plants and the factories producing confec-
tionery and tinned beverages. The Metal Box Company
with an industrial establishment in Lagos produces
cans in use by fruit canning factories in other
parts of the country. Examples such as these are
relatively very few and should be multiplied. The
Nigerian government's concern about the country's
low-key development of strong linkage relations is
reflected in the following official statement
(Nigeria, 1975, p. 149):

> The import content of the manufacturing sector
> is high. On the average 34 per cent by value
> of the raw materials is imported. For the
> high technology groups the percentage is
> much higher: basic industrial chemicals
> (87.3 per cent), glass products (92.9 per cent).

In Ghana, Ivory Coast, Mali, Upper Volta, Senegal
and Liberia, sugar mills provide both sugar and alcohol for other industries including the breweries
and the bakeries, as in Nigeria. In Ghana and
Ivory Coast, as in Nigeria, import-based paper production is using the conversion method to supply
corrugated and packaging paper containers to a
variety of other manufacturing industries. And in
Ivory Coast, Liberia and Ghana, as in Nigeria, plywood and veneers are produced for use by local furniture manufacturing firms. Altogether a few such
examples exist. This major structural weakness
of industrial development in West Africa seems to
have been officially acknowledged in most of the
countries of the region. The efforts being made to

eliminate or rectify it are considered in the last
Chapter.

SPATIAL PATTERNS ON THE WEST AFRICAN LANDSCAPE

We close this chapter with a critical look at the
spatial pattern of industrial activity in West
Africa.   Figure 4.1 presents a bird's eye view of
the industrial activity centres in West Africa.
What immediately meets the eye is the element of
strong concentration of industrial activity in a relatively very small portion of each country in the
region.   The main centres of concentration are the
coastal areas for all the countries having a sea-
board.   In the land-locked states, industrial activity seems even more concentrated, invariably
around the capital city.   In any case, the industrial concentrations are in areas where the modern
route system is best developed in the country.   As
shown in this map, such areas are either the chief
port-cum-capital complex in countries with a coastline, or the capital city in the heart of the hab-
itable section of a land-locked country.   If all the
fifteen mainland states of West Africa fall into
this spatial pattern, then it is of interest to
have a close study of the underlying factors.
     West African countries, like most of the
developing countries, are characterised by
grossly inadequate provision of infrastructural facilities.   Transport, power, potable water supply,
postal and telephone facilities as well as other
utilities indispensable for successful industrial
development are not only scantily provided but also
disproportionately concentrated in a few centres.
This pattern of infrastructure provision has remained
one enduring example of the colonial impact on black
Africa in general as has been explained in Chapter 2.
However, the fact that the problem of infrastructural
inadequacy has actually increased since independence
(some twenty years ago) is clearly indicative of the
generally unimpressive achievements of the indigenous
political powers of West African countries in the
promotion of economic development.
     The effect of this structure of modern route
system has been mainly to give the very few and relatively well served centres the considerable comparative advantage of accessibility and easier factor
mobility.   With such a head start in the economic
development race within the urban system of each
country, such favoured urban centres have been much

Figure 4.1: Industrial concentrations and major transport links of West Africa

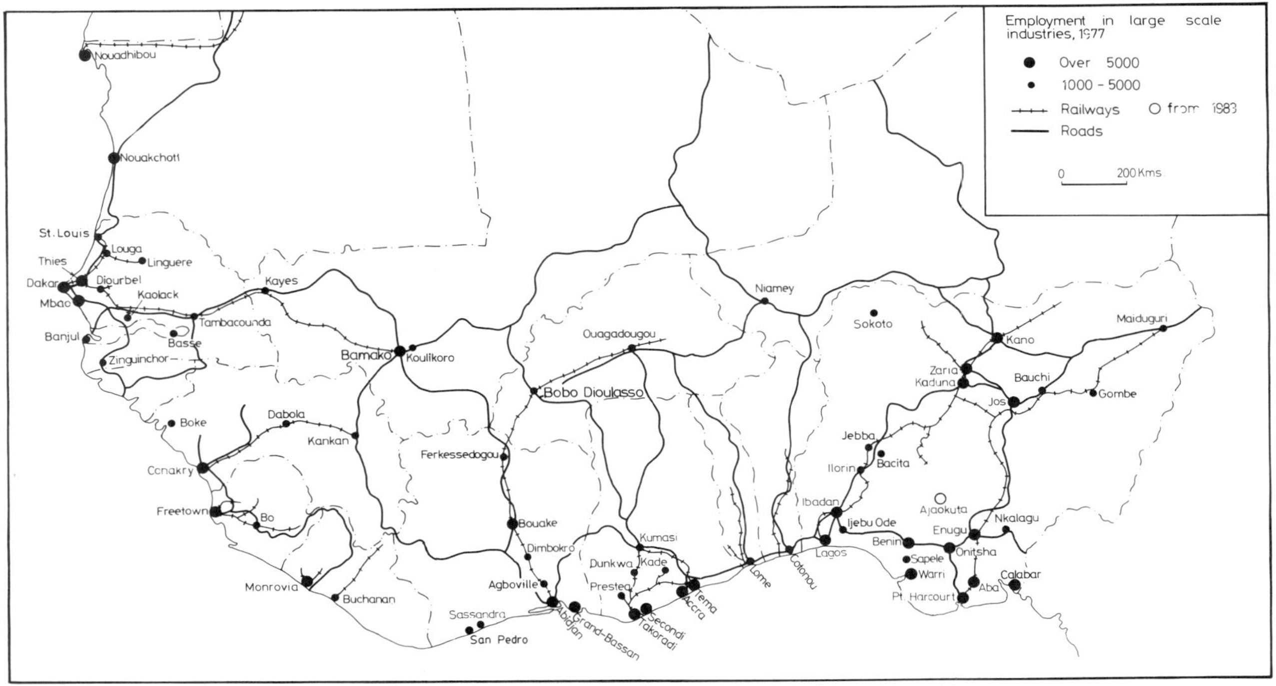

quicker in growing into big centres with brighter
prospects for trade articulation and profitable economic production. It is in such rapidly growing
population centres that central institutions
concentrate and further attract more infrastructural
facilities. A combination of such institutions and
public utilities constitutes the attractive elements
of an industrial environment. And it is in such
centres that the bulk of the medium and large scale
manufacturing units have been found   (Fig. 4.1).
     The industrial promoters' decision to locate
their plants in such relatively most favoured centres is clearly in keeping with the principle of
cost-minimisation and revenue-maximization.[8] This
is more so where the industry is (as in most cases)
of the import-substitution type needing a certain
demand threshold hardly available outside such population concentrations.
     Because the majority of such favoured centres
are the chief ports as well as capitals of their
respective countries, and also because most industrial productions in the region depend mainly on imported inputs, the concentration of industrial activities at the coast is clearly explicable on grounds
of economic rationality. Firstly, location decisions along that line are in keeping with the modern
tendency towards market location. In all West African countries except the land-locked Niger, Mali
and Upper Volta, the main concentrations of population and purchasing power are at the port-cum-
capital complex. Location of consumer goods import-
substituting industries as well as export oriented
industries at the coastal area is, other things
being equal, a sound economic practice. Secondly,
industries that are in theory material-rooted or
supply-based, but which largely depend on imported
material inputs, are strictly speaking nearest to
their material sources at the port location.
Thirdly, coastal locations in the West African context are for such import-based industries the best
point from which to combine the advantages of mat-
erial-orientation and market location. Finally,
coastal locations combine the above advantages with
those from the best infrastructural facilities and
external economies available in the country - especially in port-cum-capital cities.
     In view of these and other favourable factors,
it becomes easier to understand why West African
industrial activity is mainly concentrated at the
coastal area where the chief port and capital is
also the primate city. Mabogunje's study (1973)

Table 4.10: Percentage shares of some West African
capital cities in manufacturing establishments, 1971

Country	Capital City	Percentage Share
Gambia	Banjul	100%
Liberia	Monrovia	100%
Senegal	Dakar	81.48%
Sierra Leone	Freetown	75%
Ivory Coast	Abidjan	62.5%
Guinea	Conakry	50%
Nigeria	Lagos	35%
Ghana	Accra	30%

Source: Mabogunje, A.L.: Economic Geography Vol. 48, 1973,
p. 16

showed that by 1971, six of the then fourteen independent West African countries had 50 per cent or
more of their large scale industrial establishments
in their coastal capital cities (Table 4.10).
Banjul in Gambia and Monrovia in Liberia had each
100 per cent of the industrial establishments in
their respective countries. Dakar in Senegal had
over 81 per cent, Freetown in Sierra Leone about 75
per cent, Abidjan in Ivory Coast over 62 per cent,
and Conakry in Guinea 50 per cent. Although the
relative share of each capital city has changed
since, as new centres of industrial activity develop,
the pattern that one finds remains the same, that is,
industrial concentration continues in a few centres of
infrastructure and population concentration. Industrial location in West Africa in the late 1970s may
be summarised in one sentence, namely, that over 80
per cent of industrial plants in each country outside the capital city are generally concentrated in
less than half a dozen urban centres. In Mauritania
the other centres besides the capital, Nouckchott,
are Atar, Nouadhibou, Kaedi, Rosso and Akjoujt. In
Senegal, industrial activity outside Dakar is concentrated in Thies, Kaolack, Diourbel, M'Bao, Cayar,
Rufisque and St. Louis. In Gambia it is only in
Denton Bridge, Basse, Brikama and Kartung besides
the capital, Banjul. In Guinea Bissau, it is in
Buba, Sara, Bambadinca, Bolama and Vasela besides
the capital, Bissau. In Guinea, it is in Kankan,
Dabola, Boke, Kindia and Mamou, besides Conakry. In
Sierra Leone, a little industrial activity is located

in Waterloo, Bo and Baoma besides the primate city,
Freetown.   In Liberia, outside Monrovia, industrial
activity is now emerging in Robertsfield and Buch-
anan in particular and also around Harper and
Gbarnga.   In Ivory Coast manufacturing outside the
Abidjan port complex is in Bouake particularly, as
Table 4.11 shows.[9]   The other centres are San Pedro,
Agboville, Dimbokro, Ferkessedougou and Grand Bassam
(fig. 4.2).   In land-locked Mali, Bamako, like the

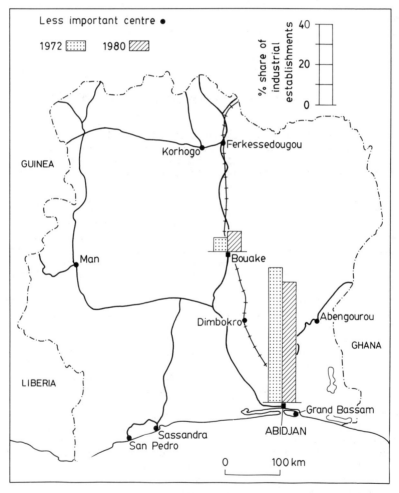

Figure 4.2:   Leading industrial concentrations in
Ivory Coast, 1972, 1980

114

port capitals of coastal states, is the centre of
commercial activity and has the best of the infrastructural facilities available. It has the bulk of
manufacturing activity. Over 80 per cent of industrial plants outside the capital are located in Segou,
Kayes, Bougouni, Mopti and Sikasso. Outside
Ouagadougou, the small amount of industrial activity
in Upper Volta is located in Banfara, Koudougou, and
Bobo Dioulasso. In Niger, besides Niamey, the capital, Maradi, Birni N'Konni and Zinder have the bulk
of the very little manufacturing activity in the
country.

Table 4.11: Geographical pattern of manufacturing
investment in Ivory Coast

Area	Investment (mil. CFA francs) in:			Percentage of national total		
	1972	1975	1980	1972	1975	1980
Abidjan	91,043	229,705	477,260	67.5	65.6	60
Bouake	13,263	29,315	53,497	9.9	8.4	7
Rest of Ivory Coast	30,527	90,994	169,127	22.6	26.0	33
Ivory Coast	134,833	350,014	650,427	100	100	100

Source: Ivory Coast, L'Industrie Ivoirienne en 1980,
Statistiques du 1.10.1974 au 30.9.80, Chambre D'Industrie de
Cote D'Ivorise, May 1981, p. 5

    In Ghana, Tema, Kumasi and Sekondi-Takoradi
together have over 80 per cent of large-scale manufacturing plants outside Accra, the capital. In
Togo, outside Lome, the capital and chief port, over
80 per cent of the country's industries are located
in Palime and Blitta.
    In Benin, Cotonou, the chief port, has the bulk
of manufacturing activity in the country, followed
by Porto Novo, the capital. Here is the only case
in the coastal countries of West Africa where the
capital city is not also the largest and industrially
most important city. The other small industrial

centres of note are Abomey and Pobe. It is only in
Nigeria that 80 per cent of industrial plants outside the capital city are found in more than half a
dozen centres. Since the creation of states in 1967
and the subsequent emergence of sub-national state
capitals and growth centres, many more than half a
dozen industrial centres can now be counted besides
Lagos. Noteworthy are Kaduna, Kano, Warri, Port
Harcourt, Sapele, Ibadan, Enugu, Jos, Zaria, Aba,
Calabar, Benin, Onitsha and Oshogbo. More will be
said about the Nigerian pattern of industrial location in Chapter 7.

Material rooting of industrial activity, which
does not often produce concentration on the landscape, is also noteworthy. Certain industrial
plants that are port-oriented in West African countries are in fact as material oriented as they can be
since they depend entirely (at least up to now) on
imported raw materials. Typical examples are flour
mills importing the bulk of wheat milled, beer
breweries importing the entire requirement of barley,
and oil refineries (outside Nigeria) importing the
bulk of the crude oil from Nigeria, Gabon or even
farther afield. Such port locations are, therefore,
not to be seen as evidence of departure from the
Weberian location model. On the contrary, they
tend to underscore the relevance, albeit limited
importance, of classical location theories. It is
probable that as technology improves in West African
countries - to the point of making the latter more
self-reliant on certain industrial inputs hitherto
imported - more of the plants in the coast-based
import-dependent industries will tend to locate
inland near the domestic resources. This, of course,
is more likely to be the case with industries using
highly weight/bulk-losing materials - paper, beer
and chemical industries, for instance.

Plant locations in keeping with this pattern of
material rooting are common in West African countries among industries using local raw materials with a
high material index. On account of their clearly
above-unity material index (1.5 for limestone-using
cement plants),[10] such industrial establishments as
sugar mills, cement, glass, ceramic and brick plants
are generally raw material rooted in West Africa.
The same is true of the bulk of processing plants -
cotton ginneries, palm oil, rubber, tobacco, hides
and skins processing establishments as well as most
mineral beneficiating plants. One general characteristic is their spatial dispersal in the search
for transport cost minimization on bulky raw

material rather than for external economies often present in activity concentrations. Thus the dispersal of the plants in these resource-based industries has a valid explanation different from that suggested by some authorities (e.g. Greenhut, 1956). Experience in West Africa shows that plant dispersal often arises in spite of demand inelasticity for their products. Indeed, a number of spatial structures found on the West African landscape are noteworthy for their apparent departure from traditional models of industrial location. The factors underlying such atypical behaviour in location decision-making may well provide part of the grounds for a careful reappraisal of industrial location theories.

Industrial establishments are increasingly appearing in peripheral areas where neither the market, the material nor even the much-needed infrastructural facilities are available. In nearly every case, the project is the investment of a single member of a community or of the community itself in which the plant locates. It is often set up by the individual as a contribution to his community welfare, or by the community as part of its own self-help programme in economic development. It is in particular intended to provide employment opportunities in the area, and to diversify the economy of a peripheral area that is essentially rural and agricultural. This departure from classical location theories is a common feature in West African countries. In Nigeria, Ivory Coast, Ghana and Benin, this aspect of industrial dispersal has particularly involved printing, bakery, animal feed, rubber and plastic, textile and meat processing enterprises. It is a spatial structure that increasing efforts in community self-help programmes are helping to throw into bold relief in most West African countries. It is one that arises from entrepreneurship probably more inclined to achieve satisfaction in social welfare terms than in private benefit-cost terms.

Another location pattern that is fast developing on, though not peculiar to, the West African scene is the city market location of industrial establishments that depend entirely on materials that lose considerable weight/bulk. Saw-milling industry, for example, is fast becoming a city-based activity. Of course, such location conforms to theory if the city is close to the resource base (the log source). But a good number of cases in Liberia, Nigeria and Ivory Coast show that the logs are hauled for upwards of 100 kilometres. The same is also largely the case with fruit processing plants. On account of the

considerable loss of weight and bulk in the course
of processing fruit like citrus, pineapples and
mangoes and of their perishable nature, plant location near the source of the fruit is more in keeping
with traditional location theory. Yet it is the
big cities that increasingly harbour saw mills and
fruit processing plants. Problems of high material
index also tend to question the location of groundnut oil mills and palm kernel crushing plants in the
main cities of West Africa rather than in the vicinity of the material sources. The groundnut oil mills
of Senegal are concentrated in Dakar, Diourbel,
Ziguinchor, Kaolack and Rufisque rather than in small
towns and rural service centres of the groundnut
zone. In Mali, groundnut mills and rice mills concentrate in Bamako, the primate city, and in Kayes,
Segou, Mopti and Koulikoro - the leading urban
centres of the country. In Nigeria the main groundnut oil mills are in Kano and the largest palm
kernel-crushing plant is in Lagos. The same is
largely true of Niamey, Maradi and Zinder in Niger.
    The major factor explaining this spatial struc-
ture (city concentration of otherwise material-
rooted industries) seems to be infrastructure. Power
supply generally not available in rural environments
of West Africa is relatively adequate in the cities
for the processing industry. Also transport facilities in the form of long-distance bulk haulage make
it relatively easy to move cheaply the bulky raw
materials to plant location at the market. By and
large, the emerging spatial structures of industrial
activity in West Africa point particularly to the
dynamics of change that must be expected from human
adjustments to constantly changing situations of the
space economy. It is this dynamic element that is
not adequately provided for in classical location
theories.

NOTES

    1. For other forms of linkages, such as horiz-
ontal, lateral and diagonal linkages/integrations,
the reader is referred to E.A.G. Robinson (1956,
pp. 108-115).
    2. In no West African country do industrial
plants employing 5,000 workers or more constitute up
to 1 per cent of the total plants. But those employing between 10 and 50 persons represent over 60
per cent of the total industrial workforce.

3. Since the most populous and industrially developed countries of West Africa are in the seven, the entire region's average is certainly below this figure.

4. Liberia (1975) <u>Manufacturing Industry Directory</u>, Monrovia (Sept-Dec), Table III.

5. Of the twenty-five countries covered, five - Nigeria, Benin, Ghana, Ivory Coast and Senegal - belong to West Africa.

6. Pearson's figures of £75 and £59 respectively for Kenya and Uganda are here converted into US dollars at the rate £1 = $2.5.

7. 67 kobo is 0.67 naira.

8. Traditional models of industrial location based on the assumption that entrepreneurs seek maximum profit through their plant location, emphasize either cost-minimizing locations (e.g. Weber's) or revenue-maximizing locations (e.g. Losch's). For a good review of these models, see D.M. Smith, <u>Industrial Location</u>, John Wiley, New York, 1970.

9. The Abidjan area has continued to have a disproportionate share of industrial concentration. However, this share and Bouake's (the next in importance outside the Abidjan-Grand-Bassam core) has gradually declined over the years as more centres develop their industrial activity.

10. Material Index $(I) = \dfrac{\text{Weight of material input}}{\text{Weight of resulting output}}$

According to Weber (1909), cost considerations require that plants be material-oriented if $I > 1$, and market-oriented if $I < 1$.

Chapter Five

FACTORS AND FORMS OF THE SPATIAL DYNAMICS OF
INDUSTRIAL ACTIVITY

This chapter focuses on certain important, though as
yet hardly well studied and documented, aspects of
the region's spatial dynamics of industrial development which the student of industrial geography and
development planning should be familiar with. Such
familiarization would involve concepts like industrial migration, industrial splashing and industrial
shift which are applied to our study area - West
Africa - though only to the extent that available
relevant data permit.

INDUSTRIAL MIGRATION

Industrial migration has been defined in different
ways by different writers. Hamilton (1967) thinks
that industrial migration, unlike population migration, rarely involves a physical movement of
plants from one area to another but usually results
from differential rates of industrial growth. Almost in line with this view is the one expressed by
Wilczewski et. al. (1978), namely that industrial
migration does not imply only physical movement of
productive capacity from one place to another but
also the extension and modernization of existing
plants at lower cost. Contrary to these views that
tend to emphasize non-physical movement, Brown
(1965), Cameron and Clark (1966) and Smith
(1970) consider industrial migration to involve the
complete transfer (relocation) of productive capacity to, or the establishment of a branch factory in,
a new location by an existing manufacturing firm.
Unlike the first set of definitions, industrial migration is actually concerned with physical movement
and tends to fall in line with population migration.
What seems to be an appropriate definition of the

120

concept has been given by Howard (1968) and adopted
by both Keeble (1971, 1976) and the present author
(Onyemelukwe, 1974b,1978c). According to Howard,'industrial migration includes both the complete relocation or transfer of a firm or factory's existing
manufacturing activity from one location to another,
and movement....of a branch unit of the firm concerned, which nonetheless maintains its manufacturing activity to some degree in its existing location'. In this sense, industrial migration can be
seen to involve the physical movement of manufacturing plants in an industry, rather than of the entire industry, and to exclude shifts in the structural (non-spatial) characteristics of the firm as
is implied in the first set of definitions above.
The concept of industrial shift is quite different
and will be taken up later in this chapter. Meanwhile we shall proceed to examine theoretically the
various factors and patterns of industrial migration
and thereafter to identify such phenomena in West
Africa.

The set of questions that can be raised at this
point is: what factors underlie industrial migration,
and what variants of migration patterns can be associated with those causal factors? These questions
relate to forces behind the moves, to the distance
and directional characteristics of such moves as well
as to the relative importance (in terms of frequency
of occurrence) of the identified movement types.

Among the many factors giving rise to the migration of manufacturing plants eight are considered
to be of particular relevance to West African countries. Whereas some have centripetal effect, some
are centrifugal and the others multi-directional.

The first factor underlying plant migration is
the need for expansion. Need for additional factory
space is in most cases growth-induced, and such expansion is rarely effected on the spot. This may be
a result of space constraint, prohibitive rental on
adjacent land space, mounting problems of congestion,
pollution and, therefore, environmental costs, and
relatively high cost of labour. A possible way out
in each case is plant migration to a relatively better location. However, since the need for expansion
is itself a sign of prosperity at a given location,
industrial firms usually go on with the expansion
programme by setting up a branch plant elsewhere instead of relocating the existing prospering plant.
This removes the risk element usually present in
having to disrupt production in the process of relocation, in losing a large proportion of trained

labour force and longstanding patronage at the original location, and in the process of starting afresh
in a new and relatively unfamiliar environment. In
other words, the uncertainty risk in relocation and
fresh start is generally greater than the risk of
taking a branch plant to a new location. Thus, in
terms of directional impact, this is clearly centrifugal - often from the more space-constrained central city location to the more open city periphery.
    The second factor of plant migration is one of
industrial infrastructure pull. In developing countries like those of West Africa, the stock of industrial infrastructure, including piped water, electricity, good transport facilities, postal and
telephone service- as well as financial institutions -
is very inadequate and usually concentrates in a few
favoured centres as shown in Chapter 4. Such concentrations favour the polarization of economic activities including manufacturing. As certain centres increase their economic growth potential
through the upgrading of their stock of infrastructure, their attraction power on industrial firms becomes more irresistible. Firms not faring well in
environmentally less favourable centres are often
much more responsive to the centripetal (pull) force
of the growing centres, if only to improve their
chances of survival by taking advantage of much increased external economies. In cases like this the
migration is generally one of plant relocation.
    Diseconomies arising from serious congestion,
particularly in centres which have experienced long
standing polarization, cause the migration of industrial plants. As traffic congestion and high population pressure on very limited urban space increase travel cost in time and money, raise floor
space rental and service charges relatively steeply,
and exacerbate effluent disposal, noise and general
environmental problems, seriously affected industrial firms may see migration through plant relocation as a way out. In keeping with Alfred Weber's
thesis, which has been confirmed by real life experiences in many a city centre,[1] industrial plants
most prone to such deglomerative forces are those
most adversely affected by the growing external diseconomies. Again, spatial response by way of plant
migration is frequently in the form of plant relocation rather than branch plant transfer.
    Fourthly, official policy intervention often
causes industrial plant migration. Such efforts may
be towards regional equalization or urban renewal.
In an attempt to reduce regional inequalities through

a number of regional planning measures involving
fiscal and financial policies as well as the provision of infrastructural facilities, the government
of the day can increase or decrease the economic
growth potential and attraction of an area. This
may lead to industrial plant movements in line with
official policy objectives. Examples in the United
Kingdom (involving movement from the London area to
peripheral and some of the depressed areas), in the
Republic of Ireland (from the Dublin area to the central,
West and North-West areas of the country), in Poland
(from the Upper Silesia and Warsaw zones to the southern
areas), and in Brazil (from the South-Central region
of Rio de Janeiro and   Sao Paulo to the North-
East and the Amazon regions of the country) are
among the real life cases outside our study region
to which we shall later return. Plant migration re-
sulting from this is generally multi-directional.

     Also in the process of urban renewal, official
efforts may be towards the decongestion of city centres and the creation of industrial estates or industrial zones (discussed in Chapter 3) to which
industrial firms move. Thus, official policy decisions leading to plant migration have both direct
effects (through these forms of regional equalization and urban planning measures) and indirect effects (especially through infrastructure provision).

     Fifthly, the factor of technological advance
has much effect on industrial plant migration, particularly in developing economies. As is often the
case in such economies, manufacturing activity is
largely based initially on large-scale imports of
material inputs some of which could be provided locally,
given the necessary level of technology. And
while the heavy leaning on imported materials continues, industrial firms find it economically ideal
to locate at the port, as has been shown in Chapter
4. But as technology improves appreciably and makes
the processing and use of local materials relatively
easy and cheap, material rooting of industrial
plants using weight/bulk-losing raw materials tends
to offer greater economic prospects than may be
available at port locations. Industrial firms may
respond by establishing branch plants near the
source of raw material. The main plant at the port
that is in most cases the market centre (if not also
the capital city) may be retained principally as the
firm's administrative headquarters and contact point
with official and foreign groups but not necessarily
as the main production point. In other words, what
is often (but by no means always) involved is branch

plant transfer rather than original plant relocation.

The sixth factor influencing industrial migration is the need for effective market penetration
and control. Especially in countries originally
largely or entirely dependent on imported manufactured goods, the importing foreign firms desirous
of retaining their hold on the market (served in the
face of increasing competition and of rising import
duties in the territory) may wish to establish a
local manufacturing plant. This is frequently encouraged by the host country being served, since it
is a kind of import-substitution strategy which the
rising import duties are meant to protect. As more
foreign firms establish their production units in
the host country, the need to establish regional
(sub-national) branch plants increases. Such branch
plants are located in parts of the same country for
purposes of retaining a considerable part of the
national market. With import duties on finished
products thus totally obviated, the foreign firm now
competes more effectively, taking advantage of its
existing facilities for product distribution in reducing manufacturing costs.

The nature of migration thus involved is that
of branch plant transfer from the initial (main) industrial plant set up within the country. If the
foreign enterprise has a manufacturing component
outside the country at its administrative headquarters, then both the "main" and the branch plants
in the host country can be taken as the overseas
branches or extensions of the manufacturing component at the headquarters, and, therefore, representing components of international migration. In that
case, of course, it is assumed that decision-making
to establish the migrant plants is traceable to the
home headquarters. If, on the other hand, the
latter has no manufacturing component (as is the
case where merchant firms preoccupied with distrib-
utive trade develop a manufacturing arm in the overseas market served), then a phenomenon other than
international industrial migration is involved, as
will be explained shortly under the concept of
industrial splashing.

A seventh factor of industrial migration is
insecurity. Industrial plants, like most other
economic units, can be subjected to locational change
by different forms of insecurity - war or civil
strife, natural disasters, and political dangers like
acts of nationalization, indigenization, or of restrictions on the export of company profits. To eliminate the risk perceived, the migration of the af-

fected industrial plant may take place. And what is usually involved is plant relocation away from the push factor.

Finally, there is the factor of the industrial entrepreneur's effort to promote economic and socio-political ends or, more generally, get psychic satisfaction. Particularly in less developed economies where considerable sections of a country are still relatively undeveloped and largely off the mainstream of economic progress known in other parts, individual entrepreneurs are known, as has been shown in Chapter 4, to set up industrial plants in their economically disadvantaged home areas. As has been argued, the main objective is not to optimise production or proceeds through the location of the industrial activity in one's home area that is lacking the necessary industrial infrastructure and climate. What the entrepreneur is hoping to achieve is two-fold: enhanced socio-economic welfare for his home community (through rural economy diversification and increased gainful employment) on the one hand, and the entrepreneur's socio-political elevation by an appreciative community on the other hand. The plant set up is frequently a branch of a major industrial activity in the cities.[2]

The point that requires to be clarified is what actually constitutes industrial plant migration in a situation such as this. No migration is involved if the plant set up in this way is the entrepreneur's only and unrelocated industrial unit. But if it is the branch of an existing industrial enterprise, then that branch is a migrant plant. In this case, the element of main plant-branch relationship is clearly present, and in a spatial framework can be seen in origin-destination terms. Also, if the entrepreneur's only industrial plant elsewhere is so relocated, then there is migration by plant relocation. Again in spatial terms the origin-destination relationship of the industrial activity is not in doubt.

The factors of industrial migration identified here relate to four categories of plant migration, viewed from a spatial angle. Those are (a) intra-city; (b) inter-city (within a region) (c) inter-regional (within a nation) and (d) international migrations. Intra-city migration mainly involves plant relocation particularly from the congested city centre to the more open and industrially more congenial city periphery where land for expansion is more handy and less expensive, transportation less constrained and pollution minimal. As can be appreciated from Figure 5.1, intra-city migration is the most frequent, and, in that sense, the most important, always kept alive by the dynamics of urban population sprawl and change in patterns of urban land use.

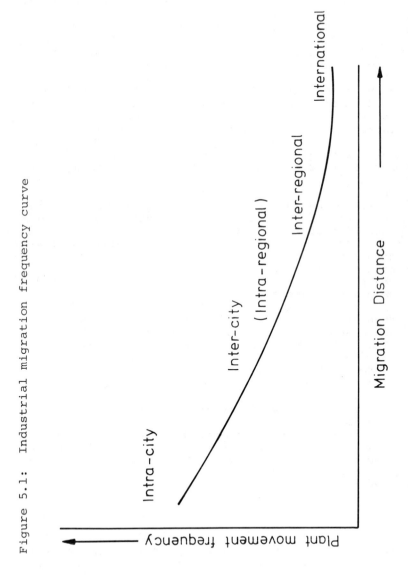

Figure 5.1: Industrial migration frequency curve

Inter-city migrations within a sub-national space involve plant relocation and branch plant transfer. Both types collectively rank quite high in terms of frequency of occurrence, though generally not as high as intra-city moves (Beacham and Cunningham, 1970).

Inter-regional migration within a single country also involves both main plant relocations and branch plant transfers. Migration through branch plant transfers is particularly prominent especially as a means of market penetration and control by main firms strategically located at the capital city, the chief port or the principal commercial centre of the country if different from the former.

International migration is generally rare, particularly among developing countries. It is one important means of industrial linkage relations of multinational corporations on a global scale, especially involving links between the developed and the less developed countries. In such linkage relations, there are far more cases of branch plant transfer to the less developed countries than plant relocation in either direction. Figure 5.1 suggests that international migration of industrial plants is the least frequent in a developing region like West Africa.

One interesting point that emerges from the general picture of industrial migration examined here is the inverse relationship between movement frequencies and migration distances: migration types occurring most frequently cover the shortest distances, and vice versa (Onyemelukwe, 1978c). Also implicit from our theoretical discussion so far is the point that growth-induced migration is more likely among older industrial firms than among the more recent establishments. An industrial firm normally requires considerable time to find its feet, attain a high level of success (in a market that is quite competitive within a capitalist economy), and hit a local/ceiling beyond which on the spot expansion is no more possible or worthwhile. Hence the proposition that if all the manufacturing firms within an economy were to be placed along a time scale, growth-induced migration would, other things being equal, be more frequent among the older firms (Onyemelukwe, 1978, p. 122).

INDUSTRIAL PLANT MIGRATION IN WEST AFRICA

A major difficulty in applying the concept of industrial migration to West Africa arises from the
gross inadequacy of information on industrial movements. No country in West Africa keeps any statistics on plant movements - which firms moved to where
and at what point in time, how much industrial labour or fixed capital is involved, and the site addresses of most industrial plants. Therefore, to
apply fruitfully the migration concept, specially
conducted field surveys are needed. One such survey was conducted in Nigeria and reported elsewhere
(Onyemelukwe, (1978c).   No other West African country has to date been closely studied. Although
Nigeria is not a statistical representation of West
African countries, it is likely that events in that
country will to a large extent mirror situations on
the wider regional scene. That study, at any rate,
may well be regarded as the first of the many
country-by-country studies which will later be
pieced together for a fuller regional picture and a
more critical appraisal of the concept and practice
of industrial migration in the African sub-region.
Meanwhile we shall focus on the Nigerian example for
what may be regarded as a preliminary appraisal.
     Rather few cases of plant migration have
been known in Nigeria. Even if the statistical
sources are updated and made quite comprehensive,
the probability of very few plants being involved
is high. The reason for this derives from one major
factor - the fact of relative recency of modern manufacturing industry in Nigeria, as in all other
countries of West Africa. It has been shown in
Chapters 1 and 3 in particular that modern manufacturing in West Africa hardly predated World War II.
Table 5.1 and Figure 5.2 provide a Nigerian illustration of this fact. Indeed, over 47 per cent of
the 746 industrial establishments covered by the
study for 1970 were less than ten years old! This
fact becomes very interesting in respect of our
search for cases of industrial migration. On the
basis of our earlier theoretical discussion of this
phenomenon, a hypothesis that countries with a short
history of industrial development have low incidence
of plant migration can be tested using the Nigerian
case. We have earlier concluded, though only on theoretical grounds, that growth-induced migration is more
likely among old than among new industrial establishments. According to the distance-moving frequency
graph (Fig. 5.1) above, it is intra-city movements

Table 5.1:   Age structure of manufacturing industry in Nigeria

Period of Establishment	Number of Establishments*	Cumulative Frequency
Before 1911	9	9
1911 - 1920	5	14
1921 - 1930	12	26
1931 - 1940	11	37
1941 - 1950	66	103
1951 - 1960	286	389
1961 - 1970	357	746

Source: Industrial Directory, Federal Office of Statistics, Lagos, 1971.

*Excluding establishments in the mining and service sectors as well as those with unspecified start-up years or size (employment) shown in the Directory.

(dominated by growth-induced migration) that tend to occur most frequently. With an overwhelming majority (over 86 per cent) of industrial establishments being below twenty years old (i.e. post-1950 establishments), growth-induced plant migrations in 1970 Nigeria were probably quite low since very few firms would have found expansion through plant movement really worthwhile. Table 5.2 shows that altogether only 42 cases of plant migration were known to have taken place in Nigeria up to 1974. The summary shown in this table represents the returns of industrial promoters' ranking of the reasons underlying their decision to move industrial plants.

Among the various factors motivating industrial plant migration through main plant relocation, government influence through fiscal measures, the provision of infrastructural facilities and the creation of industrial zones were the most important in terms of frequency of mention by industrial promoters interviewed. Need for expansion was the most important driving force behind the establishment of branch plants at new locations. This did not arise so much from lack of space for on the spot expansion as from a desire to extend services to, and retain considerable influence on, regional (sub-national) markets. For example, the Nigerian Tobacco Company, after relocating its main plant from Lagos to Ibadan,

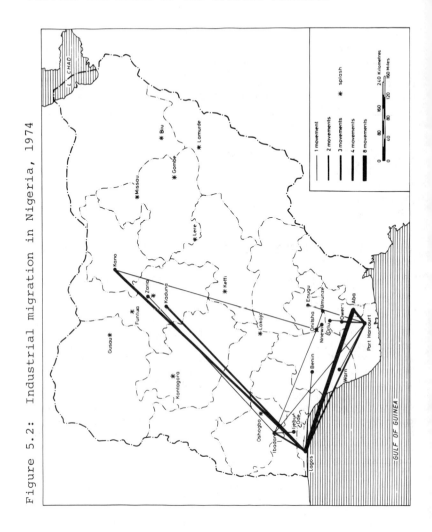

Figure 5.2: Industrial migration in Nigeria, 1974

established branches, first in Port Harcourt and
later in Zaria. The Nigerian Breweries Limited has
its headquarters in Lagos and branch plants in Aba
and Kaduna. Another branch is proposed for Ibadan.
The Nigerian Bottling Company has its main plant in
Lagos and branches in Kano, Ibadan and Ngwo (16 km

Table 5.2: Factors, types and frequencies of plant migration in Nigeria, 1974

| Reasons for Migration | Type of Movement | | | |
| | Plant Relocation | | Branch Plant Transfer* | |
	Topmost Reason	Secondary Reason	Topmost Reason	Secondary Reason
Need to expand through branch plants			13	4
Lack of space for <u>in situ</u> expansion	1	3	1	3
Better production prospects elsewhere	1	2	3	2
Desire to make impact at promoter's home area	2	1	4	5
Government influence	8	2	2	3
Security	7	2		
Total Moves	19		23	

Source: Personal field survey, 1974 (first published in <u>Industrial Change</u>, F.E.I. Hamilton (Ed), Longman, London 1978, p. 126)

*The establishment of a plant at a location other than that of the main manufacturing plant.

to Enugu). Also two tyre retreading and rubber product firms have their main plants in Lagos [3] and Onitsha respectively and branch plants in Kano, Port Harcourt, Ijebu-Ode, Ibadan and Umunze. Plant relocations in the quest for more space were particularly intra-city and typified by moves by a number of block-making plants in Onitsha, Benin and Warri, a jewellery establishment by Ottibros Limited in

Onitsha, and two bakeries, the Silas Works Limited
and the Mazi Ejidike and Sons Bread Industry, both
in Onitsha. All the moves were from the city centre
towards the city periphery. There are probably more
examples in other growth centres.

Another important set of moves observed arose
from insecurity. All the known cases arose from the
danger of civil strife, causing inter-regional migrations. Just before the Nigerian civil war began
in 1967, a number of industrial plants owned by
Nigerians of Igbo origin had to be closed down in
the northern, south-western and south-eastern parts
of the country for relocation in what was then
Biafra. A typical example was the building materials
factory relocated from Port Harcourt to Owerri, the
capital of Imo State. Also some plants were closed
down in the latter area and relocated by their non-
Igbo-speaking owners elsewhere in Nigeria. A number
of known cases were not represented in the above
table because of the non-cooperation of the industrial owners on information pertaining to, among
other issues, the origin (former location) of plant
and the reasons for relocation.

Finally, the desire to make a positive impact
on one's home area came out as another important,
albeit isolated, factor both for plant relocation and
for branch plant transfer. Six out of the forty-two
cases of plant migration were motivated by this factor. In each case, it was clear that the home district was not economically the most attractive location in which the industrial entrepreneur could
have set up his plant. The need for social identif-
ication was very strong. In most cases there was the
express need to increase a community's sense of belonging to the mainstream of national economic development through the introduction of factory employment in an otherwise agricultural (subsistence
farming) environment. A couple of cases like the
Ugofoam industry in Umunze involved the entrepreneur's sole effort in providing electricity, piped
water, health and housing facilities. The Ugofoam
industry producing foam mattresses and allied goods
was not even remotely influenced by material or market factors, since the bulk of the raw material is
imported into the area and the products of the industry are marketed in cities far from the district.

Although there could have been many more reported cases of plant migration, given a much improved access to relevant information, yet the overall incidence of plant migration in Nigeria can be
described as very low when compared with experiences

in Britain[4] (Keeble, 1978) and Poland (Wilczewski et al., 1978) which have a much longer history of industrial activity. Because of the scantiness of our data base, no conclusive statements can be made on the Nigerian experience as regards the validity or otherwise of our theoretical expectations. Among the tentative conclusions that may be reached is the point that the factor of relative recency of industrial development in Nigeria probably largely explains this low incidence of plant movement. It is probably the same in all West African countries, and it would require the study of a greater part of the West African region to reach definite conclusions on the factors and patterns of industrial migration in the African sub-region.

INDUSTRIAL SPLASHING

Can all new branch plant transfers be properly described as processes of plant migration? Examples do exist in which a couple of industrial plants are simultaneously set up in one country by a single firm hitherto not engaged in manufacturing. In situations such as those, there is no question of any such plants set up being part of an expansion process of any other industrial plant. It also happens that a number of plants emerge simultaneously or successively on a national space as a result of decisions by the non-manufacturing headquarters of the firm in a foreign country.[5] A trading firm with headquarters in Europe, for example, may decide to set up factories in its overseas market (like Nigeria) which it hitherto supplied with manufactured goods produced by other firms. The intention of doing that is primarily to hold its markets within the tariff walls of the host (overseas) country. In cases like these, there is actually no element of main plant-branch plant relationship between the origin (a decision-making non-manufacturing headquarters) and the destination (new industrial plants) in the overseas territory. In the light of our definition of industrial migration earlier in this chapter, this phenomenon cannot be correctly described as industrial migration. For instead of any physical location of branch plants in the overseas territory from an existing manufacturing unit, there is a splash of manufacturing plants, as it were from nowhere (since there is no manufacturing origin) over the host country's spatial system. This splash phenomenon has been studied and reported elsewhere

(Onyemelukwe, 1974a, 1978). A point that needs to be emphasized is that it is not and should not be viewed as a variant of industrial migration. The phenomenon of industrial splashing is common and requires to be closely studied in other parts of the world.

Examples of industrial splash abound in West African countries. Foreign and indigenous firms sometimes cause a splash of export-oriented processing plants in the effort to control a large enough catchment area and consolidate their control of the market. Many foreign merchant firms which have for many years been sending the manufactures of other firms into West African countries have increasingly been faced with difficulties. There is the problem of stiff competition from other foreign firms as well as from indigenous manufacturing enterprises in the host countries of West Africa. There is also the difficulty of operating in the face of host countries' official efforts to protect local import substituting industries within high tariff walls. To get over some of those problems, the importing merchant firms with well established bases for their distribution function may decide to set up a number of plants in the West African country being covered. None of the plants set up in any of these ways (sometimes simultaneously) can be rightly said to have migrated, having been set up by a non-manufacturing firm, or be correctly described as functionally the main plant from which the others of its kind hive off as branch plants. In Nigeria the British Cotton Growing Association set up about 13 cotton ginneries in different parts of the country where cotton is a major export crop. The objective in establishing such a spate of ginning plants was largely to control the cotton ginning industry as well as the wholesale function in the pre-export cotton market. There was no cotton ginnery in the United Kingdom headquarters of the firm from which the 13 ginneries in Nigeria could then have developed as overseas branch plants. Thus the ginneries appeared as industrial splashes across Nigeria (Fig. 5.2). Also state-sponsored industrial projects have sometimes developed as examples of industrial splash. Several plants are set up simultaneously, such that none can be said to be hiving off from, or part of the expansion process of, the other. For example, Nigeria's two oil refineries at Warri and Kaduna were set up almost simultaneously, neither being the branch of the other or even of the earlier refinery near Port Harcourt. Each arose

independently from decision-making by a non-manufacturing arm of government, the Nigeria National
Petroleum Company (NNPC) primarily concerned with
petroleum exploration and marketing. The same
structural arrangement can be identified in respect
of the country's paper pulp mills and sugar mills.
None of the three new sugar mills being constructed
is an extension or part of the Bacita Sugar Company
mills operating since 1964. Neither of the two paper
pulp mills being established almost simultaneously
at Iwopin and Itu near Calabar can be correctly described as an offshoot or branch of the Jebba paper
mills operating since the late 1960s. The expansion
programme of the Jebba Mills is at the moment being
carried out on the spot. Also the emergence of
Nigeria's steel mills represents variants of industrial splashing rather than industrial migration.
Numerous examples of industrial splashing are present in other West African countries. For example,
a number of groundnut oil mills in Senegal, palm oil
mills in Sierra Leone, cotton ginneries and rice
mills in Mali, cotton ginneries in Ivory Coast, and
rice mills in Guinea Bissau are parts of the process
of industrial splashing. Many of them are government sponsored, particularly in Mali and Guinea
Bissau. Foreign merchandise firms, like Lever
Brothers, Societe Commerciale de l'Ouest Africain
(S.C.O.A.) the Leventis Company and the United
African Company (U.A.C.) operating in those countries require to be closely studied for a fuller
characterisation of their splash activities as a
market area control strategy.

CHANGES IN THE SPATIAL STRUCTURE OF MANUFACTURING

The spatial dynamics of industrial activity in a
country can be quantitatively measured. The values
obtained in the process can, among other things,
give useful indications of development in a spatial
context and suggest possible directions of regional
economic policies and national development planning.
We have earlier observed that industrialization in
West African countries is in general quite youthful
historically as well as lopsided in its spatial incidence so far. It has also been noted that the
rate of growth of manufacturing plants and employment has over the years been quite fast in relative
terms even though the absolute magnitudes remain
hardly impressive. The fact that the sector is very
young, and changes in it come fast, raises the geo-

grapher's interest in identifying and measuring the
changes taking place, ascertaining where they are
occurring and with what possible socio-economic consequences. To that end, a number of measurement
methodologies in the literature can be applied with
good effect if the relevant industrial statistics
are available in the form amenable to such quantit-
ative analyses.

Spatial structures are generally of varied types. They vary from concentrations to dispersions.
Industrial concentrations can also take a number of
forms, and each form can be quite varied in degree.
It is helpful to ascertain by measurement varied
degrees of concentration and activity dominance a-
mong regions or any other sub-national areal units.

Two useful methods of measurement involve the
location quotient(LQ) and the coefficient of localization (CL)[6]. Each one is calculated from data for
a specific period, i.e. from cross sectional data.

Applying the location quotient technique to
West African industrial activity, we are handicapped
by lack of sub-national disaggregation of industrial
statistics in most countries. However, it would
suffice to illustrate with data on Nigeria. The
state of affairs in the manufacturing sector of the
country's 19 states is as shown in Table 5.3 in
terms of industrial work force. Compared with total
population[7] as the reference variable (obtained by
projecting the 1963 population to 1975, the industrial survey year), the location quotients are as
shown in the last column of the table. Only 3 out
of the 19 states of the country had more than their
'fair share' of manufacturing activity. Lagos was
clearly above all the other states with an LQ of 13.51
which is very reflective of its well-known position
as the industrial core of the country. Cross River
and Bendel States with 1.35 each were much more
specialised than the rest of the states, followed by
Kaduna with 1.08. Rivers State was close to having
its 'fair share' with 0.89. At the other end of the
scale were Bauchi (0.04), Borno (0.04), Niger (0.05),
Gongola (0.05), and Benue (0.06). Manufacturing in
these states was relatively insignificant. Until
the creation of states in 1976 (after this industrial survey had been conducted), all but one (Borno)
of these five states constituted part of the periphery of the older administrative units, and had little
to attract industries on any appreciable scale. By
and large, from this illustration, the location
quotient technique can be seen to be very simple to
compute and useful for making clear distinctions in

Table 5.3: Manufacturing location quotients of
Nigeria's nineteen states

State	Manufacturing Employment[+]	Total 1975 Population* ('000)	Location Quotient
Anambra	11,023	4,837	0.62
Bauchi	465	3,270	0.04
Bendel	16,888	3,310	1.35
Benue	795	3,264	0.06
Borno	531	4,031	0.04
Cross River	23,521	4,678	1.35
Gongola	786	3,504	0.05
Imo	4,364	4,939	0.24
Kaduna	24,765	5,512	1.08
Kano	19,106	7,767	0.68
Kwara	7,590	2,206	0.81
Lagos	105,086	2,112	13.51
Niger	343	1,606	0.05
Ogun	1,890	2,040	0.24
Ondo	3,690	3,671	0.27
Oyo	7,474	7,005	0.27
Plateau	4,241	2,776	0.54
Rivers	7,629	2,313	0.89
Sokoto	4,054	6,104	0.16
Nigeria	264,243	71,995	

Source: *Projected from the 1963 census figures.
[+]_Industrial Survey_ 1975, Federal Office of
Statistics, Lagos.

the relative levels of activity specialization or
share among competing sub-national areal units.[8] On
the basis of such a measure, there could be more
realistic approaches to planned minimization of
spatial disparities in development-oriented resource
allocation. Also progress in development could be
fruitfully monitored and modified in line with certain target indicator values based on this measure.
    Applying the localization coefficient computa-
tion to West African manufacturing, we are again
faced with lack of requisite data, even for Nigeria.
The latter's only industrial survey covering the 19
states of the country had the industry-by-industry
disaggregation of statistics badly mixed up. Many

states' information on employment, number of plants,
value added and gross output was mixed up to the extent that the calculation of the coefficient of localization of any specific industry is not practicable. Since the type of information required calls
for nothing short of a full census of industrial
establishments in the country - the organization of
which is hardly practicable as a private undertaking
- effective calculation and use of localization co-
efficients will have to await officially collected
industrial data satisfactorily disaggregated by industry types and by sub-national areal units.

SHIFT AND SHARE PHENOMENA

Another useful means of appreciating the nature and
degree of change in industrial structure over space
and time is the shift and share analysis. For a
guide to the use of shift and share technique, the
reader may wish to refer to discussions by Townroe,
(1969), Schatzl, (1973) and Keeble, (1976).
Here it would suffice to point out very briefly that
this method appraises quantitatively the geographical variations in the changes occurring over time
in respect of such structural variables as industrial employment, output and value added. Thus employed in a monitoring process, the shift and share
technique provides a basis for choice of policy
strategies.
    Application of this analytical technique to the
West African industrial sector is handicapped by
lack of industrial statistics in the form amenable
to shift and share analysis. In particular, the
data are in nearly every case not arranged regionally or subnationally for meaningful spatial analysis. In Nigeria where such regional groupings are
made for the 19 states, there is only one set of
such data - that for 1975 9. Without a set for
another time period, the information cannot be use-
fully applied to the shift and share analysis.
However on the basis of the old (twelve-state)
structure of the country, the industrial shift analysis was carried out by Schatzl (1974) and also by
Adegbola (1978). The two sets of data used by
Adegbola were for 1971 and 1973. In spite of the
narrowness of the gap between the two time periods,
some interesting spatio-structural features could be
discerned on the basis of the shift analysis. Table
5.4 shows the results of the analysis by Adegbola;
it can be appreciated from this table that Lagos had

Table 5.4: Shift analysis of Nigerian manufacturing industry

	Benue Plateau	East Central	Kano	Kwara	Lagos	Mid West	North Central	North East	River	South East	West	North West	Total
Employment in 1971	3,297	8,445	9,099	5,441	67,884	8,627	18,996	1,067	1,442	5,047	13,895	2,205	145,449
Employment in 1973	3,605	10,181	12,321	5,039	79,481	10,379	18,047	1,831	2,440	7,590	13,578	2,358	166,826
Actual Change	+308	+1,736	+3,222	-402	+11,597	+1,752	-979	+764	+998	+2,543	-317	+156	21,371
Total Net Shift	306	646	2,112	-2,315	-2,201	1,374	-11	364	901	1,829	-4,098	466	+7,996

Source: Adegbola, K. Manufacturing Industries , in A Geography of Nigerian Development, Oguntoyinbo, J.S et al.(eds) 1978, p. 300

the bulk of the additional employment during the
period 1971-73. Out of the additional 21,375 industrial jobs, Lagos alone accounted for 11,597 (i.e.
54.3 per cent). Next was Kano with 3,222, or 15.1
per cent; the South-eastern state accounted for
2,543, or 11.9 per cent. The last row of values
in the table shows the net shifts. All but Kwara,
Lagos, North-Central and Western States had positive
net shifts. Adegbola has rightly observed that this
strategy of state creation and the subsequent upgrading of each state capital has helped very much
to raise the industrial potential and attraction
power of the new state capitals, mainly at the expense of Lagos which had hitherto enjoyed a disproportionate share and, probably partly as a result,
developed diseconomies that are beginning to have
deglomerative impact on industrial establishments.
The change from a twelve to a nineteen-state structure has set the stage for further industrial shifts
likely to further reduce the share of Lagos.
    Finally, it is necessary to show how small
scale industries fit into the general picture we now
have of West African industries, since the illustrations of the various concepts and structures so
far have been based on data from large-scale industries employing more than ten persons per plant.[10] In
general, small scale industrial plants have much
less locational constraint on them than plants in
the "large-scale" category. This is largely because
capital is easier to mobilize, factor mobility is
much easier and cheaper, and space constraints are
much less on small-scale factory units. The latter
are, therefore, generally much more footloose or less
constrained locationally, operating even from resid-
ential apartments. By implication, the spatial
structures we have identified above are more applicable to the more locationally constrained large-scale
plants to which greater importance is attached by
each country's government and policies affecting the
space economy are directed.

NOTES

    1. The north-eastern states of the United States
have witnessed large-scale migration of cotton textile plants to the south-east mainly as a result of
growing external diseconomies.
    2. One of the classic examples of such enter-
prises shown in Chapter 4 is Chief M. Ugochukwu's
foam mattress and allied product industry at his

village, Umunze, Nigeria. Chief Ugochukwu has large
-scale tyre-retreading and allied rubber production
units in cities like Onitsha and Lagos.

3. The Onitsha branch plant of the Lagos-based
firm was partly damaged during the Nigerian Civil
War and has remained derelict since.

4. Between 1945 and 1965, 3,014 industrial plants
(accounting for 9.7% of the total industrial work
force in Britain) moved to new locations (HMSO, 1968)
Howard Report on The Movement of Manufacturing Industry in the United Kingdom, Board of Trade, London.

5. Industrial splashing is not necessarily
inter-national in scope. Although it is often so,
there are also many cases occurring within single
countries or regions, as the Nigerian examples show.

6. The Location Quotient and the Coefficient of
Localization have been well explained and appraised
by Bendevid, A. Regional Economic Analysis For Prac-
titioners, Praeger, New York 1972; and by Rweyemamu,
J. Underdevelopment and Industrialization in Tan-
zania, Oxford University Press, New York 1973.

7. It would have been more appropriate to use
total wage employment, instead of total population,
but the former was not available.

8. A drawback of this analytical technique
arises mainly from its failure to take into consideration inter-areal differences that often exist in
levels of income, tastes, needs and economic structure, among others - differences which could make LQ
values suspect. The LQ is therefore not much more
than a rough guide in decision making.

9. Prior to 1976, Nigeria had 12 states; industrial statistics then were aggregates for each of
the 12 states. There are no such data for the present 19 states.

10. Industrial statistics for small-scale
plants in West African countries hardly exist at
national or even regional levels. What exist in a
few countries are the outcome of private, localized
surveys rather than official (government) data build
-up of a time series nature. The data problem in
the small-scale industry group is making more de-
tailed and comparative studies very difficult.

Chapter Six

PROBLEMS OF ECONOMIC INDEPENDENCE THROUGH
INDUSTRIALIZATION

In a world setting where the economies of all the
countries, as open systems, constitute a matrix of
economic interrelationships, it can be argued that
no country is really economically independent. Be
that as it may, some countries are certainly much
more economically dependent than others. All the
West African countries are now well aware of the
fact that, in spite of their political independence,
they are still economically much more dependent than
the industrial countries - indeed more dependent
than a good number of Latin American and North African countries, which are also Third World states.
Developing countries in general and those of West
Africa in particular have been putting much premium
on industrialization,generally regarded as a panacea
for their economic under-development. In the present
chapter attention is focused on the problems in the
way of industrial progress towards either the ideal
situation of economic independence, or the actual
level of economic self-reliance attained in industrial countries. The problems are indeed so many and
of such varied magnitude that we can hardly do more
than refer to the very serious ones.
     The extent of economic dependence of West Af-
rican countries can be partly appreciated from the
volume and the variety of the countries' imports,
particularly imports drawn from industrial countries.
Such imports range from raw materials, intermediate
and finished capital goods and consumer goods, to
expertise of both technical and managerial types.
Besides imports of goods and skills, there is also
considerable dependence on foreign assistance re-
ceivable in a variety of forms - as grants, loans,
share capital, technical assistance as well as aids
in kind including machinery, equipment, food, drugs,
seed varieties, fertilizers, pesticides, among

others. Another very important way of appreciating
the heavy economic dependence of West African countries is by considering the economic and political
consequences of their generally unfavourable terms
of trade vis-a-vis the developed countries.
     Pursuit of industrial development has nearly
always been with a view to reducing the magnitude of
the unfavourable dependency relations with the industrial powers. But the fact remains that industrial development in West African countries has been
generally slow and sloppy - so much so that the degree
of economic dependence has not been reduced to any
appreciable extent through industrial efforts. In
some cases dependence has, in fact, increased over
the years, as local craft industry gets relegated.
One reason for the slow growth of the industrial
sector in each country is that industrialization
processes are seriously being constrained by a variety of factors. It is on such factors that we may
now focus.

TECHNOLOGY CONSTRAINTS

We have already in Chapter 1 taken technology to
refer simply to the science of, and levels of efficiency in, factor combinations. We have seen that
one major reason behind the relatively late start of
modern manufacturing in West Africa is low level of
technology - a low fund of the right types of technical and managerial skills. West African countries
have generally made a start in industrialization
since World War II. Here it is of interest to see
how low level technology is being reflected in the
relatively slow progress so far made by the industrial sector. The generally very small contribution
of the sector to each country's economy between 1960
and 1980 can be appreciated from the GDP shares
shown in Table 6.1. The slow rate of growth of the
manufacturing sector in most of the countries is
evident in Table 6.2. The growth rates for Mali and
Liberia may seem impressive at first sight. However
the point to note is that theirs is actually growth
from a very low base. On the other hand, the negative rate of change in Ghana seems to be a fair reflection of the deepening crisis in which the country's economy as a whole has been embroiled since the
mid-1960s.
     Heavy reliance on imported raw materials, in-
termediate goods, simple industrial equipment and
machinery mainly arises from the inadequacy of local

143

Table 6.1: GDP share of manufacturing sector in
West African countries, 1960, 1980

Country	% GDP in:		Country	% GDP in:	
	1960	1980		1960	1980
Benin	3	7	Mali	5	6
Cape Verde	n.a	5*	Mauritania	3	8
Gambia	x	3**	Niger	4	8
Ghana	5	3	Nigeria	5	6
Guinea	3	4	Senegal	12	19
Guinea Bissau	x	4	Sierra Leone	x	5
Ivory Coast	7	11	Togo	8	7
Liberia	x	7*	Upper Volta	8	13

x Below 3%   * For 1979   ** For 1977

Sources: Various including: (a) World Bank, World Develop-
                             ment Report 1982, p. 114
                          (b) Europa, Africa South of the
                             Sahara 1981

technical skills necessary for producing such industrial goods within each West African country. This
is more particularly the case where large-scale import of industrial raw materials that are otherwise
locally abundant is involved. A certain level of
technology is required for successful processing of
certain natural resources at costs lower than it
would normally take to import such materials in processed forms from more industrialised countries.
The problem is often more of production at relatively high costs than incapacity to process local resources. The cost constraints are even more
serious for intermediate goods requiring more than
mere processing to produce them. Among such goods
are, notably, basic industrial chemicals, concentrates such as those for soft drinks and beer production, cardboard and kraft paper, wood pulp,
thread, cordage, building materials, cured tobacco
and glass, to mention but a few. The enormous costs
of imports involved in the absence of adequate import
substitutes can be appreciated from the fact that
generally over 95 per cent by value of basic industrial chemicals and glass products being used by West
African countries is imported. It is about 90 per
cent in Nigeria, Ivory Coast and Senegal, but almost

Figure 6.1: G.D.P. Shares of manufacturing sector in West Africa, 1980

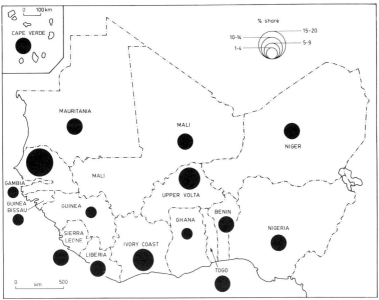

Figure 6.2: Relative importance of manufacturing by value added, 1979

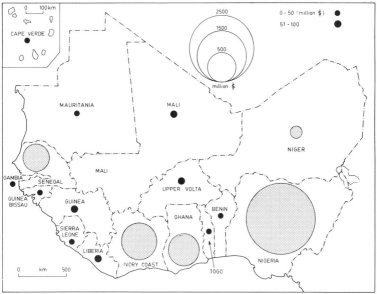

1OO per cent in Mali, Upper Volta and Niger, for example. There is a strong negative correlation of
this high dependence on imports with levels of value
added by manufacturing.

Table 6.2: Annual growth rates of manufacturing in
some West African countries, 1970-1980

Country	Growth rate per annum 1970–80
	%
Nigeria	12.0
Mali	9.2
Liberia	8.0
Ivory Coast	7.2
Senegal	3.8
Sierra Leone	3.8
Upper Volta	3.7
Mauritania	0.2
Ghana	-2.9

Sources: (a) World Bank, <u>World Development Report 1982</u>, p. 112
         (b) Europa, <u>Africa South of the Sahara 1981</u>
         p. 647

    The import of practically all machinery, equip-
ment, spare parts and machine tools in use in West
African countries adds to each country's heavy import bills which, in addition to consumer goods,
have constantly helped to keep the foreign exchange
reserves very low in most of the countries. What is
important to stress here is the point that the se-
vere foreign exchange limitations of West African
countries are largely traceable to the factor of low
technology in those countries. And until a good
deal more   foreign exchange is available for investment in real industrial production, the probability of rapid industrial growth is low. Most countries bank on the rate of foreign aid which itself
is fraught with serious problems that will be taken
up later.
    Another aspect of the cost impact of technolog-
ical constraints may be appreciated in terms of the
very high rate of machine breakdowns. The point is

that the general lack of adequate technical knowledge often leads to poor quality of machine minding,
servicing and maintenance, and, therefore, to high
frequency of plant breakdowns, expensive resort to
foreign machine menders, and to compulsory but paid
holidays for the industrial workforce (during the
process of machine repairs). Because imported spare
parts and expertise are not easy to come by, there
is often a long period of delay during which workers
must be paid and certain other overheads like rents
discharged. Thus even in the few cases where import
bills are kept low by dependence on cheaply procured
and processed local materials, costs arising from
machine breakdowns are generally high, sometimes
crippling.

A third angle from which to appreciate the ad-
verse effect of low technology is from the standpoint of industrial infrastructure. Partly as a
result of the gross inadequacy of the requisite
technology for efficient provision of such infrastructure as roads, electricity, piped water and
telecommunications, heavy dependence on foreign con-
tractors has been a very common practice in West
African countries. Foreign contracts invariably inflate the costs of projects - sometimes to more than
double what the country involved would have spent if
the right engineering manpower were locally available. The effect of high costs is not only to reduce the size and mix of infrastructure, often provided from foreign loans, but also to put the charges on them at an abnormally high rate. Poor servicing and handling of the facilities generally
obtain as well, causing constant disruptions in
facility use. West Africa was by 1971 the poorest
of the African regions in terms of infrastructure
provision.[1] The relative position of the region in
Africa has not improved appreciably ever since. Indeed, in many cases what is physically installed is
so faulty that services are often not available.
Many installed telephone lines and sets are very
frequently out of order; and power flow is anything
but constant.

Industrial production under conditions of unsteady flow of water, power and telephone services
has been very costly in West African countries like
Nigeria.[2] In the latter, power failure has for years
been a matter of daily occurrence. Dependence on the
$120 million Kainji power station since 1968 remained
quite precarious until 1979 when the gas powered
station in Sapele was brought into the national power
grid, to the partial relief of industrial firms in

147

particular. Until the completion of the gas powered
station and the full use of its 720 Megawatt capacity as well as the other new installations, Nigeria's power supply problems will remain a serious
constraint on industrial progress. In many other
countries like Ivory Coast, Liberia, Mali, Senegal,
Mauritania and Guinea, the development of much of
the available hydro electric power potential is
still under way. In Niger, Benin, Togo and Upper
Volta where hydro electric potentials are low, dependence on better-endowed neighbouring countries -
Nigeria for Benin and Niger, and Ghana for Togo and
Upper Volta - has so far been the main, albeit
hardly adequate, resort.

    We have argued that mainly on account of very
low technical efficiency within the economies of
West African countries, there is generally heavy
leaning on imports both of goods and expertise. It
has been shown in Chapter 4 that industrial production in West Africa is generally highly capital intensive - probably more so than in some other regions of Africa. Since the more industries become
capital-intensive, the more their technological demands increase, it can be appreciated why West
African countries tend to be relatively highly dependent on the technologically advanced economies -
probably more so than most other African sub-regions.
Without doubt, one direct implication of high dependence on external technical assistance is excessive
foreign exchange commitment. In other words, West
African countries, on account of their heavy leaning
on foreign technical assistance, are great exporters
of foreign exchange. Yet the countries are generally very poor, as has been amply reflected by their
Gross National Product shown in Table 2.12.

    For a region so poor, one implication of high
rate of foreign exchange commitment is inevitably a
heavy dependence on foreign assistance. Such assistance is commonly secured as loans but sometimes
as grants, technical assistance or in kind. Whichever form it takes, the fact remains that the
reality of economic dependence - which actually
weakens the basis for political independence - comes
out strongly in bold relief, diminishing the bar-
gaining power of the recipient countries. Yet the
destabilizing effect of such forms of dependence on
foreign assistance is generally not fully realized
in West Africa. Besides the heavy strain of servicing external debts, the strings sometimes attached to aid by foreign benefactors tend to compromise the economic if not also the political pos-

ition of the beneficiary. What is more, technical
aid has in most cases involved the introduction of
certain levels of technology quite unsuited to the
socio-economic circumstances and needs of the recipient countries of West Africa. Much as the donor
countries do not always intentionally seek to weaken
the economy to which they give technical assistance,
the tendency has always been to offer the type of
technology which they actually have and would con-
veniently service and sustain over the years (through
constant sale of needed spare parts, industrial
equipment and technical expertise). Thus as no technology is actually acquired, dependence by the recipient country tends to be perpetuated. It is on
account of dangers such as these that Schumacher
(1973, p. 132) has rightly insisted that there is:

> A major gap in aid and development: the virtual
> absence of organised systematic efforts to pro-
> vide the poor countries with a choice of low-
> cost, self-help technology, adapted to meet
> their needs for labour-intensive and small-
> scale development. This deficiency cannot be
> made good by accelerating conventional aid pro-
> grammes any more than, say, a housing shortage
> can be alleviated by building more supersonic
> aircraft.

Thus West African countries, like most of the developing economies, have on account of these forms of
dependency relations with the industrial economies
tended to compromise much that actually brings about
real development. Indeed, what the Intermediate
Technology Development Group[2] has said about the
less developed economies applies forcefully to West
African countries. And that is that the choice of
technology (one of the biggest single collective
decisions facing any developing country) has continued to be denied to most of the world's developing
countries. Although most of West African states are
now aware of this danger, very little, if anything,
can be done about its removal in the near future.
But even as a long term measure, any remedial strategy that does not emphasize and give practical effect to the development and adaptation of technology
appropriate to the socio-economic circumstances and
needs of the people (with emphasis on labour-intensive production functions) will run the risk of ex-
acerbating the dangers of dependency relations with
the developed economies.

DEMOGRAPHIC AND SOCIO-CULTURAL CONSTRAINTS

From our discussion so far, it will have become evident that poverty tends to perpetuate economic dependency in West Africa. Not only does it encourage the accumulation of foreign loans and indebtedness, it also frustrates savings, investment and economic production, thereby reducing the level of gross national product and the quantum of capital available for further investment in productive ventures - continuing the vicious circle of poverty. Experience in West Africa shows that, while poverty tends to perpetuate economic dependency, certain demographic and socio-cultural phenomena in the region help to perpetuate poverty itself. The economic dependency dilemma of West African countries is therefore much more deep-rooted than may be traceable to poor income, technology and industrial performance. A close look at the demographic and socio-cultural factors is worthwhile here.

The population birth rate of West Africa is one of the highest in Africa which has the highest in the world - 47 per 1,000. The death rate has declined in the region to less than 28 per 1,000 population. As can be appreciated from Table 6.3, the countries of West Africa have high ratios of dependent population (averaging 48 per cent). Such ratios are indicative of the region's youthful population and poor manpower potential. When all these are pitched against the slow-growing but relatively very low GNP per capita, the poverty problem in West Africa becomes more understandable.

Furthermore, among the relevant characteristics of the West African population are its very high level of illiteracy (over 75 per cent in the lingua franca of every country), and its high degree (over 65 per cent) of preoccupation with agriculture that is essentially subsistent in scale and rudimentary in style. Farmers all the world over are characteristically conservative. But they are much more so where they are predominantly illiterate, as in West Africa. Mass ignorance in the region's vast rural sector tends to nurture superstition and belief systems which often influence attitudes to fertility, to child birth and upbringing as well as family size, choice of diet and feeding habits. Also the individual's perception of his socio-economic problems and his approaches toward their solution are very much the reflection of his tradition-bound culture. Thus while in pursuit of socio-cultural aspirations that are largely tradition-oriented and meeting much

Table 6.3:   Dependent population of West African states

Country	Dependent Population (%) in 1980	Country	Dependent Population (%) in 1980
Benin	49	Mali	48
Cape Verde	n.a	Mauritania	48
Gambia	n.a	Niger	49
Ghana	49	Nigeria	50
Guinea	47	Senegal	47
G. Bissau	n.a	Sierra Leone	47
Ivory Coast	47	Togo	49
Liberia	50	Upper Volta	37

Source: Computed from World Bank   World Development Report 1982, Table 19, p. 146

of his needs without necessarily being subjected to the rules and preconditions of the monetized economic sector, it is not always easy for the typical sub-sistent farmer (who represents the vast majority of the population) to appreciate the need for full monetization of the economy and for its increasing orientation towards modern manufacturing. Produc-tion and savings are, therefore, hardly geared to-wards industrial development. The linkage economies which can be developed between the farm and the fac-tory are not often known, or appreciated if known. Thus even when government or private industrial pro-jects are designed to stimulate such inter-sectoral linkages, and in the process help diversify a rural economy that is predominantly agricultural and im-prove employment opportunities, lack of understanding of how to make the best out of industry-oriented de-velopment efforts often constitutes a serious drag. Hence the common experience, particularly in Ghana and Nigeria, of under-utilized capacity in agro-based industrial plants inadequately supplied with farm products obtainable in their respective local-ities. Hence the common, short-lived, resistance of farming communities of many a West African country to certain production innovations somehow in conflict with traditional norms. The stiff opposition of far-mers in parts of the oil palm belt of Nigeria to factory-type "pioneer oil mills" widely introduced during the late 1940s and early 1950s to displace the slow and inefficient manual process is very typical.

In every country of West Africa vast numbers of rural communities in particular are yet to be fully drawn into the mainstream of modern economic development that is as yet predominantly urban and slightly, but increasingly, industrial. To do this would probably require the reorientation of the majority of the people in terms of savings and investments. At the moment, a great deal of private savings (rarely made through banks or other modern institutions) gets spent on frivolities - festivals, marriages of second or third wives, funerals, parties, title taking - or on feeding unduly large families. Until such reorientation gains ground, much that can go a long way to facilitate economic development through industrialization will probably remain either untapped or misused. The various governments in West Africa have so far been directly involved in industrial sponsorship but have hardly shown sufficient appreciation of the immense potential of the mass of small farmers and low income workers in the area of large-scale project financing. Carefully planned and pursued official campaigns seem to be needed to raise mass awareness and encourage partnership and co-operative ventures capable of enhancing the earning, saving and investment potentials of the vast majority of each country's inhabitants hitherto confined to the informal sector of the economy.

ROLE OF MULTINATIONAL CORPORATIONS

Multinational corporations (MNCs) have increasingly become a major factor shaping the economies of nations, developed and developing. A few hard statistics of trade and industrial investment organized by MNCs for or with certain market economies may give indications of how important and powerful the MNCs are and how far-reaching their impact can be. By 1973, U.S.-based MNCs accounted for 80 per cent of all direct foreign investment by United States firms, exceeding $100 billion annually, over 40 per cent being in manufacturing (Hunker, 1974, p. 92). Throughout the 1970s, over 50 per cent of Nigeria's total crude oil output was bought by the United States alone, and the entire exchange was transacted by U.S.-based MNCs. Also the annual turnover of MNCs in most Third World countries far exceeds the annual budgets of the host countries. Although the impact of MNCs has been both positive and negative in both developed and developing countries (Beacham and Cunningham, 1970; Alexandersson, 1971; Hunker, 1974; Tuppen, 1983), the negative impact would appear to be greater on developing countries (Seers, 1963; Streeten, 1972; Onyemelukwe, 1974; Odife, 1976).

It is widely believed that MNCs have in large measure influenced development in West African countries, as in most Third World countries, especially by increasing investment in their host countries, thereby assisting the latter while official aid by developed countries is low or declining; by serving as a potent agent of innovation, resource development and employment generation. This they do by dint of their size, their high level of technology and organizational competence, their ability to draw from reserves outside their host country, and on account of their institutionally built-in propensity to adapt and blaze the trail of economic progress within the very difficult physical and socio-economic environments of most of their host countries. However, in the process of pursuing their private economic objectives, MNCs have clearly demonstrated that they are not the philanthropic organizations which they are sometimes naively expected to be! They have not failed to show through the conduct of their business that, according to Streeten (1972, pp. 223-4), "the creation of profitable opportunities pays little heed to social considerations, to justice, to equality, to even or balanced progress, or to national sentiments;... and their (MNCs') profit-motivated approach is incompatible with an approach emphasizing social planning." It is against this background that the constraining impact of MNCs on capital mobilization by West African countries, on employment generation and on the development of appropriate technology in the region can best be appreciated.

West African countries have been having their foreign exchange reserves drastically curtailed mainly as a result of unfavourable trade relations with developed countries operating largely through the MNCs. For about two decades now the prices West African countries receive for all their primary exports except petroleum have declined considerably relative to the prices they pay for manufactures imported from industrial market economies. In other words, the terms of trade of West African countries, as of most other developing market economies, have remained unfavourable (United Nations, 1973; Bairoch, 1975). According to Bairoch, the period 1954/55 to

1962/63 witnessed 11 per cent deterioration in the
terms of trade for Third World Countries. During the
same period, the terms of trade of the developed countries improved by 10 per cent. Also the period 1962/
63 to 1970, though marked by relative stability in
the trend of trade exchange, was equally one of unfavourable terms of trade for West African countries.
For whereas in the latter the trend was stabilized
near the lowest level reached since the end of World
War II, the developed countries' stability occurred
at the top of the curve during the same period. Furthermore, according to the International Monetary Fund
(IMF), between 1970 and 1975, the terms of trade of
non-oil-exporting Third World Countries, including
those of West Africa, fell from 100 to 80, compared
with a fall of from 100 to 88 for industrial countries
(1970 = 10 in each case). Heavily dependent on primary exports for their capital generation, West African
countries have thus remained seriously constrained in
their capital mobilization for industrial investment.
     The resolute price-raising moves by the Organ-
ization of Petroleum Exporting Countries (OPEC)
since 1973/74, besides claiming their own toll of
damage on the economy of non-oil-exporting West African countries, have been consistently countered
and sometimes neutralized by developed economies
operating largely, but by no means entirely, through
the MNCs. Among such moves which MNCs have spear-
headed against developing countries, including the
oil-importing West African countries, are radical
price increases on manufactures including machinery,
equipment and inputs exported to West Africa, and
also further drops in the prices of primary exports
(especially copper, iron ore, cocoa, coffee, palm
produce and cotton) from West Africa. The latter
was thereby being forced to make up for the downward
trend in export prices through increased production
and export of primary products (Rake, 1981/2, p. 29).
But low prices are themselves strong disincentives
to increased production. In fact, agricultural output and export volumes have since either stagnated
or declined drastically in most countries of the
region. Nigeria which sought further refuge in petroleum export, to the neglect of agricultural production, did so at the grave risk of virtually becoming a one-product economy!
     The cumulative impact of these counter moves by
developed countries, largely through the MNCs, has
been one of marked slowing down in economic growth
through industrial development especially. This trend
for all but one of the West African countries has

been seen to fit well into the wider African picture
which Robert McNamara has aptly described as "negative growth for the 141 million people in the oil-
importing countries of sub-Saharan Africa" (Rake,
Ibid.). Attempts to get over acute capital mobilization and balance of payments problems have quite
often been through foreign loans and aid, the dangers
of which have already been discussed.

The other area of conflict of MNCs with the
governments of West African countries is the MNCs' import into the region of know-how, technology and
practices inappropriate to the needs of the host countries. By importing and using machinery designed for
capital-intensive production in West African countries badly in need of labour-intensive industries
and processes, MNCs tend to frustrate meaningful
development and wider income distribution in those
countries. In the first place, such machinery is
highly demanding in technology - too sophisticated
to be quickly, if at all, understood, adopted and
reproduced by the calibre of technical manpower
available in any West African country. In other
words, technology acquisition by the latter group
is seriously inhibited and dependence on developed
countries for the operation of such capital-intensive industries tends to be unduly prolonged. Where
training schemes are provided by MNCs to accelerate
indigenous manpower development often required by
host countries, too little is generally done in
areas of high level technology or to put qualified
local personnel in positions of high-level decision-
making for effective mastery of the firms' management techniques.

Secondly, by operating capital-intensive industrial processes, MNCs reduce the chances of the host
countries for meeting their objectives of large-scale
employment generation in the modern sector of the
economy. Although it is valid to argue that MNCs
are not adopting capital-intensive production processes with the sinister motive of blocking avenues to
employment, the fact remains that unintentional harm
is nevertheless done to the economy of the host
country. This problem of employment restriction
through the application of inappropriate factor proportions in countries with very high rates of unemployment and lopsided income distribution may better be
appreciated in terms of the multiplier effects of
employment so drastically curtailed or foregone.

MNCs have often adopted measures designed to
weaken the competitive or survival efforts of firms
belonging to the host countries. For example, taking

advantage of their large size to enjoy economies of
scale reflected in low production costs, they sell
at prices with which the local firms cannot compete.
This situation tends to give rise to the increasingly
oligopolistic organization of an industry by MNCs
and the reduction of competition from indigenous
firms. The example of the soap and detergent industry
in which multinationals like Lever Brothers are dominant in West Africa is noteworthy.

Production by MNCs and other foreign firms in
their parent countries or elsewhere where even
greater scale economies accrue to them enables some
of them to practise dumping[4] in West African countries (Kilby, 1969). This practice is currently
worrying many West African countries, Nigeria in
particular; and the main sources are MNCs and other
firms based in Far Eastern countries. The consequences for manufacturing and some trading firms in
the region have been quite disastrous and very un-
settling for the economies of the affected countries.
Efforts by some of the affected countries to curb
the practice of dumping especially through heavy import restrictions or high import duties have generally left matters even more involved. Large-scale
smuggling is being encouraged, and is now rampant in
Nigeria and Benin. Also some indigenous firms tend
to get rather over-protected behind high tariff
walls and generally inflate the prices of their
qualitatively uncompetitive manufactures, thereby
further encouraging smuggling. The foreign firms
which, in addition to their substantial advantages
over the local firms, find themselves so protected
within the tariff walls, naturally take full advantage of such official dispensation to multiply their
gains or secure their oligopolistic position at the
expense of the host economy. This common phenomenon
in West Africa is by no means peculiar to the region
(Johnson, 1967; Streeten, 1972).

Although West African countries are aware of
the fact that the net impact of MNCs on their economy
is negative, they often do not have the political
power or the technical ability to control MNCs effectively. Ghana's and Nigeria's efforts, for instance, to control them through the holding of majority equity shares in each firm have not yielded
the desired result. Through the manipulation of the
firm's dependence on external sources of machinery,
spare parts, certain inputs and expertise, MNCs in
Nigeria have continued to be in effective control of
their locally based business, their minority equity
share notwithstanding. The multinational oil corp-

orations now hold no more than 40 per cent of the
equity shares in their Nigeria-based business. But
the expected local investment of their proceeds ac-
cruing from the sale of 60 per cent of their equity
shares to the Nigerian government and people has not
materialized. Rather than expand into other aspects of the Nigerian economy, the firms resort to
capital divestment (Odife, 1976), to the discomfit-
ure of the host country.
        Attempts to control MNCs' activities through
the United Nations agencies have so far not been
very successful. Perhaps the best way the West
African countries can effectively contain some of
the destabilizing impacts of MNCs might be by acting
in concert within a supranational framework such as
the Economic Community of West African States
(ECOWAS). This would enable the countries to evolve
some regulations governing the operations of MNCs in
member countries. It would also help eliminate competitive concessions which have hitherto tended to
favour the MNCs and weaken the economies of the West
African countries granting them. Herein, then, lies
a raison d'etre for ECOWAS.

IDEOLOGICAL ISSUES

There is a lot that can be done by the people of
West African countries toward the improvement of the
economic position of their states, in spite of op-
posing external forces like the ones already highlighted. The point is that, however potentially economically strong a country may seem, it requires the
practical demonstration of a strong public will to
effectively forge economic strength out of the positive policy measures of the state. Such a public
will tends to issue more freely and spontaneously if
the state's political economy has a clearly identified and popular ideology,[5] which is hardly the
case in the region. In countries like Guinea, Mali
and Guinea Bissau where socialist policies have in
varying degrees of intensity been officially pursued,
it has largely been a problem of containing the new
wine of socialism (however defined) in the old capitalist wine-skin fashioned, fixed and handed down
from colonial times. In such circumstance, success
has as yet been partial, perhaps more in Guinea
Bissau and Guinea than in Mali; and the issue of a
popular ideology is seemingly problematical everywhere. Absence of a popular and development-oriented ideology tends to be reflected throughout West

Africa in poor attitudes to paid employment, particularly in state-owned establishments; in low
ethical standards especially in private businesses;
and in the low patronage of indigenous as opposed to
foreign industrial productions. In all West African
countries the state is directly investing in industrial projects particularly for purposes of developing the industrial sector and strengthening the
state's economic resilience. The prevalent poor
attitude to work in such state-sponsored enterprises
has been one main reason why most state projects
have been utter failures in most countries. The examples of Nigeria, Ghana, and Mali are cases in
point.

In Nigeria, many state projects have been huge
failures. Some are perennially being sustained with
state subventions. Current demand in the country is
that government relinquish its direct responsibility
for manufacturing to profit-oriented private entrepreneurs. Examples of state-sponsored industrial
failures or liabilities include the Jute and Canning
Factories of the old Western Nigeria Government,
located at Badagry and Ibadan respectively, the
Calabar Cement industry of the Cross River State,
the Ceramic industry of the old Eastern Nigeria
government at Umuahia, and the Jebba Paper Mills of
the Central Government, to mention but a few.

In Ghana, many industrial projects begun under
the socialist programme of Kwame Nkrumah are still
to be fully rehabilitated. They include the Bambo
and the Coir Fibre Factories at Axim, the Denu
Groundnut Processing Factory, a Glass Factory, a
Brick and Tile Factory, a Paper Conversion Mill, a
Steel Works, and the Oppon Valley Rattan Factory, to
mention but a few. The 1975-80 development programme
hoped to put those and many other sick projects on
the path of industrial progress through the "removal
of production bottlenecks" (Ghana, 1977), among
other things, by the Ghana Industrial Holding Corporation. It did not make much headway.

In Mali, most of the industrial plants are
state-operated, or run by societies commissioned by
Modibo Keita. Most of those have been plagued by
crippling problems that are mainly bureaucratic. By
1974 about 28 of such establishments lost around
18,000 million Mali francs in bad debts. Up till
1976 rehabilitation was still problematic owing to
lack of funds and to the bureaucratic difficulties
largely associated with officials' poor attitude to
state projects. However, some rehabilitation has
since been possible, though slow, thanks to external

158

funding from France in particular.

There is generally a low level of patriotism associated with indigenous industrial production. In
fact, there is, particularly in Nigeria, considerable
antipathy towards home-made industrial goods. A
clear predilection for imported equivalents exists.
The reason often given for the low patronage of domestic industries is quality differential in favour
of imported goods. Such an opinion, though often
based on facts, is not always correct. Many cases
abound where home-made goods of high quality sold
much faster than would normally have happened simply
because a "made in England" tag was put in place of
"made in Nigeria"! Without the will to struggle and
survive as a people - a will that could be reflected
in genuine patronage of domestic manufactures - the
consuming public in many a West African country has
been contributing in no small measure to the slow
progress of the industrial sector. But it must be
noted that many indigenous firms in the private sector often display very low ethical standards that
tend to provide justification for public prejudice
against indigenous industrial enterprises. However,
it is here that the task of governments to ensure
quality control and fair prices as well as the full
protection of the consuming public becomes crucial
in the interest of both the industrial sector and
the national economy at large. It is perhaps in
doing that, in the provision of badly needed industrial infrastructure and investment climate as well
as in seeing to the obtaining of appropriate technology, that state authorities are likely to make
their major contributions towards industrial progress and the greater economic independence of West
African countries.

NOTES

1. Poor infrastructure provision must be seen
as one important evidence of failings by national
governments of West Africa to facilitate development,
the slow and unsteady start of which has been so
much blamed on colonialism.
2. The radical decline in the GDP share of
Nigeria's manufacturing sector has been largely accounted for by these constraints vis-a-vis several
institutional bottlenecks undermining private investment in the sector.
3. The Intermediate Technology Development
Group was set up in Britain in 1966 as a limited
liability company (with Schumacher as Chairman).

The main objective is the provision of self-help
technology for rural development in less developed
economies. It has since 1968 been undertaking research into basic technologies for rural development.
    4. Dumping is the practice of selling products
in a foreign market at prices below what are acceptable in the domestic market.
    5. A set of beliefs and programmes systematic-
ally articulated as the embodiment of a people's
developmental aspirations constitutes their ideology.

Chapter Seven

INDUSTRIALIZATION IN NIGERIA: A CASE STUDY

In this chapter the Nigerian example is used to illustrate a number of points already referred to in a
wider regional context. The choice of Nigeria may
be justified on a number of counts. In the first
place, the country has attained the highest level of
industrial development in West Africa and therefore
provides illustrative material for the various
stages that West African countries have undergone.
Secondly, the country also provides perhaps more
evidence than any other West African country to illustrate many of the problems that bedevil industrial development efforts in the West African region.
Finally, this case study affords the author the opportunity to share some of his Nigerian experiences
with the reader.

THE INDUSTRIAL RESOURCE BASE OF NIGERIA

For the three main factors of economic production -
land, labour and capital - Nigeria's potential is
immense if viewed from the long-term standpoint of
West African industrial development.

Land
Within the 913,000 square kilometres of Nigeria's
land area, there is a coastline stretching for a
little over 700 kilometres for port and coastal
transport services and for coast-oriented industrial
and other economic activities. All the major ecological zones of West Africa whose natural endowments
are conducive to agricultural resource development
and industrial growth are well represented in Nigeria.
There are over 100,000 km^2 of tropical rain forest,
about 80,000 km^2 of derived savanna, and over 720,000
km^2 of pure savanna (Guinea, Sudan and Sahel savanna).

Out of these over 70 million hectares(661,000 km^2) of cultivable land exists, nearly 50 per cent of which has yet to be brought under cultivation. And in the different parts of that vast area for agricultural development, all types of tropical crops and livestock can be produced.

Notable among the perennial rivers of the country are the rivers Niger, Benue, Sokoto-Rima, Kaduna, Gongola, Ogun, Oshun, Anambra, Katsina-Ale, Yobe, Hadejia and the Cross river. Together with Lake Chad, those rivers constitute the main water sources of existing and future irrigation schemes in the country; together with the coastal lagoons, they provide the inland fisheries of the country (Fig. 7.1).

Nigeria is endowed with good solar radiation, as the country is situated within 14 degrees of the equator and so receives the direct rays of the sun for most of the year. Studies by Davis (1966) and Oguntoyinbo et al. (1978) have shown that the annual radiation level in Nigeria ranges from 110 Kg-cal. in the delta area of the south to 100 Kg-cal. in the extreme north-west about the latitude of Sokoto. Power generation from the solar radiation has good economic potential.

Labour

Labour supply in Nigeria is rather enigmatic, in the sense that the country has been witnessing both a surplus and a shortage of manpower: problems of growing labour surplus are reflected by unemployment and underemployment, and problems of acute manpower shortage are evident in almost every subsector of the economy. A labour force sample survey by the Nigerian government in December 1974 showed that the level of unemployment ranged from 5 per cent in Maiduguri to 22 per cent in Calabar. A considerable proportion of the unemployed in those centres were, and have continued to be, school leavers. The level of enrolment in secondary, technical and vocational schools throughout the country during 1970-73 was as shown in Table 7.1 and has continued to rise. There was an average of 351,000 enrolled per year in secondary schools, and 16,000 in technical schools. An earlier (1966-67) Labour Force Sample Survey in the country showed that young persons with primary but below school certificate level of education constituted about 60 per cent of the unemployed persons found in the survey (Nigeria, 1975c, p.382). The fact is that most of the entrants who complete their education still lack the skills required by a good

Figure 7.1:   Nigerian fisheries

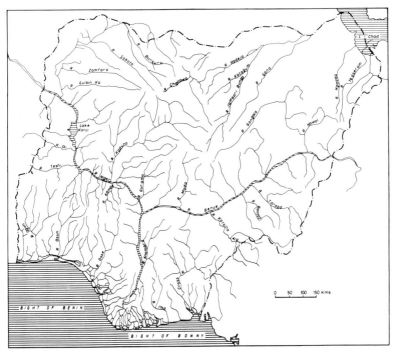

number of jobs.   Thus while so many posts remain
vacant or filled with unqualified hands, given their
special technical demands, many unemployed young
people roam the streets of Nigerian cities and towns.
With the current education programme of the country
which has so much emphasized quantity rather than
quality, the unemployment situation in the 1980s
will probably be much worse than in the 1970s.   Many

163

Table 7.1:   Secondary, technical and vocational
education enrolments, 1970-73

Year	Enrolments in:		Total
	Secondary	Technical & Vocational	
1970	310,054	13,641	323,695
1971	343,313	15,203	358,516
1972	400,803	15,950	416,753
1973	*	19,427	-
Average	351,390	16,055	366,321

Source: Annual Abstract of Statistics, 1975, Federal Office
of Statistics.

* not available.

more inadequately trained young people are likely to
be unemployed in the modern sector of the economy
where skilled hands are in very high demand.   According to government estimates (Nigeria, 1975c), by
1981-82 the out-turn from primary schools will have
increased to about 2 million - three times the annual out-turn before 1975 - and about 70 per cent
will probably secure admission in post-primary institutions.
     It may be arguably maintained that the calibre
of manpower directly relevant to the industrial sector is normally above the mere post-primary and secondary levels and should be looked for among graduates of universities and technical institutes.
Even so, the problem is essentially the same, if not
worse, in the area of senior-level manpower.   Many
posts at that level remain unfilled even though the
problems of unemployment and of inappropriate job
placements increasingly bedevil Nigerian graduates.
This is even more so in the technically highly demanding manufacturing sector.   Hence in consideration of the special technical and managerial manpower needs of the latter sector among others, the
Nigerian government in 1975 estimated that the country's senior-level manpower needs of 49,210 during
1976-80 could be met only to the tune of 43,550.
The shortfall envisaged was 5,560.   However, events

164

have shown that the shortfall is likely to be much
higher as enrolments in Nigerian universities have
fallen below the set target. At any rate, there
continues to be acute shortage of the right calibre
of technical manpower badly needed in the manufacturing subsector. The current emphasis on technical
education requiring the setting up of universities
of technology and the improvement of existing colleges of science and technology is likely to improve
the manpower situation in future. Table 7.2 gives
factual indications in that respect. The new efforts to increase the technical content of secondary

Table 7.2: Enrolment in Nigerian colleges of
technology* and universities, 1975/76-1980/81

	Colleges of Technology	Universities
1975/76	11,993	31,511
1976/77	17,452	38,877
1977/78	19,880	41,417
1978/79	29,829	45,201
1979/80	35,777	57,772
1980/81	41,097	70,704

* including Polytechnics

Source: Annual Abstract of Statistics for several years;
also see Fourth National Development Plan, 1981-85, National
Planning Office, Lagos, 1981.

and post-secondary education in the country also
augur well for the future manpower needs of the
country, albeit in a fairly distant future. It is
important to note that this issue of lopsided educational structure, generally seen as a colonial
legacy, deserved a quick political solution within
the first post-independence decade. Nothing appreciable was done until the latter 1970s!
     The manpower structure of the industrial sector
in Nigeria from 1971 to 1974 was as shown in Table
7.3; it has not changed significantly since, particularly in the relative sizes of the various employment cadres. The groups of industrial workforce
that require closer attention are the professional
and managerial group and the operatives group, but
more particularly the former. There was an average

Table 7.3:   Employment structure of Nigerian
industries 1971-74

Year	Employment cadre of Nigerian work force				Total
	Professional	Clerical	Operatives	Non-Nigerian unclassified	
1971	4,110	17,582	121,298	2,455	145,445
1972	5,117	23,382	136,232	2,739	167,470
1973	5,632	24,632	129,250	2,333	162,010
1974	7,340	29,625	135,674	2,651	168,408
Average	5,550	29,625	130,538	2,545	160,833

Source: Nigeria, Annual Abstract of Statistics,
1975, pp. 28-33

of 5,550 Nigerians in the professional and managerial cadre of Nigeria's manufacturing. This is a very low figure for a country as large as Nigeria, amounting to an average of 5 per industrial establishment. Although undifferentiated, the bulk of the non-Nigerian employees probably belong to the professional and managerial group. That being the case, the situation in which foreigners constitute about a third of the professional and managerial personnel is clearly indicative of excessive economic dependence hardly consistent with true national development. Also since industrial operatives are mainly of the intermediate and lower technical grades, a work force of a mere 130,538 operatives seems small and indicative of a weak industrial sector in a country with a total active population of over 27 million (IIO, 1973; Nigeria, 1975c, p.370). Appreciating the technical and organizational manpower problem of Nigeria, the Nigerian government has set up, among other things, the centre for Management Development and Industrial Training Fund. According to Okunrotifa (1978), this demonstrates government commitment to create a conducive environment for training at the level of the individual enterprise and organization.

Capital

Nigeria is easily the richest West African country.
Our earlier examination of the country's natural
endowments (land) shows the vastness and variety of
her sources of capital. The non-renewable and renewable natural resources which abound have been subjected to varying degrees of exploitation to produce
the bulk of Nigeria's capital for economic development. Only brief indications can be given here as
regards the extent of capital mobilization on the
basis of which the country's industrial development
largely operates.

Nigeria's oil reserves at the end of 1975
totalled about 2,700 million tonnes. At the present
rate of about 1.0 million barrels per day, the life
of the country's oil industry is likely to be between 40 and 50 years, assuming that the estimates of
winnable reserves are correct. At any rate the im-
mensity of this natural resource is not in doubt for
the rest of this century. Table 7.4 shows the production of petroleum and natural gas during the
second half of the 1970s and the first half of the
1980s. Nigeria has much greater reserves of gas
than of crude oil. For every barrel of crude oil,
the country is estimated (World Bank, 1974) to have
an average of 750 cubic feet of gas. Until 1984
when the first petrochemical complex of the country
will have been commissioned, a very considerable
part of the gas resource will continue to be flared
- a waste which is a pointer to the inadequacy of
the country's technical manpower.

Coal reserves are fairly large; some 236 million long tons (Swardt and Casey, 1963);[1] they are
as yet the only ones known in West Africa. However,
the coal is generally of low quality both in calor-
ific value and for coke making. Production has
since the late 1960s been drastically reduced (Table
7.5) as a result of the civil war of 1967-1970 and
of the subsequent switch from coal to diesel-powered
railway trains. Large reserves of lignite also
exist; combined with coal reserves, they constitute
a reasonable resource base for the manufacture of
industrial chemicals and for the generation of thermal electricity.

Among the metallic minerals, iron ore is by far
the most important in the country both in size and
for industrial development. Reserves estimated to
be over 250 million tonnes of low-medium grade ore
(45-50 per cent ore content) are found in the Agbaja
Plateau south-west and south of Lokoja and in the
Udi Plateau around Nsude south-west of Enugu. These

Table 7.4: Production of crude oil and natural gas, 1975-80

	Unit	Year 1975	1976	1977	1978	1979	1980
Crude Oil	Mil. barrels	651.315	757.652	765.297	692.269	840.864	753.228
Natural Gas	Mil. cub. metres	402	632	500	380	1,378	1,070

Source: OPEC, Annual Statistical Bulletin, 1980, pp. 4-48.

Figure 7.2: Mineral resources and hydro-electric power distribution

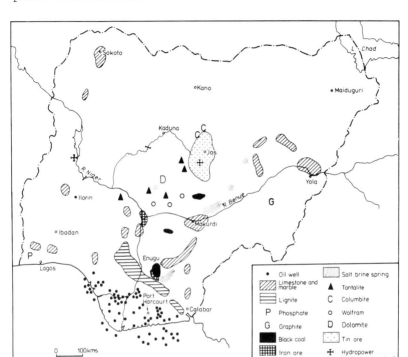

reserves have been the main resource base for Nigeria's iron and steel complex now under construction at Ajaokuta south-west of Lokoja. Considerable import of ore,[2] particularly from Brazil and Liberia will however be undertaken until about 1984 when local ore reserves become the main source for the direct production process by the steel complex at Aladja, near Warri.

Of the non-metallic rock minerals in the country limestone is the most important and has been accessible for exploitation in many different sedimentary rock regions of the country. About 400,000 tonnes will be used at Ajaokuta every year, mainly taken from Jakura near Lokoja and Ubo near Okene. In conjunction with the almost ubiquitous clay, limestone has been copiously available as material for the country's many integrated cement plants.

From the Nigerian forests, particularly the

Table 7.5:   Coal production in Nigeria, 1957-79

Year	Production ('000 tonnes)	Year	Production ('000 tonnes)
1957	831	1969	17@
1958	944	1970	59
1959	757	1971	195
1960	573	1972	343
1961	609	1973	327
1962	636	1974	304
1963	579	1975	249
1964	702	1976	299
1965	743	1977	267
1966	643	1978	264
1967	97[+]	1979	166
1968	–		

[+] For January - March only   @ From Okoba coal mine only

Source: Annual Abstract of Statistics (various years)

tropical rainforest and the derived savanna belts,
more than 100 timber-yielding species abound; but
so far less than a quarter of this number has yet
been under commercial exploitation. The vast majority of the species are hard-wooded, notably
mahogany, khaya ivorensis, agba, obeche, wawa,
African walnut among others. A few relatively soft-
wooded species of commercial value include the silk
cotton tree and such exotic species as gmelina
arbores and the eucalyptus tree. In spite of largely uncontrolled tree felling, considerable reserves of timber trees still exist to form the basis
for a wide variety of industrial activities. The
possibility of natural forest regeneration or re-
placement with choice exotic species (like gmelina,
teak and the eucalyptus plant) has been established
through years of experimentation (King, 1968).
    Agricultural resources embrace crops and live-
stock. For industrial development purposes, attention will here be focused on the major agricultural
items directly usable for industrial production. It
is, however, important to note that those left out
as not directly involved in the manufacturing subsector are of considerable importance, even if indirectly, in improving the food and physical health
welfare of the industrial workforce and indeed of

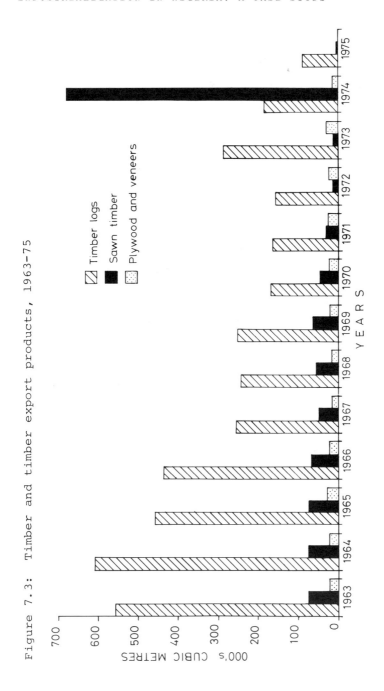

Figure 7.3: Timber and timber export products, 1963-75

the entire population of the country.

Nigeria has immense potential for agriculture, considering the land space available for cultivation especially outside the few areas with very high man/land ratio, and also in view of the generally favourable climates and soils in the various ecological zones shown in Figure 7.4. Table 7.6 shows agricultural products that have for many years been exported for foreign exchange but which can be very fruitfully used in domestic industries, given the necessary technology, industrial climate and market. Although production has declined quite sharply since the late 1960s, particularly in respect of palm oil and benni-seed, largely as a result of national preoccupation with petroleum, the prospects of much increased production, at least to pre-1967 levels, are bright. Stepping up production to such levels is made necessary by the great need not only to widen the foreign exchange scope of the economy

Figure 7.4: Major ecological zones of Nigeria

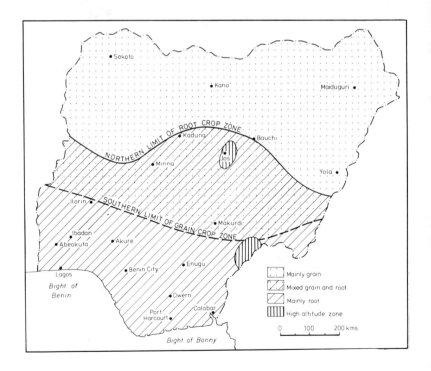

Table 7.6:   Agricultural products purchased* mainly for export

Year	Products (in thousand tonnes)					
	Cocoa	Ground nuts	Palm Kernels	Palm Oil	Seed Cotton	Benni Seed
1960–61	156	631	432	194	154	28
1961–62	187	699	439	177	84	21
1962–63	198	889	360	131	149	22
1963–64	220	803	421	152	132	20
1964–65	299	693	410	150	133	24
1965–66	185	998	458	167	129	24
1966–67	268	1,047	422	132	151	16
1967–68	239	693	222	33	181	13
1968–69	218	779	194	5	166	13
1969–70	219	658	236	14	195	18
1970–71	309	287	296	26	115	6
1971–72	257	307	308	32	111	3
1972–73	241	559	269	21	143	4
1973–74	224	44	230	14	86	3
1974–75	184	162	302	25	140	4
1977–78	188	140	117	47	115	2
1978–79	185	n.a	173	n.a	117	n.a

* by the Produce Marketing Boards from the country's output

Sources: (i) Annual Abstract of Statistics, 1975 and Digest of Statistics, Oct. 1977, Federal Office of Statistics, Lagos.

(ii) Central Bank of Nigeria, 1980 Report.

beyond crude oil, but also to provide a firm resource base for an effective industrial development. The impact of local industrialization on produce exports can be appreciated from Table 7.7 which shows a markedly declining trend in exports. However, there is potential for much improved levels of production and export.

Viewed in GNP terms, what Nigeria has altogether been able to command, out of which investments in industrial enterprises have been planned and implemented since independence, rose rapidly during the 1970s, particularly the later half of the decade (Table 7.8).

Table 7.7: Nigeria's export of major commodities, 1975/76-1979/80

Commodity	Unit	Export in:				
		1975/76	1976/77	1977/78	1978/79	1979/80
Groundnuts	'000 tonnes	–	2.0	0.8	–	–
Groundnut oil	'000 tonnes	–	–	–	–	–
Groundnut cake	'000 tonnes	7.0	29.0	8.2	–	–
Cocoa beans	'000 tonnes	195.0	219.0	165.2	205.6	219.1
Palm kernels	'000 tonnes	171.0	472.0	185.5	58.3	55.1
Rubber	'000 tonnes	61.0	34.0	24.6	33.2	37.5
Hides & skins	'000 tonnes	3.0	2.0	1.9	1.3	1.0
Tin ore & metals	'000 tonnes	5.0	3.0	1.6	1.5	1.5
Crude petroleum	'000 tonnes	81,677.0	95,872.0	100,016.3	88,225.9	105,271.5
Timber, logs, plywood	'000 cub. met.	107.0	28.0	11.1	0.2	0.2

Source: (a) Federal Office of Statistics. Also see Fourth National Development Plan 1981-85, Vol. I. p. 21.

Table 7.8:   Gross National Product at 1977/78
factor cost

Year	GNP (₦ '000 million)
1970/71	4.8
1975/76	26.8
1976/77	29.1
1977/78	31.4
1978/79	31.7
1979/80	34.5

Source: Nigeria (1981) Fourth National Development Plan
1981-85, Vol. I, National Planning Office, Lagos, p. 14

MAJOR FACTORS AND PATTERNS OF INDUSTRIAL DEVELOPMENT

Industrial activity of modern factory type was hardly known in Nigeria before the present century.
Table 7.9 based on surveys of the Federal (Nigeria)
Office of Statistics shows that less than ten industrial plants employing ten or more persons were
active by 1910.   In fact, up till the end of World
War II, Nigeria had hardly a recognizable industrial
sector.   As has been reported elsewhere (Onyemelukwe
1978a), manufacturing industry was predominantly
processing in character.   As shown by that report,
there were 26 plants involved in finishing functions
out of a total of 47 industrial establishments known
(by the Federal Office of Statistics) to be existing
before 1945, the remaining 21 belonging to the processing group.   It was the latter that had a much
more profound impact on the Nigerian economy because
it served the entire export crops sector of the
economy rather than a circumscribed consumer market.   The processing of agricultural products and the beneficiation of minerals like tin ore
was found to be a very necessary preliminary to
profitable export trade.   Since these natural resources could not normally bear the cost of long-
distance transportation, commodity valorization had
to be locally undertaken to ensure easier transport-
ability and a more comfortable trading margin.   Thus
it can be argued that one major factor that assisted
the development of modern industrial activity, albeit the processing type, was the country's export

175

trade in her natural resources.

Another related factor that helped very much to bolster manufacturing industry was increased overseas demand for tropical agricultural products, particularly during the Korean War of the early 1950s. The consequent increases in the price of Nigeria's exports had the effect of raising the incomes, savings and investing capabilities of a good number of Nigerians. There was thus for the first time a reasonably large stock of capital funds in the hands of many at the same period. The Second World War shortages of manufactured goods being imported in exchange for Nigeria's raw material exports had underlined the need for the local production of those goods that did not involve higher level technology than could be locally managed. Furthermore, the increasing level of political consciousness and eventual political independence found practical expression in private and public efforts to invest in manufacturing activity of an import substitution nature. The glamour, prestige and satisfaction of factory production involving much more than mere processing of raw materials quickly caught the fancy of some of the financially well-placed cash crop farmers and middlemen. Above all, the total transfer in 1960 of political decision-making to Nigerians paved the way for official policy measures creating the necessary climate for industrial development in Nigeria. The erstwhile colonial government had hitherto discouraged industrial development by deemphasizing technical education and over-dramatizing the economic advantages of export-oriented resource exploitation. The Nigerian educated elite who had felt ignored and left in the cold by the colonial administration, strove to be in the vanguard of the struggle for political independence. They saw Britain's attitude to local industrialization as repressive. It was not, therefore, a surprise that as soon as they (the educated elite) got hold of the reins of political power in a newly independent Nigeria, industrialization was made the cardinal development policy objective. In the context of the First (1962 -68) Development Plan, industrialization was seen as capable of immensely contributing "both directly and materially to national economic growth" (Nigeria, 1962, p. 60). The fervour with which this objective was declared, in spite of obvious technological and infrastructural constraints, was enough to encourage considerable private participation in industrial activity. And before 1970 the relatively high growth rate of industrial establishments and employment had

Table 7.9: Structure of manufacturing industry in Nigeria by type and age, 1900-1970

Industry Type for	Number of establishments by:							
	Before 1911	1911 to 1920	1921 to 1930	1931 to 1940	1941 to 1950	1951 to 1960	1961 to 1970	Total in 1970
Food, drink tobacco	1	0	2	5	18	98	92	216
Textiles, clothing	2	2	3	3	6	20	49	85
Leather	1	2	0	0	2	9	15	29
Wood & Furniture	0	0	2	0	15	45	43	103
Paper, pulp paper boards	0	0	0	0	1	0	12	13
Printing & Publishing	4	–	2	1	14	35	15	71
Basic industrial Chemicals	0	0	0	0	0	2	4	6
Chemical products	0	0	2	0	4	11	31	42
Rubber products	1	1	1	0	0	21	8	31
Plastic products	0	0	0	0	0	2	8	10
Clay & Glass products	0	0	0	0	0	7	10	17
Cement	0	0	0	0	0	2	3	5
Non-metallic mineral prod.	0	0	0	0	1	1	7	9
Iron & Steel basic products	0	0	0	0	0	1	1	2
Fabricated metal products	0	0	0	1	2	20	38	61
Radio, T.V., Electrical prod.	0	0	0	0	0	0	6	8
Ship building	0	0	0	0	2	1	2	5
Motor Assembly	0	0	0	0	0	4	1	5
Jewellery	0	0	0	0	0	0	1	1
Miscellaneous products	0	0	0	1	1	4	10	16
TOTAL*	9	5	12	11	66	286	357	746

* Exclude establishments in mining and services sectors also listed at source.

Source: Nigeria (1971) <u>Industrial Directory</u>, Federal Ministry of Industry, Lagos.

become very evident (Tables 7.9 and 7.10 and Fig. 7.5). As shown in Table 7.9 the number of industrial establishments rose from 66 in 1950 to 746 in 1970. Also, as shown in Table 7.10 employment in the manufacturing sector nearly quadrupled: from 64,965 in 1964 to 244,343 in 1975.

Table 7.10: Growth of manufacturing employment, 1964-76

Year	Employment
1964	64,965
1965	73,921
1970	128,519
1972	167,626
1974	175,299
1975	244,343
1976	214,280

Sources: (a) Digest of Statistics (for various years)

(b) U.N. (1979) Yearbook of Industrial Statistics.

By and large, the need to valorize low quality and bulky materials destined to overseas industries and the political and economic necessity for a good measure of self-reliance through import substitution have been very important factors in the stimulation of industrial growth in Nigeria. Also, the local abundance of resources crucial to industrial modernization - particularly water power, petroleum, coal, limestone and such farm and forest resources as cotton, palm produce and timber - has helped to provide a base for industrial progress. Nevertheless, the pace of progress has from the beginning been seriously constrained by the low fund of technical and managerial skills available in the country. It is probable that until the level of technical training and competence is raised substantially, the country's industrial sector will continue to be weak and hardly capable of meeting the challenges posed by the economy's susceptibility to undue exploitation. What remain to be examined in this section are some of the major structural characteristics of the country's industrial sector, which reflect the factors and problems so far identified.

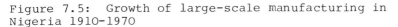

Figure 7.5: Growth of large-scale manufacturing in Nigeria 1910-1970

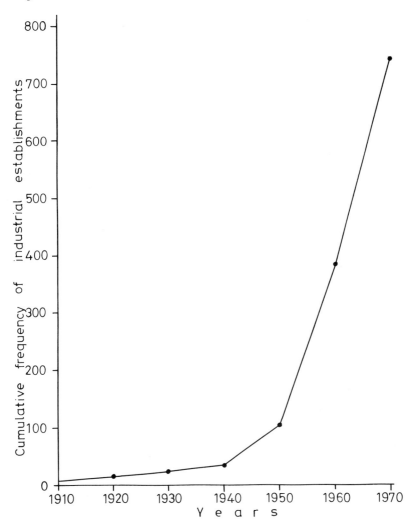

Following the International Standard Industrial Classification system, Nigeria's industries are put under eight major groups (31-39), each of which, except ISIC 39, is made up of a number of subsets representing specific industrial types. It is to the major group codes that this discussion refers, as shown in Table 7.11. We are at present interested in changes occurring in these industrial groups, to see whether such changes do reflect the factors discussed above. To begin with, it is of interest to see how the industries have been faring over the years in terms of growth measured by number of establishments, employment, gross output and value added as well as in spatial terms.

Table 7.11: Growth of industrial establishments, by group, 1964-75

ISIC Code	Industrial Group	Total No. of Establishments in: 1964	1965	1970	1972	1974	1975
31	Food, Beverages, Tobacco	106	111	171	290	250	294
32	Textiles, Clothing Leather	48	56	98	162	161	173
33	Wood & Furniture	55	49	125	216	195	276
34	Paper, Printing & Publishing	40	41	78	94	95	123
35	Chemical & Petrochemical products	75	74	94	109	110	122
36	Non-metallic Mineral products	25	24	26	49	66	110
37/38	Basic metal & Fabricated metal products	68	75	95	122	150	163
39	Other industries	6	8	17	18	18	23

Source: Digest of Statistics (for the various years)

In Table 7.11 changes in industrial growth are presented in terms of number of establishments per industrial group from 1964 to 1975. Evidently, there were considerable positive changes in the entire manufacturing sector as in each industrial group. For instance, there was a 305 per cent rise in the number of industrial establishments, from 423 in 1964 to 1284 in 1975. The wood and furniture in-

dustry (ISIC 33) with a 502 per cent increase from
the 55 establishments of 1964 to the 276 of 1975,
made the most remarkable progress during the period.
This was followed by the non-metallic mineral products industry (ISIC 36) with a 440 per cent increase,
and by the textile, clothing and leather industry
group (ISIC 32) of 360 per cent. But in absolute
terms, the food industry (ISIC 31) with 294 establishments in 1975 came out as clearly the most dominant in the country. All those relatively fast
growing industrial groups have probably been the
most locally dependent in terms both of raw material procurement and of labour recruitment. This
largely explains their relative progress and prominence compared with the basic metal and fabricated
metal products industries (ISIC 37 and 38) which together showed less than a 240 per cent increase in
number of establishments between 1964 and 1975. The
same can be said more forcefully in respect of chemical and petrochemical products industries (ISIC 35)
which depend considerably on imports of both inputs
and expertise. It has been estimated (Nigeria,
1975c p.149) that up to 1975, 87.3 per cent (by
value) of the basic industrial chemical inputs were
being imported for Nigerian industries.

     In some important respects, mere numbers of in-
dustrial establishments do not help very much in
appreciating the real changes and progress associated with the industrial sector of an economy. For
one thing, the developmental impact of industrial
groups cannot be properly assessed on the basis of
mere additions of industrial establishments without
relating such numbers to size of work force. Since
one major objective of Nigeria's industrial policy
is to generate employment and, thereby, raise per
capita income, industrial structure by size of employment is very relevant here, if only for its
policy implications. Table 7.12 shows how the various industrial groups fared between 1964 and 1975.
Overall, employment in the entire manufacturing sector almost quadrupled - from nearly 65,000 in 1964
to over 244,000 in 1975. However, considerable differences existed among the various industrial groups.
Whereas employment in the textile, clothing and
leather industry group during that period more than
quintupled (from 10,340 in 1964 to nearly 67,000
strong in 1975), and more than quadrupled in the
food, beverage and tobacco industry (from slightly
over 13,000 strong in 1964 to over 57,000 in 1975),
it barely doubled in the wood and furniture industry
and tripled in the rest of the specific industry

Table 7.12:   Total employment by industrial group
1964-1975

ISIC CODE	Total industrial employment in:					
	1964	1965	1970	1972	1974	1975
31	13,260	15,317	25,882	35,767	30,664	57,061
32	10,340	14,608	41,376	50,917	55,676	66,904
33	10,799	9,962	11,725	15,007	14,728	21,517
34	6,274	6,074	9,556	13,138	12,946	17,510
35	9,992	10,896	17,609	21,232	26,034	29,364
36	4,504	4,949	5,518	8,236	9,012	14,854
37/38	9,499	11,608	15,793	21,276	24,483	35,864
39	317	507	1,060	2,053	1,671	1,265
31-39	64,965	73,921	128,519	167,626	175,299	244,343

Source: Digest of Statistics (for the various years)

groups.   Thus although the wood and furniture industry did have the highest rate of increase of industrial establishments during the period, it made much
less impact in employment terms.
     The structural characteristics of manufacturing
are also fruitfully examined in terms of gross output to see the relative importance of the component
industrial groups as well as the extent of progress
made over a given period.   Table 7.13 shows the
values of gross output by manufacturing in Nigeria
for 1974 and 1977.   Between these two years, wood
and wood products industries made the most remarkable progress; the 1977 value of ₦136 million was as
much as 240 per cent above the 1974 value of ₦40
million.   The least increase was recorded by the
food, beverage and tobacco industry (110 per cent).
But it was this industrial group that made the largest contribution (in absolute terms) to the total
gross output by the manufacturing subsector in both
1974 and 1977, as in the intervening years, and may
on this account be considered as the largest component of the manufacturing industry in the country.
It was followed by the textile, clothing and leather
industries and by chemical, pharmaceutical and other
chemical products industries in that order.   Not

Table 7.13: Gross output of manufacturing by
industrial group, 1974-77

Industry Group	Gross Output (₦ millions) in:			
	1974	1975	1976	1977
Food, Beverages and Tobacco	440	683	795	924
Textile, Clothing and Leather	313	528	552	683
Wood and Wood Products	40	92	99	136
Paper and Paper Products	87	151	201	242
Chemical, Cosmetic, pharm- aceutical and other chemical products	146	371	571	571
Rubber and Plastic Products	78	122	166	205
Electrical Products	34	48	82	83
Other industries	339	615	1,348	1,637
TOTAL	1,477	2,611	3,814	4,382

Source: Annual Abstract of Statistics, 1981, p. 87

only is this point of dominance reflected in the
distribution of industrial employment already examined: it is also forcefully buttressed by the relative sizes of industrial value added shown in Table
7.14. Figure 7.6 shows the geographical variation
of industrial plants, workforce and gross output in
1975.
       By and large, a major structural characteristic
of Nigeria's manufacturing is the preponderance of
import substitution activity. The policy of import
substitution was originally aimed at increasing self
reliance and curtailing foreign exchange outflow.
However, in spite of considerable progress in the
volume of output the success of this policy strategy
has not been impressive. This is mainly because import substitution industrialization is largely assembly-type in essence. This involves a great deal
of importation of parts and components to be

Figure 7.6:   Distribution of manufacturing establishments, workforce and gross output, 1975

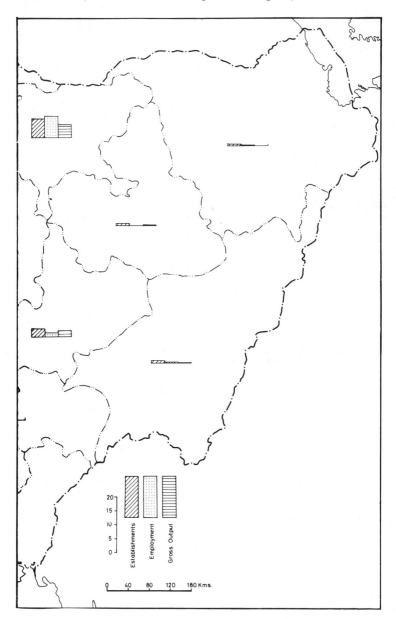

Figure 7.7: Distribution of capital goods plants, employment and gross output, 1975

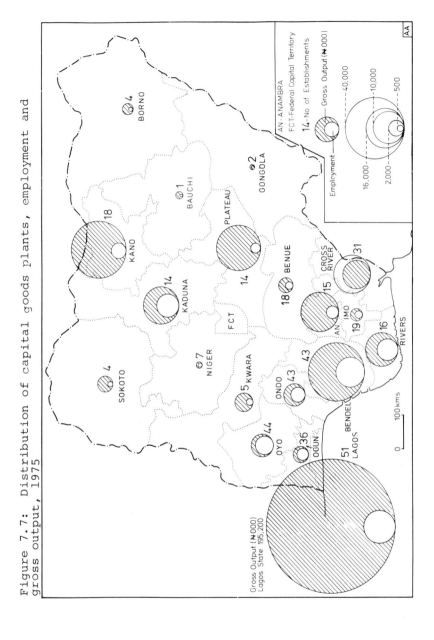

assembled.[3] It implies considerable dependence on
external markets, and in large measure defeats the
main objective of import substitution, namely, minimization of external influence and foreign exchange
outflow.

Very little export-oriented production outside
the industrial processing subsector has as yet been
developed. As can be appreciated from Table 7.15
the main items of export are shown as basic manufactures which include organic chemicals, cosmetics

Table 7.14: Value added by major industrial groups,
1972, 1975

ISIC Code	Industrial Group	1972		1975	
		Value Added:		Value Added:	
		(₦'000)	% of Total	(₦'000)	% of Total
31	Food, beverages & tobacco	169,891	28.98	328,914	27.75
32	Textiles, clothing & leather	78,777	13.44	237,501	20.04
33	Food & Furniture	115,905	19.78	44,077	3.82
34	Paper, printing & publishing	22,515	3.84	71,355	6.22
35	Chemicals & Petro-chemical products	112,797	19.25	249,242	21.03
36	Non-metallic Mineral products	22,146	3.78	46,986	2.99
37/38	Basic Metal and Fabricated metal products	61,381	10.43	197,964	16.70
39	Other Industries	2,690	0.46	5,294	0.45
31-39	Total	586,077	100.00	1,185,334	100.00

Source: Summary of Industrial Survey 1975, Federal Office
of Statistics, Lagos

and metal containers. Each individually constituted
an insignificant proportion of the total exports and
would certainly have been much less important if the
Table included items of first stage processing.
Among the unclassified goods are simple products of
small scale industry as well as printed matter.
However, the bulk of manufactured exports during the
years shown were essentially goods of second stage
processing. There has not been any substantial
change in the share of finished export products since
1978. However the 1975-80 development plan period

Table 7.15: Nigeria's exports of manufactured goods

Commodity	Value of (F.O.B.) manufactures exported in:			
	1975 ('000 US $)	1976 ('000 US $)	1977 ('000 US $)	1978 ('000 US $)
Petroleum products	43,076	70,373	30,499	28,726
Residual fuel oils	26,864	51,087	20,748	18,803
Basic manufactures	49,902	43,135	34,732	43,700
Goods not classified by kind	24,927	39,522	54,280	130,702
Cocoa butter & paste	39,965	28,821	88,412	42,087

Source: U.N., <u>1980 Yearbook of International Trade Statistics</u>,
Vol. I, p. 721.

witnessed a number of concerted efforts towards official encouragement of export-oriented manufacturing.
The inauguration in 1978 of the Nigerian Export
Promotion Council (NEPC) is one evidence of an increasing official effort to bolster the export-
oriented industrial subsector of the country. The
NEPC has recently concluded a nationwide survey expected to identify and locate active and potential

exporters of industrial and other products and services as well as bring to the general notice all the
facilities which government is putting at the disposal of export promoters. From the returns of the
survey a national directory of industrial and other
exporters will be compiled to serve both the domestic
and foreign markets.

The main factor underlying the poor performance
both of the import substitution and the export-oriented subsectors of Nigeria's manufacturing is indeed
the low level, hitherto, of technological and managerial know how. It seems that substantial progress
in these two subsectors will have to await large-
scale manpower development in the technical and organizational fields, as is beginning to develop in
the emerging heavy industry subsector[4] expected to
be dominated by steel production.

THE IRON AND STEEL INDUSTRY IN NIGERIA

An iron and steel industry has all along been regarded as basic to full-scale industrial development in Nigeria. The first (1962-68) post-Independence development plan of the country had a proposal for the establishment of an iron and steel plant
and the production of steel before 1970. However, a
number of factors, including very limited resources
and manpower as well as political problems which
undermined the badly-needed national unity of purpose (both in finding the necessary funds and skills
and in choosing a suitable location) frustrated the
efforts in that direction until the last years of
the 1970s. The oil economy helped very much to provide the necessary foreign exchange, ad the political
stability which the military regime of the 1970s imposed provided the atmosphere for firm decisions on
steel plant locations. A great deal has happened
since, and by 1985 Nigeria will probably be in a
good position to export steel, albeit to a circumscribed market in West Africa.

The natural resource base for the steel industry
comprises iron ore, coal, limestone, dolomite, fresh
water and natural gas mainly. All of these exist in
Nigeria, though not in adequate volume for iron ore,
scrap and coal. Iron ore exists in the Itakpe area in
the vicinity of Lokoja and in the Udi Hills south-
west of Enugu; however, on account of the low iron content (between 40 and 55 per cent of pure ore) at the
reserves, heavy ore importation has been built into
the project. At present Brazil and Liberia supply

ore to the country for the Aladja steel plant.   The
country's 16.2 per cent equity share in the iron ore
project of Guinea is an effort to guarantee an adequate
supply of ore.   By 1985 Nigeria will be importing 4
million tonnes of high grade iron ore from Guinea.
Nigeria's coal is not qualitatively adequate
for iron ore smelting, and again coal importation is
expected, at least until technological modifications
on local coal become economic enough to make such
imports unnecessary.   Meanwhile local coals are expected to be supplied from the Lafia-Obi area north of
Makurdi and the Udi Hills in and around Enugu.   The
right types of limestone abound in the country.
About 400,000 tonnes of limestone needed annually at the
Ajaokuta steel complex will come mainly from nearby
sources - at Jakura near Lokoja and at Ubo near
Okene, the nearest town to Ajaokuta.   About 240,000
tonnes of dolomite will be used annually at Ajaokuta.
These are obtainable at Osara and at Burum in the
Federal Capital Territory.   Finally, natural gas
abounds in the delta area of the country and lends
itself to effective use in modern steel making involving electric arc furnaces.
The location of the main steel plants of the
country, namely at Ajaokuta and at Aladja near Warri,
has been influenced by the presence of some of these
basic inputs, notably iron ore and gas.   In other
words the two major steel plants are essentially resource rooted - in keeping with classical location
theory (Weber, 1909, 1929).   While the Ajaokuta mills
are attracted by ore and, to some extent limestone,
neighbouring key materials, the Aladja steel mills
are materially-rooted (to natural gas being piped
from Ughelli near Warri) as well as coast-based for
easier access to imported ore and scrap.   However,
the three steel rolling mills now under construction
at Oshogbo, Jos and Katsina - all of which will depend heavily on the Aladja steel mills for billets -
cannot in any sense be described as resource-oriented.
Their locations have been based on political considerations for even industrial distribution among the
various social and political cores in the country.
The economic implications of this political decision
seem to have been considered (perhaps erroneously) as
not very serious in view of the political gains also
involved.   For such a basic industry as steel (less
basic industries could have been so employed without
so much risk), uneconomic location can have far-
reaching negative consequences for the country's
wider economy, since most industrial production based
on steel cannot compete effectively with its   rivals

dependent on cheaper steel products from other sources.

The Ajaokuta complex is expected to have two rolling mills backwardly integrated to it. These rolling mills are planned to come into production soon after the main complex takes off in 1983.[5] To ensure its success, such allied developments as modern transport linkages by rail and river and telecommunications as well as a functional urban centre are under way simultaneously with the Ajaokuta steel complex. A standard-gauge rail network is being developed to connect Ajaokuta with Port Harcourt and Enugu, and with Oturkpo, Makurdi, Lafia and Itakpe. The river Niger on the right bank of which Ajaokuta is situated is being dredged; a river port to handle bulky and heavy traffic for the steel complex is under way. It is expected that the new city emerging in the wake of the steel project will have 800,000 people by 1995.

The Aladja steel plant based on the direct reduction process, which can afford to depend on electricity and gas rather than coal, came into production on November 29, 1981. It has an annual capacity for 2.5 million tonnes of steel comprising bars, wire rods, light sections and billets which will be supplied to the steel rolling mills integrated (backwardly) to it.

The effects of iron and steel development in the country are certainly going to be great when all the mills go into full production. Direct employment by all the mills is expected to be around 30,000. But when all the other allied projects are considered, it is expected that 100,000 jobs will be accounted for altogether. The multiplier effects of all these hold out high hopes indeed.

Finally it is important to draw attention to this steel project as one good example where North-South relations are expected to produce positive results, especially in terms of manpower development and technology extension. Russia, Western Germany, Italy, Rumania, India and Japan have been contributing (and also gaining) immensely in these and other directions,[6] and one hopes that the present trend in manpower development in Nigeria will be sustained for some years to come after the projects have been fully commissioned.

THE SPATIAL PATTERN OF NIGERIAN INDUSTRY

A noteworthy feature of the country's industrial
landscape is the location of most large-scale manufacturing plants in a manner consistent with economic
efficiency. Some are so material-rooted (supply-
based) as to minimize production costs while taking
the reasonably high demand potential of Nigeria's
relatively large domestic market as given. Such industrial units are typified by the integrated cement
plants, especially those at Nkalagu, Ewekoro, Kalam-
baina near Sokoto, Ukpila near Okene in Bendel State,
Shagamu and Ashaka in Bauchi State. The Calabar
Cement Company (CALCEMCO), which deviates from this
pattern, located as it is some 30 kilometres from
the main source of limestone, has from the beginning
been up against crippling costs (Onyemelukwe, 1972).
The integrated cane sugar mills at Bacita as well as
those still being constructed are material-rooted in
view of their very high material index.
    Many large scale industrial units producing con-
sumer goods for the domestic market have been mainly
market-oriented or demand-based in their location.
The objective has apparently been to minimize cost
of contact with the bulk of consumers, as well as to
command appreciable influence over the market area
served. Typical of such industries are the breweries
and the soft-drinks bottling plants. They are characteristically located in large population centres - Lagos,
Kaduna, Kano, Abeokuta, Aba, Benin, Onitsha and
Ilesha for the breweries; and Lagos, Ibadan, Kano,
Port Harcourt, Aba, Ngwo near Enugu, Onitsha and
Benin for the soft drinks bottling.
    The cotton textile mills, which, unit by unit,
constitute the largest employers of industrial labour,
are also generally city-based. But their location
has not always been influenced by the market factor.
In some cases the overriding location consideration
is more the factor of government ownership and desire for effective control than the market factor.
For example, four of the five cotton textile mills
owned or controlled (through majority equity participation) by the former Northern Nigerian government
were initially (and are still) mainly producing wax
printed textiles, the market of which is mainly in
southern Nigeria. Wax printing is generally believed
to be more cheaply produced near its market centre
than at its main material source. However, to be
able to control effectively both manufacture and
product distribution, the former Northern Nigerian
regional government preferred locations in Kaduna,

Kano and Gusau (within its administrative jurisdiction) to market locations in the distant southern
Nigerian markets. Kaduna Textile Limited (KTL)
mainly producing grey cloth largely for the traditional <u>riga</u> attire of the Muslim North seems most
advantageously located - in its source area for
cotton as well as in the heart of the <u>riga</u> market.
However, most of the wax-printing plants in the
country are located in the main market for cotton
prints. Examples are the cotton textile mills in
Lagos, Aba, Asaba and Onitsha.

The clinker-grinding cement plants in Lagos and
Port Harcourt are city based; so are the sugar cubing
plants in Ilorin and Ibadan depending on the Bacita
mills for raw sugar. Also the country's steel rolling mills are city-based and footloose. But the
integrated mills at Ajaokuta are strictly ore-rooted
and the reduction plant at Aladja gas rooted as described earlier.

The few heavy industrial establishments, especially in the chemicals and metal products groups,
are characteristically city-based. Being essentially
assembly-type and depending on the city markets,
particularly the ports for the materials being assembled, the question of material rooting seems to
make sense only in respect of port locations - the
nearest to the external sources of material used.
The importance of Lagos in respect of these industries may therefore be appreciated mainly on those
grounds.

PROBLEMS OF INDUSTRIALIZATION IN A NATIONAL DEVELOP-
MENT CONTEXT

Industrialization in Nigeria has largely been constrained by the low level of technology which char-
acterizes West Africa and, indeed, most developing
economies. Although efforts to improve the industrial sector have featured manpower development in the
technical fields, the improvement of infrastructure
in cities, and the organization and encouragement of
industrial export promotion, a great deal remains to
be done in the area of effective integration of the
various sectors of the economy - particularly the
urban and the rural sectors. Doing this requires,
among other things, a comprehensive resource inventory
and an evaluation on the basis of which the development potentials of the various activity subsectors
and spaces can be appreciated and in the light of
which proper resource allocation and linkage relations

can be effected, given goodwill from all sides.

It is the rather low level of public will and commitment to national development (which should emphasize equity in the spatial distribution of enhanced socio-economic welfare) that constitutes another major drag, with serious implications for the industrial sector. This is evident not only in the increasing gap between the few centres of growth and the vast rural and urban peripheries, but also in the very weak linkage relations between them. Until many parts of the much-disadvantaged areas of the country are brought into effective linkage relations with the few growth centres - through the creation of the badly needed economic and social infrastructure and the encouragement of industrial and other economic activities for which such areas have economic promise if not comparative advantage - the country will continue to be held down in its industrial take-off. This point needs to be seen in its proper political context since many of the economic goals, not least those of industrialization, are inevitably mediated through political decision-making processes. Nigeria has immense natural resources. But it takes more than material resource endowment to achieve appreciable industrial progress. This is where the human factor (in terms of technical and organizational skills, political objectives and general attitude to development) is crucial. And there, as in most other West African countries, lies the country's most critical problem to which remedial policy measures should speedily be directed.

NOTES

1. Since the 1963 survey, more coal reserves have been discovered in Okoba and Obi, Plateau State, and current estimates are over 400 million tonnes.
2. To guarantee adequate supplies of high grade iron ore, Nigeria has taken up a 16.2 per cent share in the Guinea Iron Project.
3. The breweries, the chemical, the basic metal and the fabricated metal products industries are all heavily import dependent and essentially assembly-type.
4. In this subsector of heavy industries have already featured cement, glass, pulp and paper, petroleum refining, nitrogen fertilizer and car/truck/tractor assembly industries. A number of petro-chemical projects are about to begin.
5. Phase I of the steel project will begin in 1983 with a steel capacity of 1.3 million tonnes;

phase II will increase annual capacity to 2.6 million tonnes, and phase III to 5.2 million tonnes.

6. Through the sale of machinery, equipment and expertise, many economic benefits accrue to the developed countries involved - benefits that mean very much in these years of economic recession and acute unemployment.

Chapter Eight

CONCLUSION: INDUSTRIAL POLICY ISSUES IN NATIONAL
AND SUPRANATIONAL DEVELOPMENT CONTEXTS

What has been said and observed in the foregoing
chapters has overtly and implicitly drawn attention
to a number of policy issues to which this final
chapter addresses itself. Having identified certain
problems confronting West African countries in their
bid to develop their industrial sector and bring
about more rapid national development in each country, it remains to consider the policy implications.

POLICY ISSUES IN NATIONAL CONTEXTS

One pervasive problem identified in this study is the
gross inadequacy of technical and managerial skills
critical for strong industrial foundations and sustained progress towards industrial self-reliance.
It is a problem that each country has identified as
very serious and having far-reaching consequences.
It is also one with clear policy implications. What
are the policy implications and how have the countries of West Africa been addressing themselves to
these? The major policy implication is manpower
development. The second is technology adaptation at
a level consistent with the socio-economic circumstances of the people. And the third is attitudinal
reorientation of the people towards greater accept-
ance and patronage of, as well as support for, the
entrepreneurial efforts and innovations of the indigenes of each country. Let us take a closer look
at each of these three policy issues.
     Developing the right type of manpower for real
industrial progress is one practical approach to the
solution of problems of poor technology and excessive
dependence on external powers. This involves training
in the basic and applied sciences as well as in the
organizational and managerial fields. The advance-

ment of Western education in West African countries
has since the colonial times given little attention
to the technical content of education, emphasis
being on the non-technical aspects which equip the
recipient for clerical, civil service and other non-
technical routine functions. Thus accepting the
policy of manpower development should, in the West
African context, involve the removal of the colonial
legacy of official preference for non-technical education. Doing that effectively involves first, the
development of science from the very beginnings in
the pupils' formal education in primary schools;
secondly, adequate provision of the necessary equipment for teaching and practical work in science at
all levels of formal education beginning in the
primary school; thirdly the proliferation of purely
technical institutions at post-primary and post-
secondary school levels including the universities;
fourthly, the sponsorship of suitably qualified candidates to overseas training programmes likely to
expose them to types of technology appropriate to
the needs of the sponsoring country; and finally,
the tailoring of local technical training schemes
into the applied sciences of industries active in or
proposed for the country - that is, through well or-
ganised and monitored attachment of trainees to industries for requisite practical experience.

Some West African countries, like Nigeria,
Ivory Coast, Ghana and Benin, have in varying degrees
been pursuing their manpower development along some
of these lines. One common approach being adopted
is that of overseas training. However, in no country can the effort so far made be considered adequate for the country's manpower needs in the near
future, let alone in the long term. Within the last
eight years, Nigeria and Ivory Coast have each sponsored several hundreds of secondary school leavers
on overseas technical courses in the hope that those
involved would serve as the technical specialists -
the backbone of technical manpower - of tomorrow in
their country's industrial economy. But as the
Nigerian experience has shown, the calibre of trainees sponsored has generally been very low, perhaps
too low to achieve the expected objective.
Fresh from school and as yet virtually uncommitted
to, if aware of, the technology needs of their country, some of the sponsored students see in the overseas programme the opportunity of going overseas at
no personal cost. Many change course no sooner than
they arrive overseas, even at the risk of losing
their scholarship. The majority of those who go on

to complete the training complain of being exposed
to training programmes only tangentially related to
the problems they hope to grapple with back home at
the end of their training. It is probable that the
right calibre of trainees for such overseas programmes would be found among more mature students,
particularly graduates of polytechnics, colleges of
technology, and universities. In addition to students
and fresh graduates, technical workers with some experience in local industries, including the managerial functions, would probably be more suitable candidates for overseas training schemes. At any rate,
it is important that the candidates for such overseas programmes are those who not only appreciate
the needs of their country as regards technical manpower but are also capable of selective acquisition
of technical expertise consistent with those needs,
as well as being able to give effective leadership
in the adaptation of foreign technology. Furthermore, there is little that students of the less developed countries, like those of West Africa, can
learn in Western industrial countries outside those
industries which are essentially capital-intensive.
Much better exposure to labour-intensive technology
(particularly intermediate technology) would be secured in such countries as India, China, Taiwan and
Korea where greater emphasis has been laid on the
type of technology required by West African countries.
Nevertheless, this does not replace the need for high
level technology obtainable in technologically highly
developed countries, if only for the development of
appropriate technology for the emerging capital-intensive heavy industries in West Africa.
     The need to emphasize and fully develop the
tailoring of local training schemes to local industrial activities can hardly be over-emphasised, particularly as it relates to foreign industrial firms
operating in West African countries. The whole
question of technology transfer has received considerable attention, though the claims to it often
made by multinational industrial corporations
through their employment of local hands have not been
convincing. West African governments can more effectively utilise such industrial firms by ensuring the
development of attachment schemes, the appointment of
indigenes to supervisory and managerial posts and by
a close monitoring of progress in these directions.
     It is within this framework that foreign tech-
nology adaptation may be best pursued with good effect in the West African countries concerned. Without a good grounding in the basic scientific prin-

197

ciples, technology which is essentially applied
science is difficult to develop. After all, it was
by virtue of a good foundation in such basic principles - through generations of science education -
that Japan and, later, India, were able to adapt the
technology of the more advanced countries. It requires a good grasp of the relevant principles to
dismantle and assemble machines and successfully
copy the technology involved. Policy effort in West
African countries should emphasise the issue of a
broad base in science education for purposes of successfully adapting (rather than blindly adopting)
foreign technology as well as developing what West
African countries can proudly describe as indigenous
technology.

There is need for official policy to work towards a build-up of massive support for industrial
innovation by indigenous entrepreneurs. Mass support
can be got through mass education or public enlightenment woven around a simple ideology of national
survival and self-reliance. Also support for indigenous initiative and enterprise can be developed
through instruments of economic policy. It was earlier argued that one major constraint on indigenous
industrial progress has been the superior competitive-
ness of foreign manufactured goods. It has been shown
that most West Africans encourage foreign competition
by preferring imported manufactures even when local
manufactures are of comparable quality. It has also
been shown that official efforts to curb foreign competition are quite frequently undermined through
large-scale smuggling of foreign goods (otherwise
kept behind high tariff walls) into the West African
country concerned. All these are issues that call
for hard and realistic policies to ensure much greater
encouragement of domestic industrial efforts than now
exist.

Policy measures for such purposes may well be
directed towards drastic reductions in industrial
costs so as to ensure that local industries produce
more cheaply and sell at competitive prices, thereby
attracting more local patronage.

Doing this has many implications for local material resource development and management. It requires that the agricultural sector be modernized to
provide a firm resource base and be in effective linkage with the industrial sector. When this happens,
the degree of dependence on foreign inputs and the
import bills of local manufacturing firms are likely
to be lowered. The current official support for a
green revolution in Nigeria is the kind of policy

measure which, if successfully translated in practical terms, may lower production costs and encourage
local patronage. There is need for each West African
country to pursue similar policy measures with a
sense of purpose and urgency. By modernising their
agricultural sector, West African countries are
laying the foundations for progress in the industrial
sector. The growing drift of the youthful population
of the rural sector to the cities has been a major
constraint on progress in the labour-intensive agriculture so characteristic of West Africa. Thus the
success of a green revolution or the like needs to be
predicated on the retention of the rural youth in the
rural sector - on small scale industrial and craft
activities that can be effectively combined with agriculture. The current efforts by some countries
like Nigeria to provide universally free education is
laudable but can have very disastrous consequences in
the rural sector unless the right types of jobs to
which such education can be applied are made available in the rural environment. Failure to do so will
have the effect of preparing the educated youth for a
massive drift to the cities where opportunities for
such employment are believed - however misguidedly -
to be brighter. Official policy effort must therefore strive to promote rural industrialization, if
only to help diversify and sustain the economy of the
rural sector critical for successful industrialization.

While there is some gain in protecting domestic
industries, there is more to lose through over-
protection. Thus rather than try to keep out foreign
competition with high tariff walls - and in the process discourage the development of initiative and
competitive competence and encourage lethargy and
mediocrity - policy efforts should be directed more
to facilitating competition with foreign manufacturers. This can be pursued through the provision of a
congenial industrial environment featuring adequate
infrastructural facilities and by reducing bureaucratic and fiscal bottlenecks which have hitherto constituted serious constraints on domestic manufacturing enterprises.[1] Most West African countries have
shown great enthusiasm for boosting their industrial
economy but have done little through the provision of
the necessary infrastructure and social services.
Direct investment in manufacturing industry has generally been vigorously pursued by state governments
without providing adequate infrastructural support.
Industrial infrastructure provision is everywhere in
West Africa the monopoly of the government. Elec-

tricity, roads, railways, port facilities, water
supply, sewage disposal and telecommunications systems are all public utilities characterised by high
capital/output ratio and indivisibilities, such that
they are socially most beneficially handled by government. In developed countries, industries and
other economic activities are assured of much more
reliable and efficient infrastructural facilities at
prices low enough to allow for full use of the facilities without raising production costs unduly.
And so easily available are the facilities that they
are generally taken for granted. But in developing
lands, not least in West Africa, such facilities are
rarely available. Because the available infrastructure is largely concentrated in very few centres,
most industries have had good reason to gravitate to
those few favoured growth centres. Thus by deciding
the spatial pattern of infrastructure, government
has been the major factor affecting the spatial pattern of manufacturing activity in West Africa. Since
over-crowding in a few cities is already a major constraint on the national development roles of West
African primate and other cities, policy measures for
stemming congestion problems can be effectively applied through a more equitable spread of industrial
infrastructure, not only among cities and towns, but
also in the rural areas of each country. Without
doubt, policy measures for substantial improvements
in the quantity, quality and spatial pattern of industrial infrastructure would engender local manufacturing and increase its competitive power <u>vis-a-
vis</u> foreign industrial rivals.

West African governments are probably likely to
make a more effective contribution to industrial progress through the provision of adequate infrastructure than by direct participation in these industrial
activities that fall within the scope of private indigenous entrepreneurs. For one thing, it is economically and socially more prudent to have excess
capacity in infrastructure than in industrial plants.
An economy, in other words, loses less by setting up
an infrastructure well ahead of its full demand than
by establishing industrial projects with a high degree of capacity under-utilization owing to inadequate
infrastructural provision. Long-term infrastructure
development is among the priority strategies that
West African governments must swiftly embark upon in
support of domestic industries.

In the area of natural resource exploitation and
use, the point has been made that fuller resource development and management are still to be undertaken

in most West African countries. Since all the countries of the region are export-oriented in the exploitation of their natural resources so far developed, and since for about two decades the terms of
trade (with the exception of oil) have remained unfavourable to the region, West African countries
would be better off by internalizing the industrial
use of a greater part of their natural resources.
Although the need for foreign exchange underscores
the need to continue the export of natural resources,
the destabilizing impact of unfavourable terms of
trade calls for policy reorientation. Without drastically reducing the present level of raw material
exports, each West African country can afford to retain a considerable proportion of its natural resources for local industrial uses. Policy in this direction should therefore seek to broaden the base of
natural resource development. For example, Nigeria,
which now depends very largely on crude oil, can afford to redevelop her agricultural economy so badly
neglected during most of the 1970s. As agricultural
output increases, the rate of crude oil exploitation
and export should be reduced. This certainly extends
the life of the oil industry. Extension of the life
of the crude oil into the more distant future provides the country with a greater reserve of crude oil
for fuller industrial uses at a future time when the
much-needed high level technology will have been developed in the country. The same can be said about
the Liberian iron ore export which can be scaled down
as more of the renewable agricultural and forest resources of the country are developed for export. The
current recession in the world's iron and steel industry makes this policy strategy even more desirable
and urgent.

Ghana has been exporting her bauxite which she
does not even process into alumina. There is need to
reduce the rate of bauxite exploitation and export
and make up for the eventual drop in foreign exchange
through the intensification of agricultural resource
development. The more the life of any non-renewable
resource is extended, the greater chance there is for
its more effective use in the country as the level of
technology increases over time, other things being
equal. The same argument seems to hold for Guinea's
bauxite reserves and Togo's phosphate exploitation.
Although a similar argument applies, in theory, to
Mauritania's iron reserves as well as to Niger's
uranium industry, there is in practice little support
for the argument in view of the serious physical
(climatic) constraints on each country's agricultural

sector.

Policy effort toward the intensification of renewable resource exploitation for increased domestic use will require expanding the industrial sector and making it more local resource-based than it has been hitherto. Technology adaptation and development to that end can therefore be seen as a major policy objective. The more this objective is achieved, the more self-reliant the economy is likely to be, and the less it is likely to be constrained by external forces emanating from the industrially developed regions.

The history of national development planning in West African countries is replete with failures arising mainly from poor co-ordination. Many of such types of failure suggest that development planning is to some people of the region little more than an act of faith. It is, for instance, not enough to expect that strong linkage relations between the agricultural and the industrial sectors will develop on their own. There is need to co-ordinate and monitor the development of such linkages. And to do that requires among other things the provision of relevant infrastructural facilities in the rural areas - good road networks and good storage and produce marketing facilities required for the bulking, the preservation and the distribution of resources between farms and factories. Since most agricultural products are highly perishable, it requires well organized infrastructural provision to sustain the delicate balance between massive production and factory use of such perishable resources.

The required policy guidelines to streamline national development objectives and facilitate the co-ordination of intersectoral functional relationships are yet to be articulated in the region. In the absence of effective guidelines and co-ordination efforts, serious and far-reaching system effects can negate the objectives of national development planning. West African countries often experience this. Viewed in the context of industrialization as a national development process, the point being made is that it takes more than industries to industrialize (Rostow, 1960). It requires careful planning and intersectoral co-ordination to use effectively the industrial sector as the main engine of national economic development. And it is by calculated and earnest policy efforts rather than by mere pious hopes that such development objectives can be successfully achieved in practical terms.

SOME POLICY ISSUES IN SUPRA-NATIONAL CONTEXTS

A major constraint on industrial progress in West
Africa is the narrowness of the domestic markets of
the constituent countries. Small market size has
the effect of limiting the production capacity of
domestic-oriented industrial units. By implication,
small market size negates economies of scale without
which industrial goods cannot compete effectively.
The constraints of narrow domestic markets on industrial activity have serious effects on the compet-
itiveness of industrial firms within most West
African countries, though it is certainly more serious in smaller countries like Benin, Niger, Liberia,
Guinea Bissau, Gambia and the Cape Verde Island
group.[2]
     One important and noteworthy policy implication
of this common phenomenon in West African countries
is the organization of supra-national regional markets. It is a policy which can only be given practical effect through a consensus, especially among
contiguous states. Contiguity is an important,
though not a necessary, precondition for evolving a
regional common market or an economic community.
However, it facilitates the development and spatial
organization of common services. It provides a
framework favourable to the maximization of complem-
entarities between member states and reduces the
negative impact of intervening opportunities, often
engendered by having a non-member state serving as a
wedge between member states. On these and other
grounds, supra-national markets or economic communities have more often than not been fashioned out of
contiguous states.
     West African countries have since their indep-
endence demonstrated their awareness of the need for
such international organizations. A number of experiments of varied structures, objectives and geographical scope have been tried. Figure 8.1 presents
the series exclusive to West African states and organized within the region. Of the five, the largest
is the Economic Community of West African States
(ECOWAS), and the smallest is the Mano River Union.
The other three organizations have a range of three
to six state members.
     In setting up these organizations, problems de-
riving from the political, cultural, legal and economic legacies of colonialism in West Africa have
constituted major obstacles. Among the strong elements of such legacies are the diversities of official
languages, currencies and political loyalties, all of

Figure 8.1:   Supra-national economic groupings in
West Africa

which have tended to strengthen the claims of separate political identity and sovereignty within externally imposed artificial boundaries. However, over
the years, the people of West Africa have come to
learn from both their illusions and the narrow perception of their major problems. The current attempt
to forge an all-embracing economic community is perhaps so far the most realistic. This region-wide
arrangement has been quite pragmatic in its approach
to issues which tend to compromise the sovereignty
of member states. It is also realistic in the sense
that the region-wide organization encourages rather

than precludes the development of sub-regional
groupings within its geographical framework. Hence
the co-existence of ECOWAS and the Mano River Union,
for example, the latter embracing Liberia and Sierra
Leone (Guinea has lately joined). ECOWAS aims, among
other things, to evolve a common market; bring about
free movement of people, services and capital among
states; harmonize agricultural policies; promote
common projects; develop common economic and monetary
policies; and reduce disparities in levels of development among member states. But more particularly,
ECOWAS aims to forge a large enough market for the
development of economically more viable industrial,
agricultural and mining projects which have hitherto
been restrained in each member state by the narrowness of the domestic market.

Thus far ECOWAS has yet to translate most of
its objectives into actions, particularly those of
promoting common projects, of developing common economic and monetary policies and of reducing disparities in levels of development among member states.
Examples of economic co-operation that have occurred
so far are very few and far between. Among such are
the Benin-Nigeria joint effort in cement production
in Benin, and the Guinea-Nigeria joint venture in
iron ore mining in Guinea. In the latter project
Nigeria has a 16.2 per cent share in the project for
the development of her steel industry. Clearly these
partnership projects have been worked out on a bilateral basis rather than in the spirit and to the
letter of the ECOWAS protocol. Also the siting of
Nigeria's steel reduction plant along the coast at
Aladja near Warri can be seen as designed to facilitate contacts with other ECOWAS states both for the
collection of ore (from Liberia and Guinea) and for
the distribution of steel products as intermediate
goods to industries in the rest of West Africa (particularly in Ivory Coast, Ghana and Senegal). But
the fact remains that the choice of Aladja was entirely Nigeria's rather than a collective decision
by ECOWAS. It is probable that the practical trans-
lation of the ECOWAS objectives to the extent of influencing industrial locations directly must await a
time when the full implications of such major steps
are appreciated and the modalities for effecting them
are worked out. The recent episode involving the ex-
pulsion of some 1.5 million West African aliens from
Nigeria on grounds of illegal stay in the country
points to the kind of problems which ECOWAS member
states did not fully appreciate and guard against.
It is likely that the determination of member states

to avoid a repeat of such a traumatic experience will further delay the implementation of the objectives of joint industrial projects and the more even spread of economic development.

Other supra-national efforts have included the Organization for the Development of the Senegal River (Organisation pour la mise en valeur du fleuve Senegal) which was formally constituted in 1974 to develop the resources of the Senegal River basin. Within an integrative framework expected to bring immense benefits to the three member states - Mali, Senegal and Mauritania - the organization has set for itself the accomplishment of the following in its first decade of existence:

(i)   145 MW capacity hydro-electric dam project at Manantali in Mali;
(ii)   an irrigation dam at Diama between Senegal and Mauritania;
(iii)   a river-maritime port at St Louis in Senegal;
(iv)   a river port at Kayes in Mali; and
(v)   harbour installations and the provision of ground sills along the Senegal river.

All these were originally estimated to cost about 800,000 million CFA francs.

The Economic Community of (Francophone) West Africa (Communaute Economique de l'Afrique de l'Ouest) was formed by six francophone states - Ivory Coast, Mali, Mauritania, Niger, Senegal and Upper Volta in 1974 as an off-shoot of the defunct Customs and Economic Union of Central Africa (L'Union Douaniere et Economique de l'Afrique Centrale - UDEAC). It was designed to promote trade, harmonise customs practices and use a part of the customs revenue to promote the equitable development of the economy of member states. Finally, the Entente Council (Conseil de l'Entente) was formed in 1959 by Ivory Coast, Upper Volta, Niger and Benin but later joined by Togo; the Entente was designed to promote economic development among member states, especially by sponsoring specific development projects and by guaranteeing external loans and investments.

Clearly these smaller groupings of West African states are less unwieldy to organize. Yet it has not been easy to achieve the objectives they have set themselves, partly because of the lack of the advantages associated with the large size reflected in ECOWAS. Positive policy efforts by each member country are required to make the organizations work effectively. To that end, the countries need to go beyond the ceremonial signing of protocol agreements required for a full inauguration of each community. They also need to include efforts towards geographical specialization, particularly in the field of manufacturing. It is when industrial units produce for the entire region or for a good part of it, rather than for a small national market, that the advantages of large scale production begin to have substantial positive impact on the industrial sector and, in the final analysis, on the general economic development of member countries.

Unless these institutional arrangements are given such practical expression, the chances of individual West African countries successfully industrializing are very slim indeed.

West African countries have problems of communication through imposed foreign languages - French, English and Portuguese. They have diverse currency orientations. The insularity of one of the states (Cape Verde Islands) as well as the fact that three states (Niger, Mali and Upper Volta) are landlocked, together pose most formidable problems in industrialization. However, there seems to exist in West Africa a strong common will to hang together in spite of all the odds; and there is the more successful experiment to learn from in the European Economic Community (EEC) which was initially faced with similar difficulties. The Economic Community of West African States as well as the smaller groupings within the region seem now, more than ever before, to have a good chance of providing a firm basis for real progress in industrial and overall economic development. It is within the framework of such a supra-national organization as ECOWAS that West African countries can best hope to industrialize.

West African countries need to keep their regional organizations alive and effective in order to be able collectively to hold their own in a world of widening inequalities of political power and economic opportunities.

NOTES

1. During the last years of the military rule in Nigeria, import duties on some industrial raw materials like steel wire were higher than duties on imported finished steel products - clips and nails! The local manufacturers were as a result put in great difficulty.

2. The entire West African market, seen in terms

of aggregate purchasing power, is smaller than New York State's! Industrialization of West African countries must aim at serving a larger market through competitive production.

BIBLIOGRAPHY

Aboyade, O. (1968) Industrial Location and Economic
    Policy, The Nigerian Journal of Economic and
    Social Studies, Vol. 10, No. 3, pp. 275-302
Adegbola, K. (1978) Manufacturing Industries of
    Nigeria, in A Geography of Nigerian Development,
    Oguntoyinbo, J.S. et al. (eds.), Heinemann
    Educational Books, Nigeria, pp. 291-301
Afigbo, A.E. (1972) The Warrant Chiefs: Indirect
    Rule in South-eastern Nigeria, 1891-1929,
    Longman, London
Africa (1974) Africa Magazine, Economic Intelligence
    Unit, London
Akintola, F.D. Mineral and Energy Resources, in A
    Geography of Nigerian Development, Oguntoyinbo,
    J.S. et al. (eds.) Heinemann Educational Books,
    Ibadan, 1978
Aluko, S.A., Oguntoye O.A. and Afonja, Y.A.O. (1972)
    Small-scale Industries, Western State of Nigeria,
    University of Ile, Nigeria
Alexandersson, G. (1971) Geography of Manufacturing,
    Prentice-Hall, Englewood Cliffs
Allan, W.A. (1965) The African Husbandman, Edinburgh
Bairoch, P. (1975) The Economic Development of the
    Third World since 1900, Methuen, London
Barth, H. (1865) Travels and Discoveries in North and
    Central Africa, 1849-1855, London
Bauer, P.T. (1954) West African Trade, Cambridge
    University Press
Beacham, A. and Cunningham, M.J. (1970) Economics of
    Industrial Organization, Pitman & Sons, London
Best, A. and Blij, C.G. (1977) Africa Survey, John
    Wiley & Sons, London, New York
Bovill, E.W. (1958) The Golden Trade of the Moors,
    London

Brown, C.M. (1965) Industry in the New Towns of the
    London Region: Study in Decentralization,
    University of London M.Sc. Dissertation
Cameron, G.C. and Clark, B.D. (1966) Industrial
    Movement and the Regional Problem, University
    of Glasgow Social and Economic Studies, Oc-
    casional Paper 5
Christaller, W. (1933) Central Places in Southern
    Germany, American edn of English translation,
    Englewood Cliffs, NJ, 1966
Church, Harrison (1980) West Africa, Longman, London
Clark, C. (1966) Industrial Location and Economic
    Potential, Lloyds Bank Review, Vol. 82, pp. 1-17
Cole, H.B. and Cassell, A.B. (eds) (1970) Liberian
    Trade and Industry Handbook, Utrecht
Davis, J.A. (1966) Radiation and Evaporation for
    Nigeria, Unpublished Ph.D. Thesis, University
    of London
Denham, D., Clapperton, H. and Oudney, N. (1828)
    Narrative of Travels and Discoveries in Northern
    and Central Africa in the Years 1822, 1823, and
    1824, London
Denti, E. (1973) Africa's Labour Force 1960-80, in
    Employment in Africa: Some Critical Issues, ILO,
    Geneva, pp. 19-41
E.C.A. (1973) Statistical Yearbook Part III
E.C.A. (1979) Survey of Economic Conditions in
    Africa, Parts I & II, Addis Ababa
F.A.O. (1981) Production Yearbook, Vol. 35
Florence, S. (1948) Investment, Location and Size of
    Plant, Cambridge University Press
Florence, S. (1953) The Logic of British and American
    Industry, Routledge, London
Ghana (1977) Five-Year Development Plan 1975/76-1979/
    80, Ministry of Economic Planning, Accra
Gleave, M.B. and White, H.P. (1971) An Economic
    Geography of West Africa, Bell, London
Gnielinski, S. von (1972) Liberia in Maps, University
    of London Press
Greenhut, M. (1956) Plant Location in Theory and
    Practice
Haggett, P. (1965) Location Analysis in Human Geo-
    graphy, Methuen, London
Hamilton, F.E.I. (1967) Models of Industrial Location,
    in Models in Geography, Chorley, R.J. and
    Haggett, P. (eds.), Methuen, London
Helleiner, L.G. (1966) Marketing Boards and Domestic
    Stabilization in Nigeria, New Haven, Yale Univ-
    ersity Press

Hirschman, A.O. Strategy of Economic Development,
    New Haven, Yale University Press
Howard, R.S. (1968) The Movement of Manufacturing
    Industry in the
Hunker, H.L. (1974) Industrial Development, Toronto,
    London
ILO (1973) Employment in Africa: Some Critical
    Issues, Geneva
Johnson, H.G. (1967) The Possibility of Income
    Losses from Increased Efficiency or Factor
    Accumulation in the Presence of Tariffs,
    Economic Journal, (March) pp. 151-154
Keeble, D.E. (1971) Planning in South-eastern England,
    Area No. 3, pp. 69-74
Keeble, D.E. (1976) Industrial Location and Planning
    in the United Kingdom, Methuen, London
Kilby, P. (1969) Industrialization in an Open Economy
    1945-66, Cambridge University Press
King, F.S. (1968) Agri-silviculture (The Taungya
    System), Bulletin of the Department of Forestry,
    Ibadan, No. 1
Kriessel (1968a) Cotton Marketing in Nigeria CSNRD/
    NIGER, Ibadan
Kriessel (1968b) An Evaluation of Statutory Marketing
    in Nigeria, CSNRD/NIGER, Ibadan
Mabogunje, A.L. (1965) Urbanization in Nigeria -
    Constraints on Economic Development, Economic
    Development and Cultural Change, Vol. 13,
    pp. 413-419
Mabogunje, A.L. (1968) Urbanization in Nigeria,
    University of London Press
Nigeria (1962) National Development Plan, 1962-68,
    Lagos
Nigeria (1970) Second National Development Plan
    1970-74, Federal Ministry of Information, Lagos
Nigeria (1971) Industrial Directory, Federal Ministry
    of Industry, Lagos
Nigeria (1975a) Industrial Survey, Federal Ministry
    of Industry, Lagos
Nigeria (1975b) Annual Abstract of Statistics, Federal
    Office of Statistics, Lagos
Nigeria (1975c) Third National Development Plan 1975-
    80, Federal Ministry of Economic Development,
    Lagos
Nigeria (1977) Digest of Statistics, Federal Office
    of Statistics, Lagos
Nigeria (1981) Fourth National Development Plan
    1981-85, The National Planning Office, Lagos

Odife, D.O. (1976) The 1977 Budget and the Second
    Phase of Indigenization: A Note, The Nigerian
    Journal of Economic and Social Studies, Vol. 18,
    No. 3, pp. 451-60
O'Connor, A.M. (1978) The Geography of Tropical Af-
    rican Development, Pergamon Press, London
Oguntoyinbo, J.S., Areola, O., Filani, M.O. (1978)
    A Geography of Nigerian Development, Heinemann
    Educational Books, Ibadan
Okunrotifa, P.O. (1978) Education and Manpower Dev-
    elopment, in Oguntoyinbo, J.S. et al. A Geo-
    graphy of Nigerian Development, Heinemann
    Educational, Ibadan, pp. 193-207
Onwuejeogwu, M. (1975) The Social Anthropology of
    Africa: An Introduction, Heinemann, London
Onyemelukwe, C.C. (1966) Problems of Industrial
    Planning and Management in Nigeria, Longman,
    London
Onyemelukwe, C.C. (1974) Economic Underdevelopment:
    An Inside View, Longman, London
Onyemelukwe, J.O.C. (1972) Cotton Textile and Cement
    Industries in Nigeria: A Geographical Appraisal
    of Factory Location and Product Distribution,
    Department of Geography, University of Ibadan,
    Monograph
Onyemelukwe, J.O.C. (1974a) Industrial Location Policy
    as Development Strategy in Nigeria: Problems of
    Application in Cross-sectoral Context, The
    Nigerian Geographical Journal, Vol. 17, pp.
    151-63
Onyemelukwe, J.O.C. (1974b) Industrial Migration:
    The Nigerian Example in West Africa (Paper
    presented at the Symposium of the IGU Study
    Group on Industrial System, London School of
    Economics, London)
Onyemelukwe, J.O.C. (1978a) Structural and Locational
    Characteristics of Manufacturing, in A Geography
    of Nigerian Development, Oguntoyinbo, J.S. et
    al. (eds), Heinemann Educational, Ibadan, pp.
    261-73
Onyemelukwe, J.O.C. (1978b) Rural Industrialization
    in Nigeria, West African Technical Review,
    (June) pp. 67-71
Onyemelukwe, J.O.C. (1978c) Industrial Migration in
    West Africa: The Nigerian Case, in Industrial
    Change, Hamilton, F.E.I. (ed.), Longman,
    London, pp. 119-131
Onyemelukwe, J.O.C. (1979) Paper Industry: The West
    African Scene, Nigerian Journal of Forestry,
    Vol.   pp. 44-47

Onyemelukwe, J.O.C. (1980) Natural Resource Management for Stable Industrial Development in Nigeria, Geoforum, Vol. II, No. 4, pp. 419-427

OPEC (1980) Annual Statistical Bulletin pp. 46-48

Pearson, D.S. (1969) Industrial Development in East Africa, Oxford University Pre-s, Nairobi

Rake, A. (ed.) (1978) New African Yearbook, Economic Intelligence Unit, London

Rake, A. (ed.) (1981) New African Yearbook, Economic Intelligence Unit, London

Robinson, C.H. (1896) Hausaland of Fifteen Hundred Miles Through Central Sudan, London

Robinson, E.A.G. (1956) Structure of Competitive Industry, Cambridge University Press

Rostow, W. (1960) The Stages of Economic Growth, Cambridge

Scott, D.R. (1963) The Location of Metropolitan Industries, Quarterly Journal of Economics, Vol. 10, pp. 247-68

Schatzl, L. (1973) Industrialization in Nigeria: A Spatial Analysis, Munchen

Schmitt, M.O. (1962) Foreign Capital and Social Conflict in Indonesia 1950-58, Economic Development and Cultural Change, Vol. 10, pp. 284-293

Schulze, W. (1981) Liberia, in Africa South of the Sahara, Europa Publications, pp. 571-2

Schumacher, E.F. (1973) The Work of the Intermediate Technology Development Group in Africa, in Employment in Africa: Some Critical Issues, ILO, Geneva, pp. 131-148

Seers, D. (1963) Big Companies and Small Countries: A Practical Proposal, Kykos, Vol. XVI, fasc. 4

Smith, D.M. (1966) A Theoretical Framework for Geographical Studies of Industrial Location, Economic Geography, Vol. 42, No. 2, pp. 95-113

Smith, D.M. (1970) Industrial Location: An Economic Geographical Analysis, Wiley, New York

Smithies, A. (1941) Optimum Location in Spatial Competition, Journal of Political Economy, Vol. 49, pp. 423-39

Streeten, P. (1972) The Frontiers of Development Studies, Macmillan, London

Swardt, A.M.J. de and Casey O.P. (1963) The Coal Reserves of Nigeria, Geological Survey of Nigeria, No. 2, Kaduna

Townroe, P.M. (1969) Industrial Structure and Regional Economic Growth - A Comment, Scottish Journal of Political Economy, Vol. 16, pp. 95-8

Townsend, J. (1968) Scale, Innovation, Merger and Monopoly, Pergamon Press, Oxford

ᵬ

BIBLIOGRAPHY

Tubman, W. (1944) Liberian Government Paper quoted
    by Cole, H.B. and Cassel, A.B. (eds.), Liberian
    Trade and Industry, Monrovia
Tuppen, J. (1983) The Economic Geography of France,
    Croom Helm, London
Udo, R.K. (1978) A Comprehensive Geography of West
    Africa, Heinemann, London
United Nations (1979) Yearbook of Industrial Stat-
    istics
Weber, A. Theory of the Location of Industries,
    University of Chicago Press
Wilczewski, R., Lijewski, T. and Kortus, B. (1978)
    Spatial Industrial Changes in Poland since 1945,
    in Industrial Change, F.E.I. Hamilton (ed.),
    Longman, Harlow, pp. 80-98
World Bank (1980) Yearbook of International Trade
    Statistics, Vol. 1
World Bank (1974) Nigeria: Options for Long-term
    Development, Johns Hopkins University Press,
    Baltimore
World Bank (1982) World Development Report, Oxford
    University Press, New York, London
World Bank (1982) World Bank Atlas: Gross National
    Product and Growth Rates, 1982

GLOSSARY

I   <u>Industry</u>   In this book industry which often
means different things in different contexts
refers specifically to manufacturing which, in
essence, is factory-level processing of raw materials and transformation of processed or produced objects into distinct products. As a
secondary sector activity, manufacturing ex-
cludes mining and quarrying which belong to the
primary sector, and repair work (like the repair of cars or clocks) which is essentially a
service or tertiary function. Mining and repair services are erroneously embodied in industrial statistics by some studies.

II   <u>Linkages</u> in the present context refer simply to
forms of interaction between production units
and involving shifts of materials or services
from one production unit to another. In this
sense <u>inter-industry</u> linkages refer to such
interactions between units belonging to different industrial groups - e.g. between textile
industry and chemical industry, or between steel
industry and shipbuilding industry. <u>Inter-sec</u>-
toral linkages refer to interactions between
firms in different sectors - for example between
firms in primary and secondary sectors, or between secondary and service sectors.

III   <u>Localization Coefficient</u> is a measure for determining the degree of local concentration of
a particular activity (an industry type in this
context) compared with the distribution of industry as a whole. It can be computed by using
such relevant variables as fixed capital inves-
ted, value-added by manufacturing or employment.
Degree of localization is obtained by adding up

the positive differences between the percentage
share of each region in a given industry and
the percentage share of the region in the entire national activity (i.e. total manufacturing
industry), and dividing the sum by 100. Values
of the localization coefficient range from 0 to
1. A zero value signifies non-concentration of
the particular industry being studied. It means
that the distribution of workers in that industry coincides completely with the distribution of industrial workers in general (i.e.
dispersion). But a value of 1 indicates extreme differentiation or over-concentration:
all the industry being studied is concentrated
in one region.

IV Location Quotient is a measure (ratio) of the
relative specialization of a given activity in
a unit area, like a region, in a country. This
is obtained by comparing the share (ratio) of
the unit area with that of the larger area (say,
the ratios of the region and of the nation) to
arrive at a new ratio. Hence the location
quotient is a ratio of ratios. Variables like
employment, value or weight of products and
capital are commonly used, depending on the objective of the exercise. Whichever unit of
measure chosen is related to a reference variable or a general base which is often the population of the unit area. However, for a more
refined analysis, the most relevant part rather
than the whole of the population may be used as
the reference variable - the active population
rather than the entire population, for example.
It is important that there is a close association between the critical variable being in-
vestigated and the reference variable even
though they can be expressed in very different
terms (like output and population, value added
and employment). If employment in a selected
industry is used as the critical variable, it
can be expressed as a ratio of the total employment as well in the region as in the nation.
Thus quantitatively expressed

$$\text{Location Quotient (LQ)} = \frac{\dfrac{I_r}{R_r}}{\dfrac{I_n}{R_n}}$$

216

Where I_r = employment in industry I in region r;

I_n = employment in industry I in the nation;

R_r = reference variable value for region r;

R_n = reference variable value for the nation.

Values obtained fall between zero and infinity. If LQ = 1, then the region's share of industry I is neither more nor less than its fair share of the industrial activity I in the country. There is specialization or more than a fair share of industry I in region r to the extent that LQ ⊳ 1. If LQ ⊲ 1, then region r has less than its fair share of industry I and is therefore unspecialized in that industry.

V   <u>National/Regional Development</u> is concerned with processes of change (particularly change of a structural nature) toward the enhancement of a people's socio-economic welfare and the average individual's scope for self-fulfilment and higher quality of life. It involves a society transformation through its methods of economic production, its institutions, social rules as well as the workaday attitudes of its members - to the extent that makes the society more positively responsive to desired modern changes. Development in this context embraces not only economic growth measurable in concrete (e.g. GDP/GNP) terms but also the not so measurable qualitative changes reflected in the average individual's level of living, all occurring in socially desired directions.

VI   <u>Technology</u> refers simply to the science of factor combinations. To the extent that it reflects varied levels of efficiency in the combination of factors of production, technology can be described as low level or high level (rudimentary or modern) or even intermediate.

INDEX

220

223